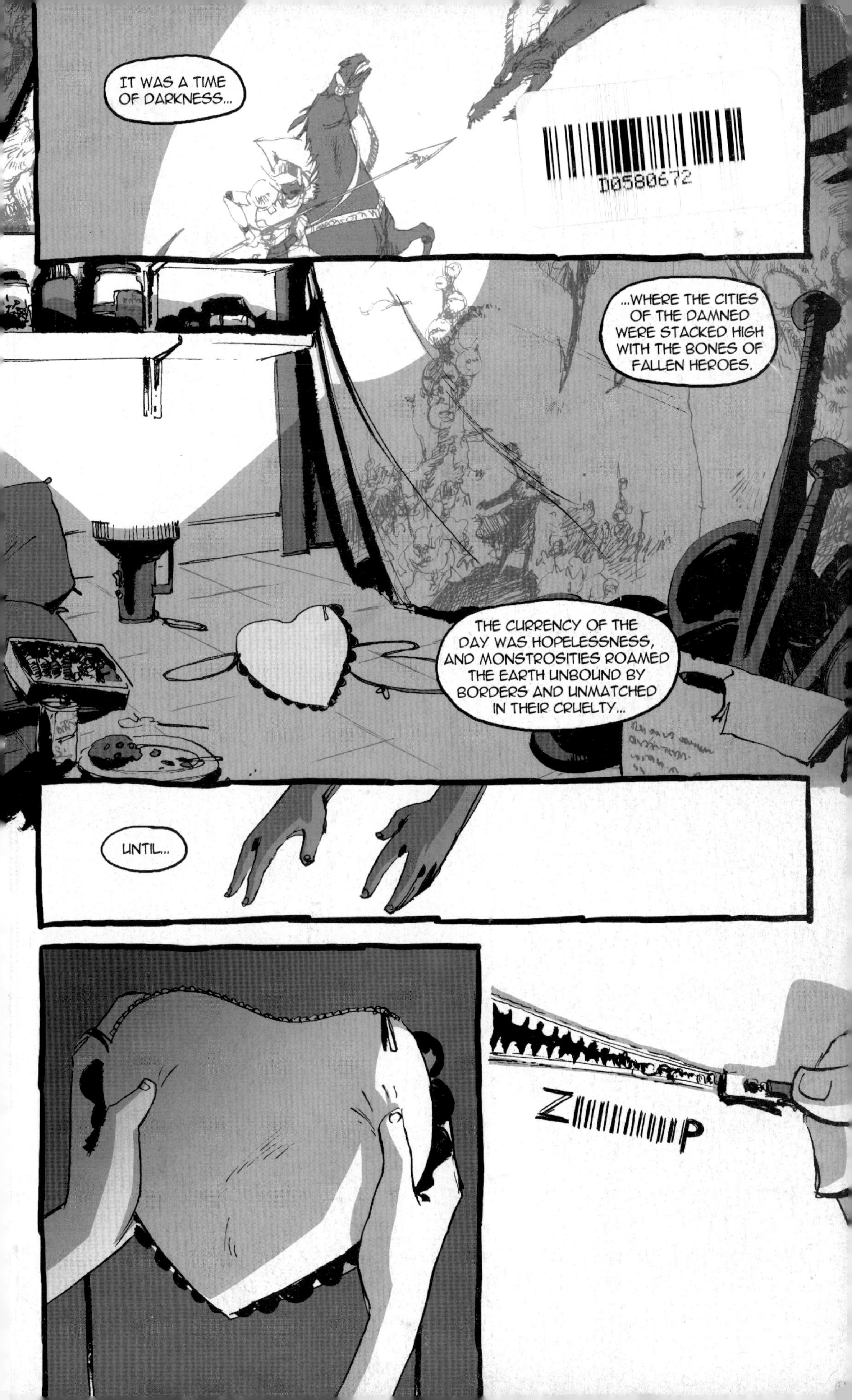
IT WAS A TIME OF DARKNESS...
...WHERE THE CITIES OF THE DAMNED WERE STACKED HIGH WITH THE BONES OF FALLEN HEROES.
THE CURRENCY OF THE DAY WAS HOPELESSNESS, AND MONSTROSITIES ROAMED THE EARTH UNBOUND BY BORDERS AND UNMATCHED IN THEIR CRUELTY...
UNTIL...
ZIIIIIIIIIIIIP

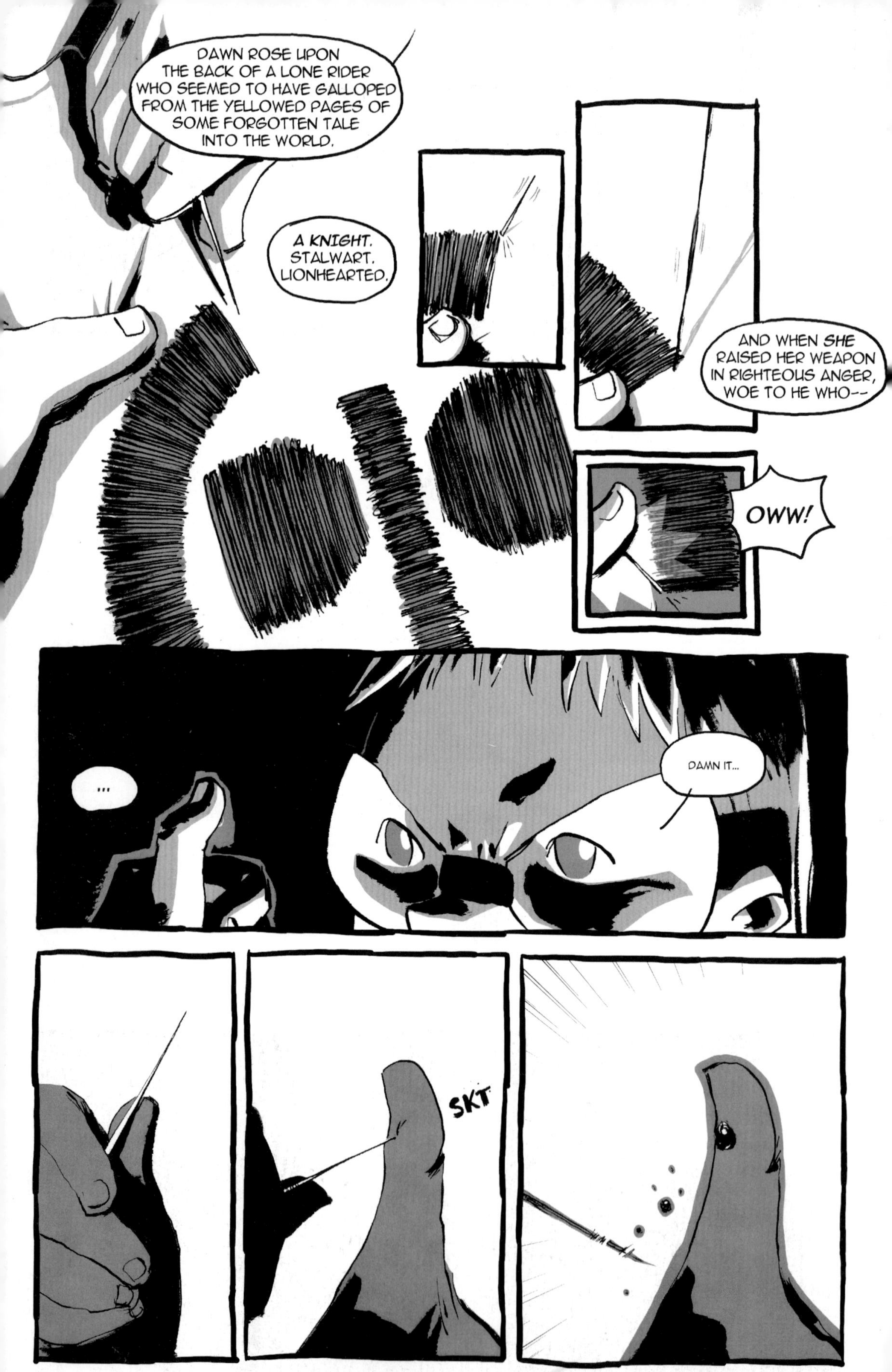
DAWN ROSE UPON THE BACK OF A LONE RIDER WHO SEEMED TO HAVE GALLOPED FROM THE YELLOWED PAGES OF SOME FORGOTTEN TALE INTO THE WORLD.
A KNIGHT. STALWART. LIONHEARTED.
AND WHEN SHE RAISED HER WEAPON IN RIGHTEOUS ANGER, WOE TO HE WHO--
OWW!
...
DAMN IT...
SKT

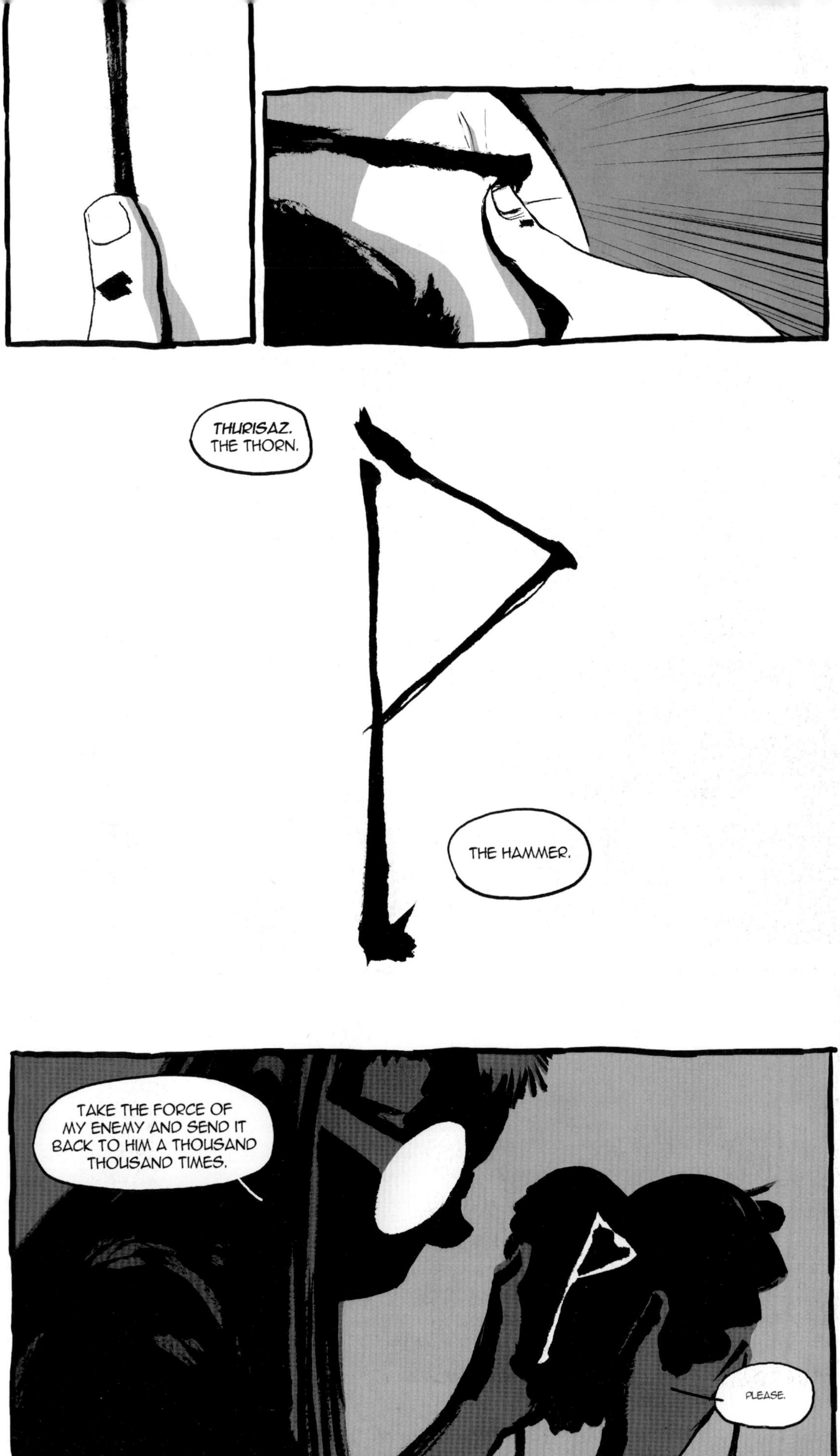
THURISAZ. THE THORN.
THE HAMMER.
TAKE THE FORCE OF MY ENEMY AND SEND IT BACK TO HIM A THOUSAND THOUSAND TIMES.
PLEASE.

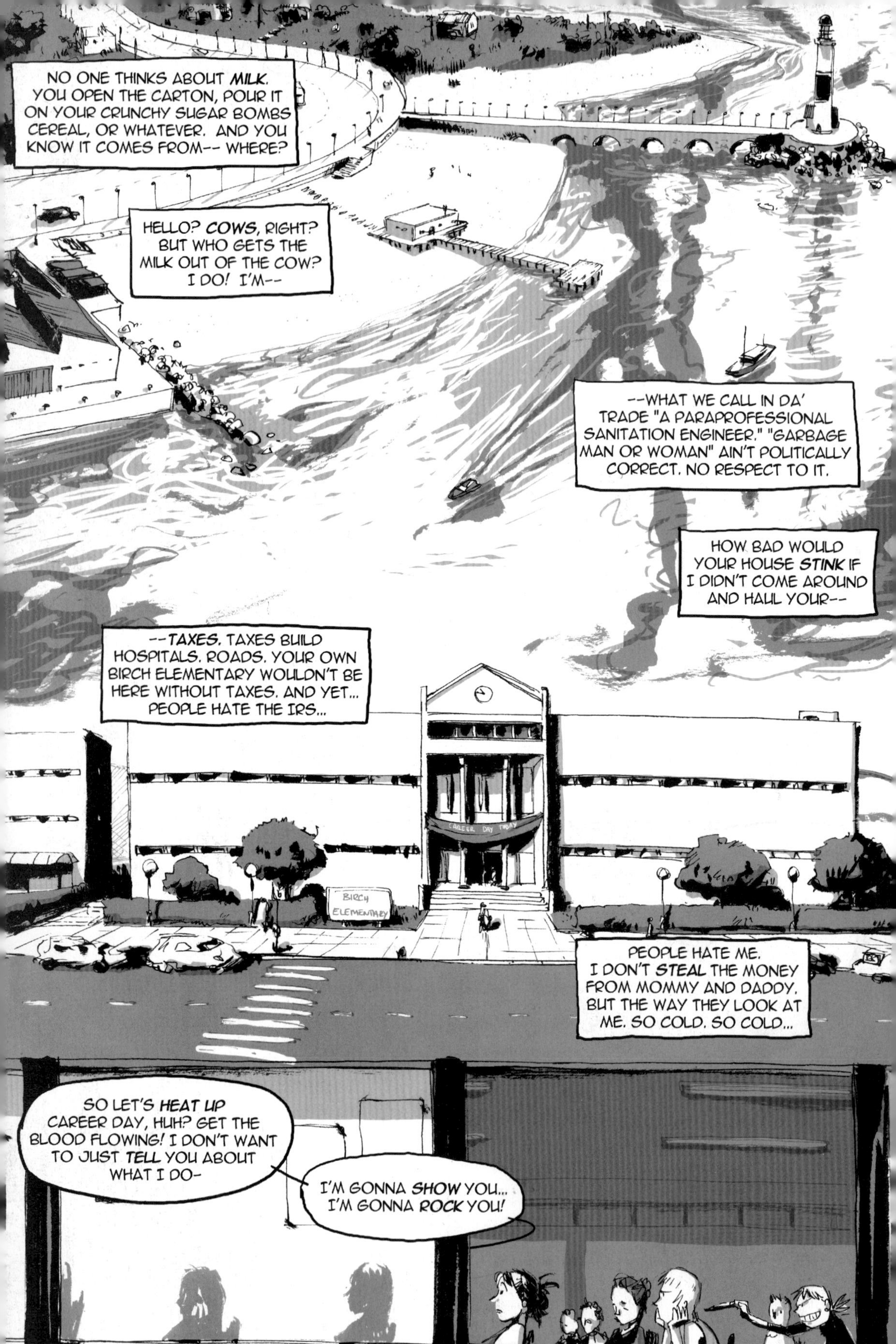
NO ONE THINKS ABOUT MILK. YOU OPEN THE CARTON, POUR IT ON YOUR CRUNCHY SUGAR BOMBS CEREAL, OR WHATEVER. AND YOU KNOW IT COMES FROM-- WHERE?
HELLO? COWS, RIGHT? BUT WHO GETS THE MILK OUT OF THE COW? I DO! I'M--
--WHAT WE CALL IN DA' TRADE "A PARAPROFESSIONAL SANITATION ENGINEER." "GARBAGE MAN OR WOMAN" AIN'T POLITICALLY CORRECT. NO RESPECT TO IT.
HOW BAD WOULD YOUR HOUSE STINK IF I DIDN'T COME AROUND AND HAUL YOUR--
--TAXES. TAXES BUILD HOSPITALS. ROADS. YOUR OWN BIRCH ELEMENTARY WOULDN'T BE HERE WITHOUT TAXES. AND YET... PEOPLE HATE THE IRS...
CAREER DAY TODAY
BIRCH ELEMENTARY
PEOPLE HATE ME. I DON'T STEAL THE MONEY FROM MOMMY AND DADDY, BUT THE WAY THEY LOOK AT ME. SO COLD. SO COLD...
SO LET'S HEAT UP CAREER DAY, HUH? GET THE BLOOD FLOWING! I DON'T WANT TO JUST TELL YOU ABOUT WHAT I DO-
I'M GONNA SHOW YOU... I'M GONNA ROCK YOU!

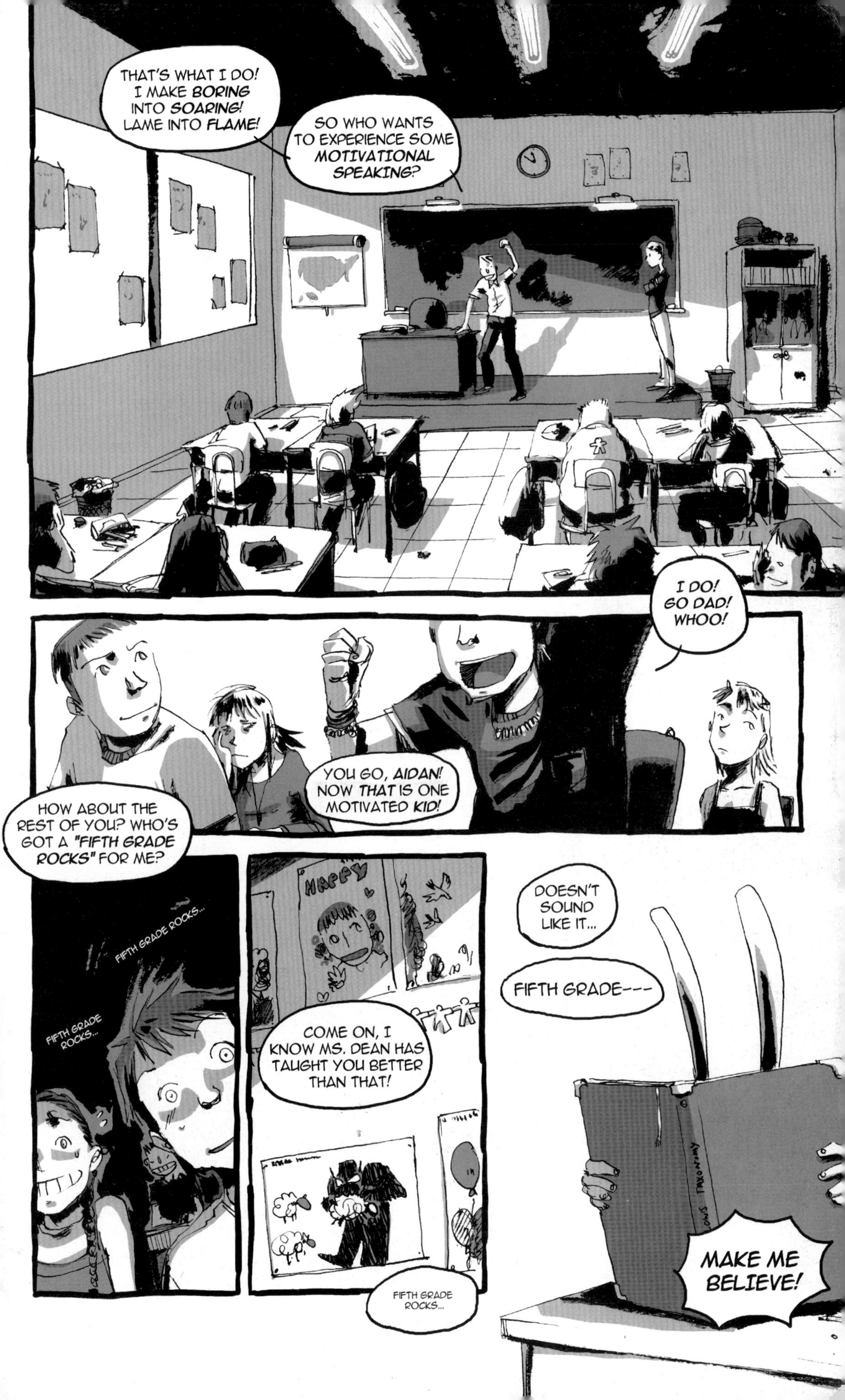
THAT'S WHAT I DO! I MAKE BORING INTO SOARING! LAME INTO FLAME!
SO WHO WANTS TO EXPERIENCE SOME MOTIVATIONAL SPEAKING?
I DO! GO DAD! WHOO!
YOU GO, AIDAN! NOW THAT IS ONE MOTIVATED KID!
HOW ABOUT THE REST OF YOU? WHO'S GOT A "FIFTH GRADE ROCKS" FOR ME?
FIFTH GRADE ROCKS...
FIFTH GRADE ROCKS...
HAPPY
COME ON, I KNOW MS. DEAN HAS TAUGHT YOU BETTER THAN THAT!
FIFTH GRADE ROCKS...
DOESN'T SOUND LIKE IT...
FIFTH GRADE---
MAKE ME BELIEVE!

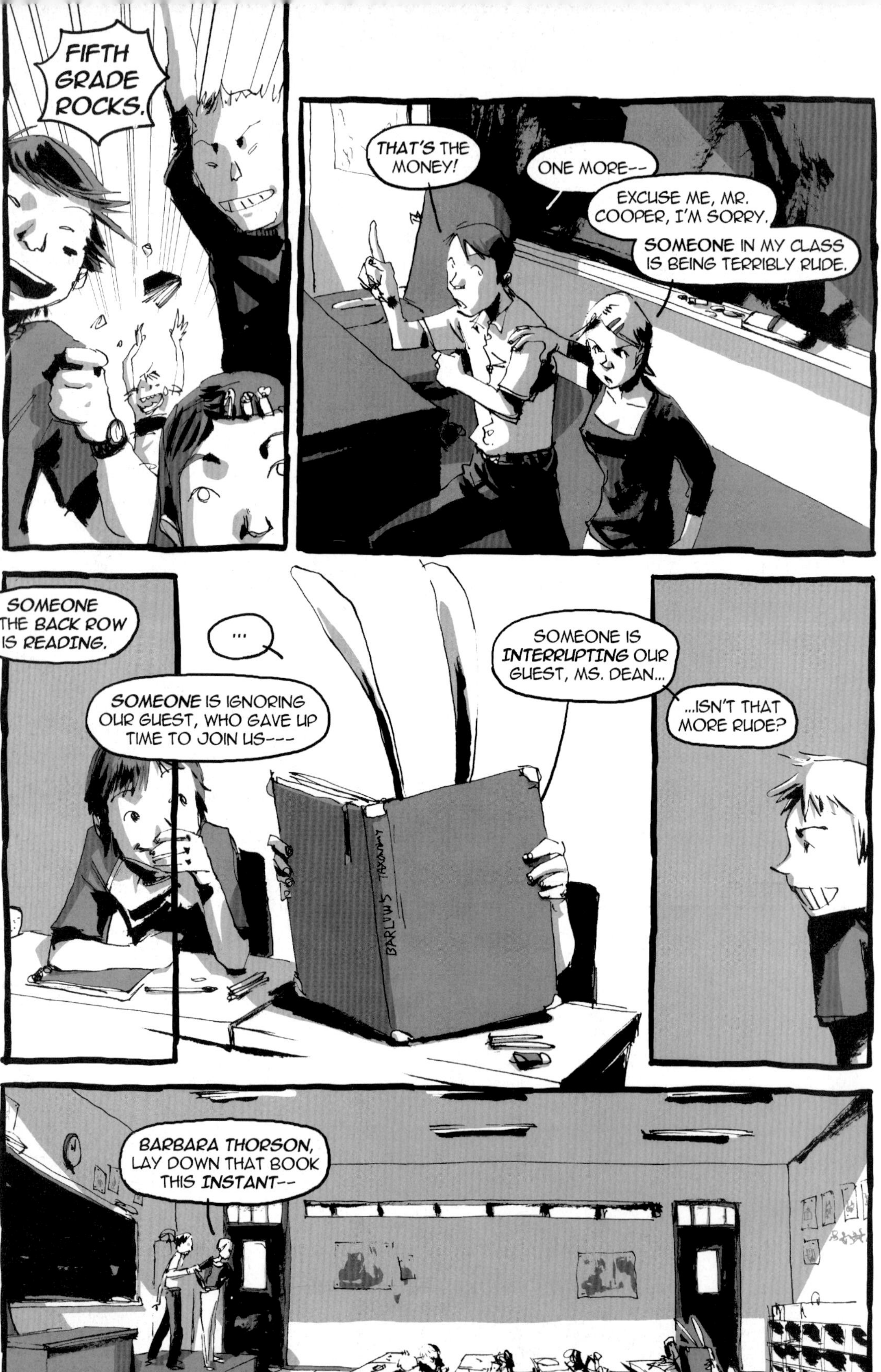
FIFTH GRADE ROCKS.
THAT'S THE MONEY!
ONE MORE--
EXCUSE ME, MR. COOPER, I'M SORRY.
SOMEONE IN MY CLASS IS BEING TERRIBLY RUDE.
SOMEONE IN THE BACK ROW IS READING.
...
SOMEONE IS IGNORING OUR GUEST, WHO GAVE UP TIME TO JOIN US---
SOMEONE IS INTERRUPTING OUR GUEST, MS. DEAN...
...ISN'T THAT MORE RUDE?
BARBARA THORSON, LAY DOWN THAT BOOK THIS INSTANT--
EASY MS. DEAN, IT'S NOT THE FIRST TIME I'VE PLAYED A "TOUGH CROWD."

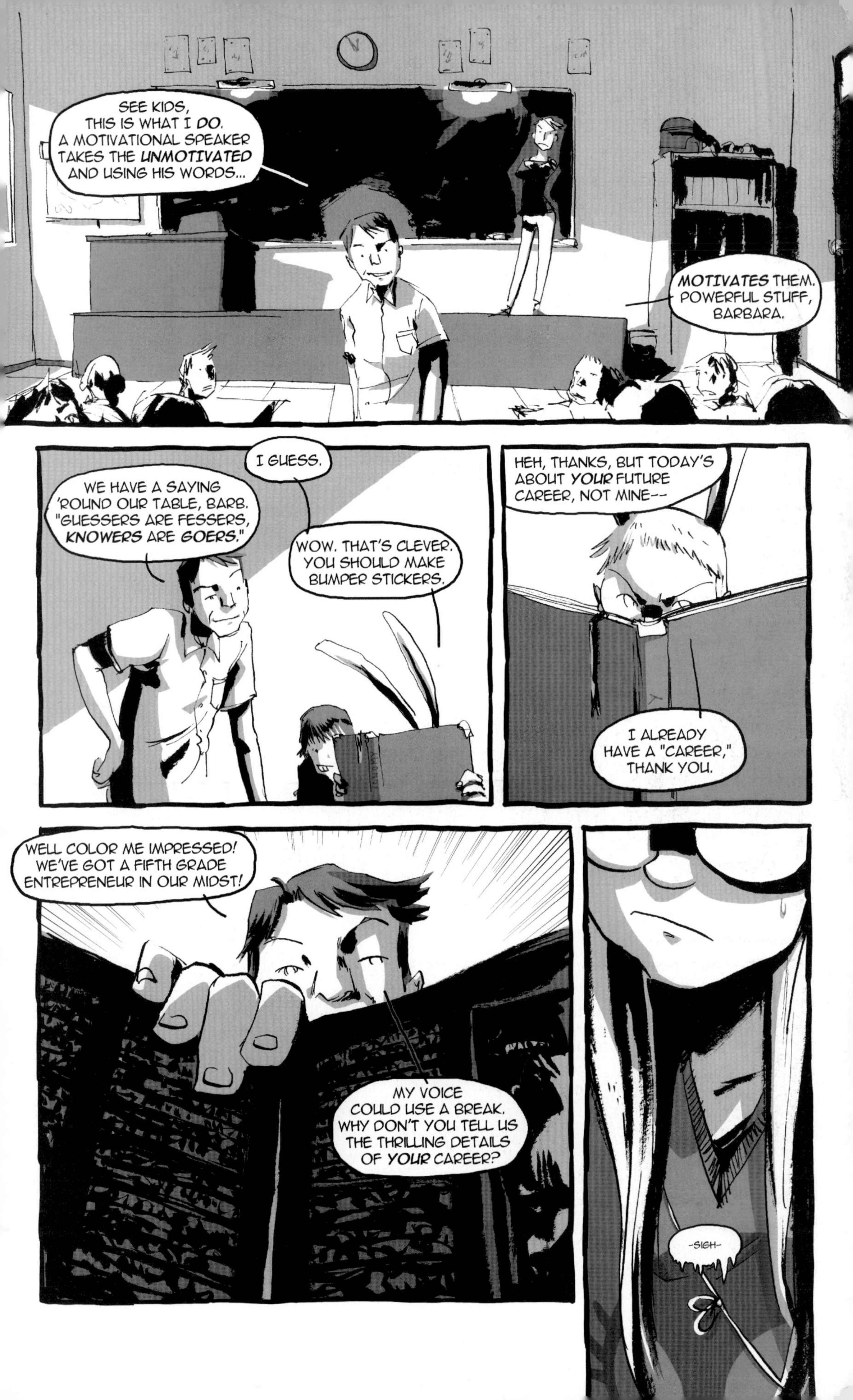
SEE KIDS, THIS IS WHAT I DO. A MOTIVATIONAL SPEAKER TAKES THE UNMOTIVATED AND USING HIS WORDS...
MOTIVATES THEM. POWERFUL STUFF, BARBARA.
I GUESS.
WE HAVE A SAYING 'ROUND OUR TABLE, BARB. "GUESSERS ARE FESSERS, KNOWERS ARE GOERS."
WOW. THAT'S CLEVER. YOU SHOULD MAKE BUMPER STICKERS.
HEH, THANKS, BUT TODAY'S ABOUT YOUR FUTURE CAREER, NOT MINE--
I ALREADY HAVE A "CAREER," THANK YOU.
WELL COLOR ME IMPRESSED! WE'VE GOT A FIFTH GRADE ENTREPRENEUR IN OUR MIDST!
MY VOICE COULD USE A BREAK. WHY DON'T YOU TELL US THE THRILLING DETAILS OF YOUR CAREER?
-SIGH-

IKG CHAPTER 1: THE HAMMER

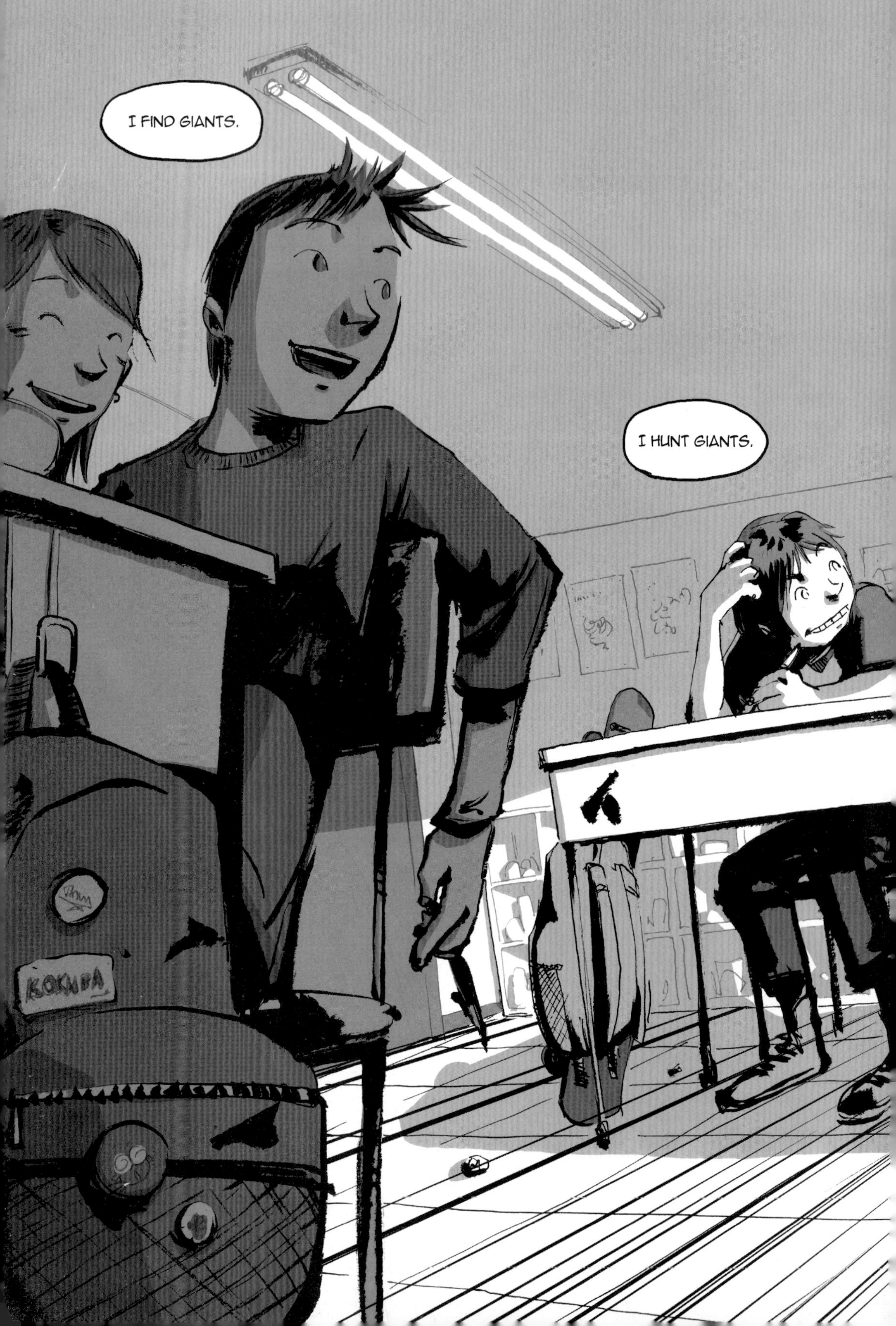
I FIND GIANTS.
I HUNT GIANTS.

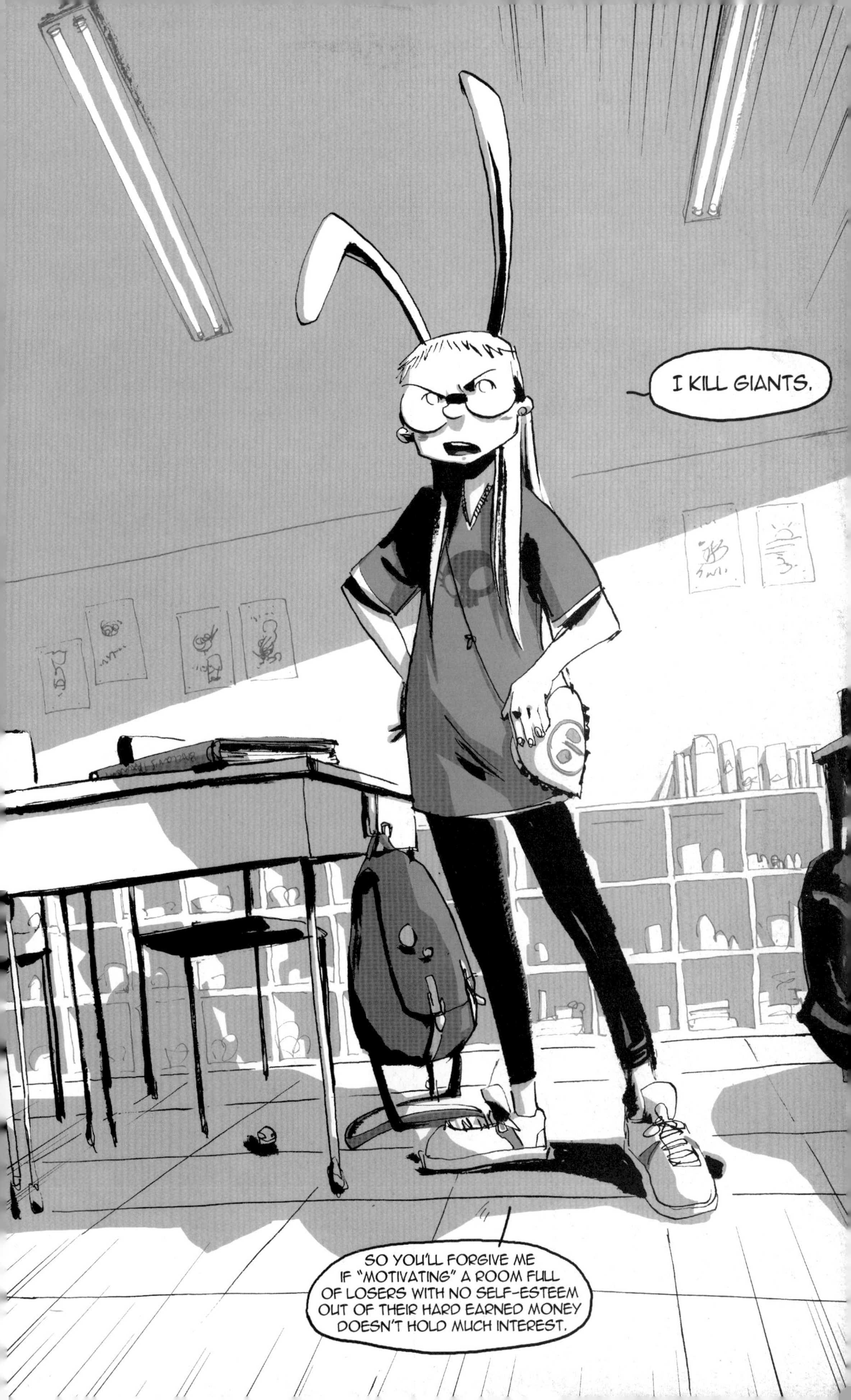
I KILL GIANTS.
SO YOU'LL FORGIVE ME IF "MOTIVATING" A ROOM FULL OF LOSERS WITH NO SELF-ESTEEM OUT OF THEIR HARD EARNED MONEY DOESN'T HOLD MUCH INTEREST.

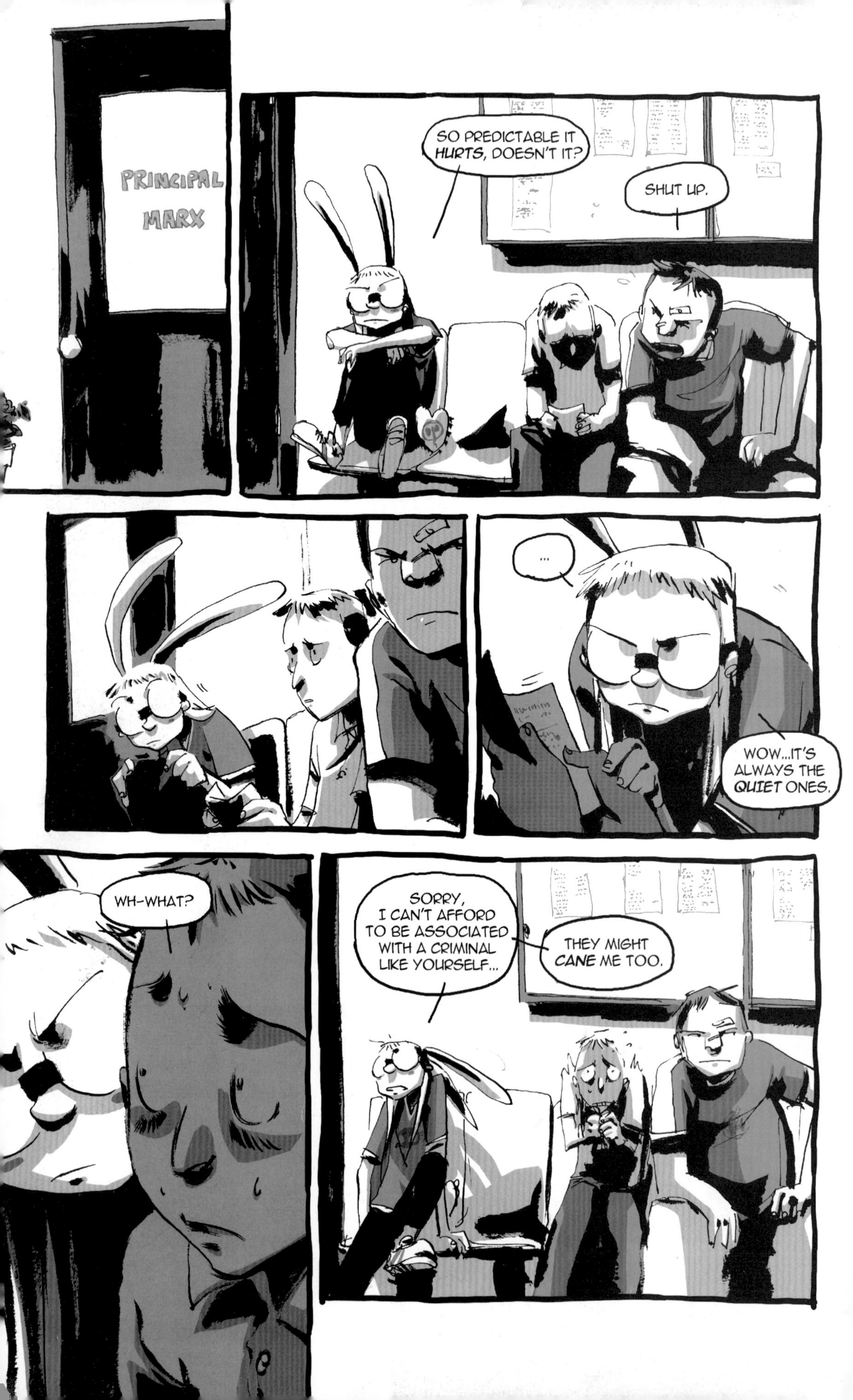
PRINCIPAL MARX
SO PREDICTABLE IT HURTS, DOESN'T IT?
SHUT UP.
...
WOW...IT'S ALWAYS THE QUIET ONES.
WH-WHAT?
SORRY, I CAN'T AFFORD TO BE ASSOCIATED WITH A CRIMINAL LIKE YOURSELF...
THEY MIGHT CANE ME TOO.

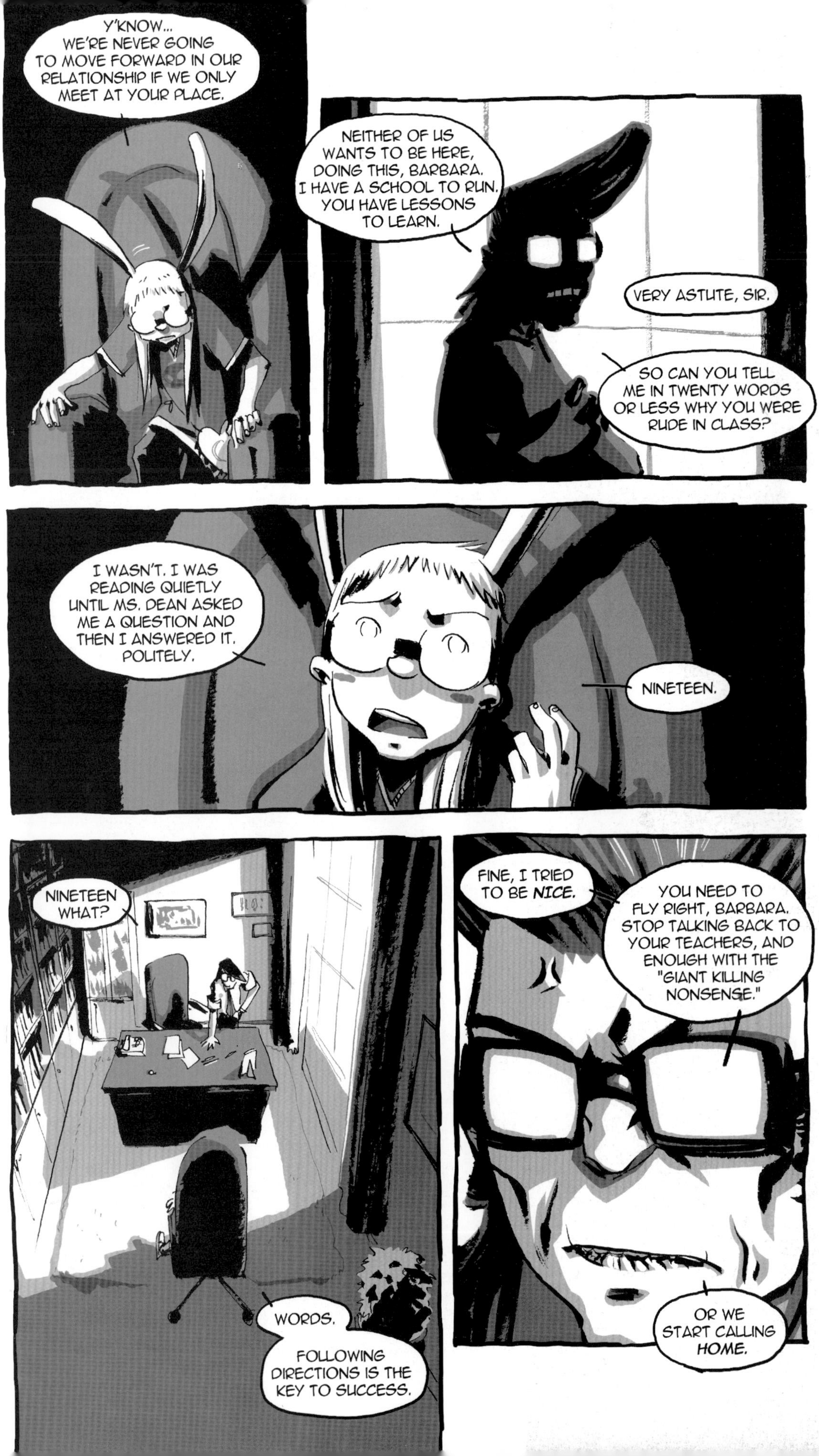
Y'KNOW... WE'RE NEVER GOING TO MOVE FORWARD IN OUR RELATIONSHIP IF WE ONLY MEET AT YOUR PLACE.
NEITHER OF US WANTS TO BE HERE, DOING THIS, BARBARA. I HAVE A SCHOOL TO RUN. YOU HAVE LESSONS TO LEARN.
VERY ASTUTE, SIR.
SO CAN YOU TELL ME IN TWENTY WORDS OR LESS WHY YOU WERE RUDE IN CLASS?
I WASN'T. I WAS READING QUIETLY UNTIL MS. DEAN ASKED ME A QUESTION AND THEN I ANSWERED IT. POLITELY.
NINETEEN.
NINETEEN WHAT?
WORDS.
FOLLOWING DIRECTIONS IS THE KEY TO SUCCESS.
FINE, I TRIED TO BE NICE.
YOU NEED TO FLY RIGHT, BARBARA. STOP TALKING BACK TO YOUR TEACHERS, AND ENOUGH WITH THE "GIANT KILLING NONSENSE."
OR WE START CALLING HOME.

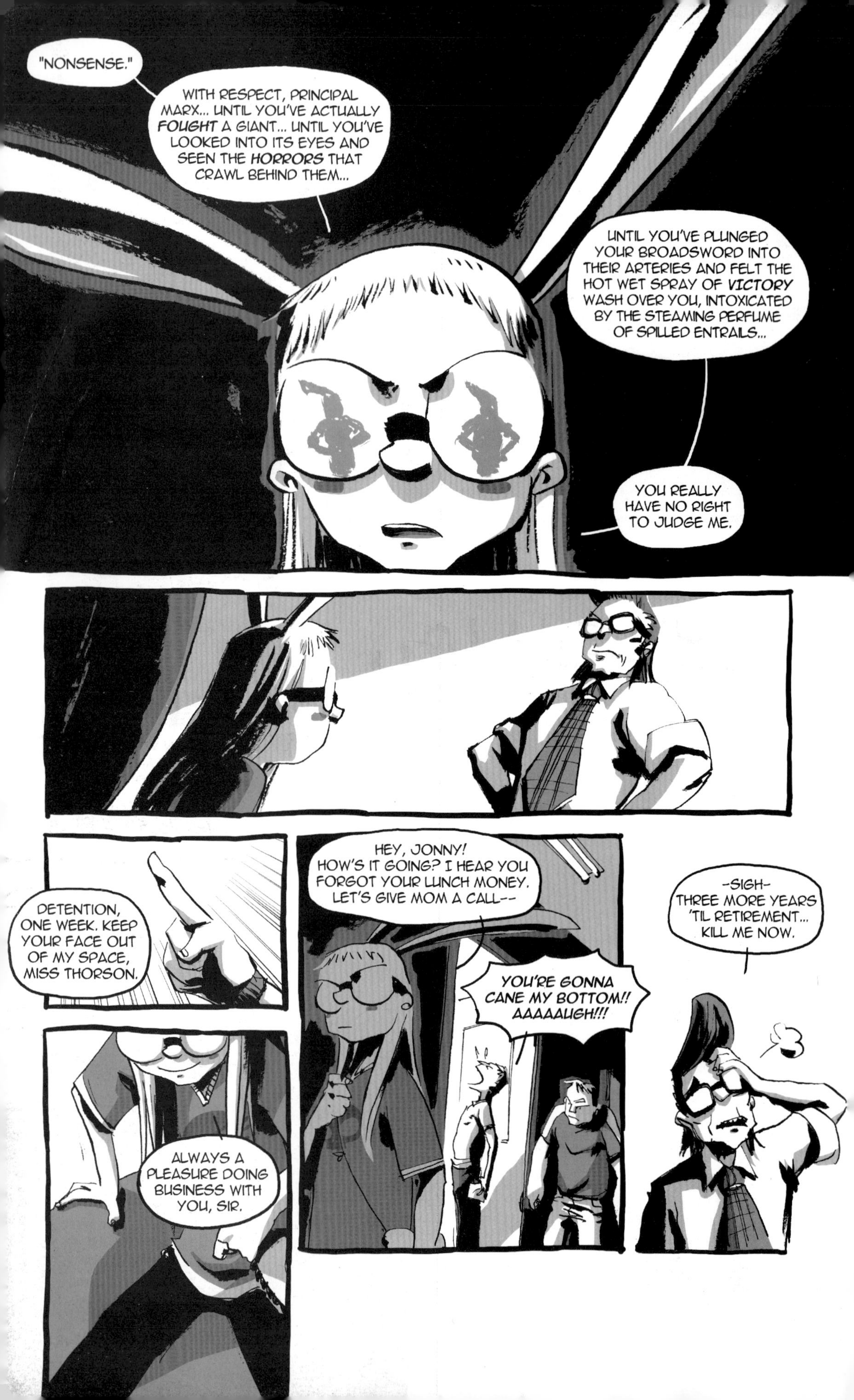
"NONSENSE."
WITH RESPECT, PRINCIPAL MARX... UNTIL YOU'VE ACTUALLY FOUGHT A GIANT... UNTIL YOU'VE LOOKED INTO ITS EYES AND SEEN THE HORRORS THAT CRAWL BEHIND THEM...
UNTIL YOU'VE PLUNGED YOUR BROADSWORD INTO THEIR ARTERIES AND FELT THE HOT WET SPRAY OF VICTORY WASH OVER YOU, INTOXICATED BY THE STEAMING PERFUME OF SPILLED ENTRAILS...
YOU REALLY HAVE NO RIGHT TO JUDGE ME.
DETENTION, ONE WEEK. KEEP YOUR FACE OUT OF MY SPACE, MISS THORSON.
ALWAYS A PLEASURE DOING BUSINESS WITH YOU, SIR.
HEY, JONNY! HOW'S IT GOING? I HEAR YOU FORGOT YOUR LUNCH MONEY. LET'S GIVE MOM A CALL--
YOU'RE GONNA CANE MY BOTTOM!! AAAAAUGH!!!
-SIGH- THREE MORE YEARS 'TIL RETIREMENT... KILL ME NOW.

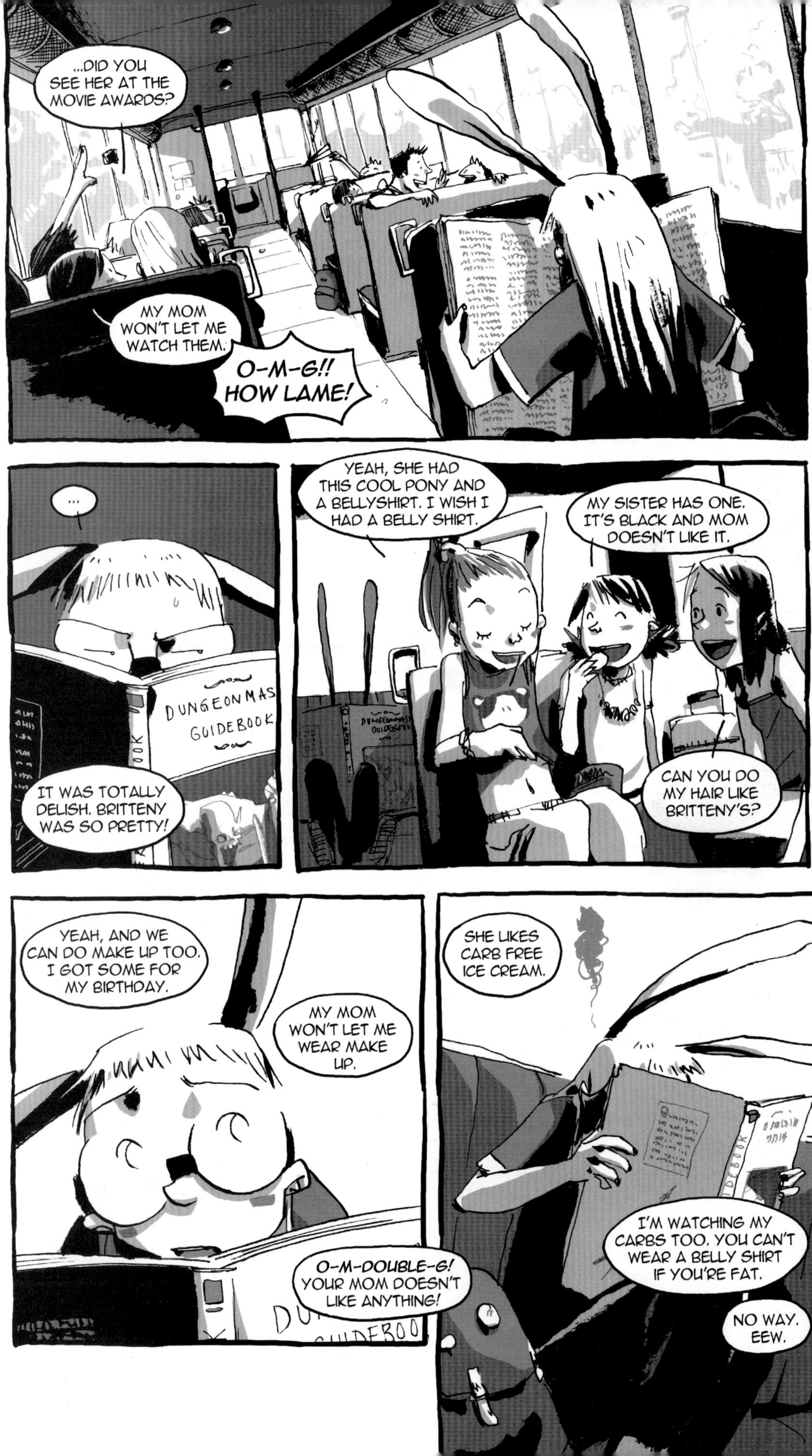
...DID YOU SEE HER AT THE MOVIE AWARDS?
MY MOM WON'T LET ME WATCH THEM.
O-M-G!! HOW LAME!
...
IT WAS TOTALLY DELISH. BRITTENY WAS SO PRETTY!
DUNGEONMAS GUIDEBOOK
YEAH, SHE HAD THIS COOL PONY AND A BELLYSHIRT. I WISH I HAD A BELLY SHIRT.
MY SISTER HAS ONE. IT'S BLACK AND MOM DOESN'T LIKE IT.
CAN YOU DO MY HAIR LIKE BRITTENY'S?
YEAH, AND WE CAN DO MAKE UP TOO. I GOT SOME FOR MY BIRTHDAY.
MY MOM WON'T LET ME WEAR MAKE UP.
O-M-DOUBLE-G! YOUR MOM DOESN'T LIKE ANYTHING!
SHE LIKES CARB FREE ICE CREAM.
I'M WATCHING MY CARBS TOO. YOU CAN'T WEAR A BELLY SHIRT IF YOU'RE FAT.
NO WAY. EEW.

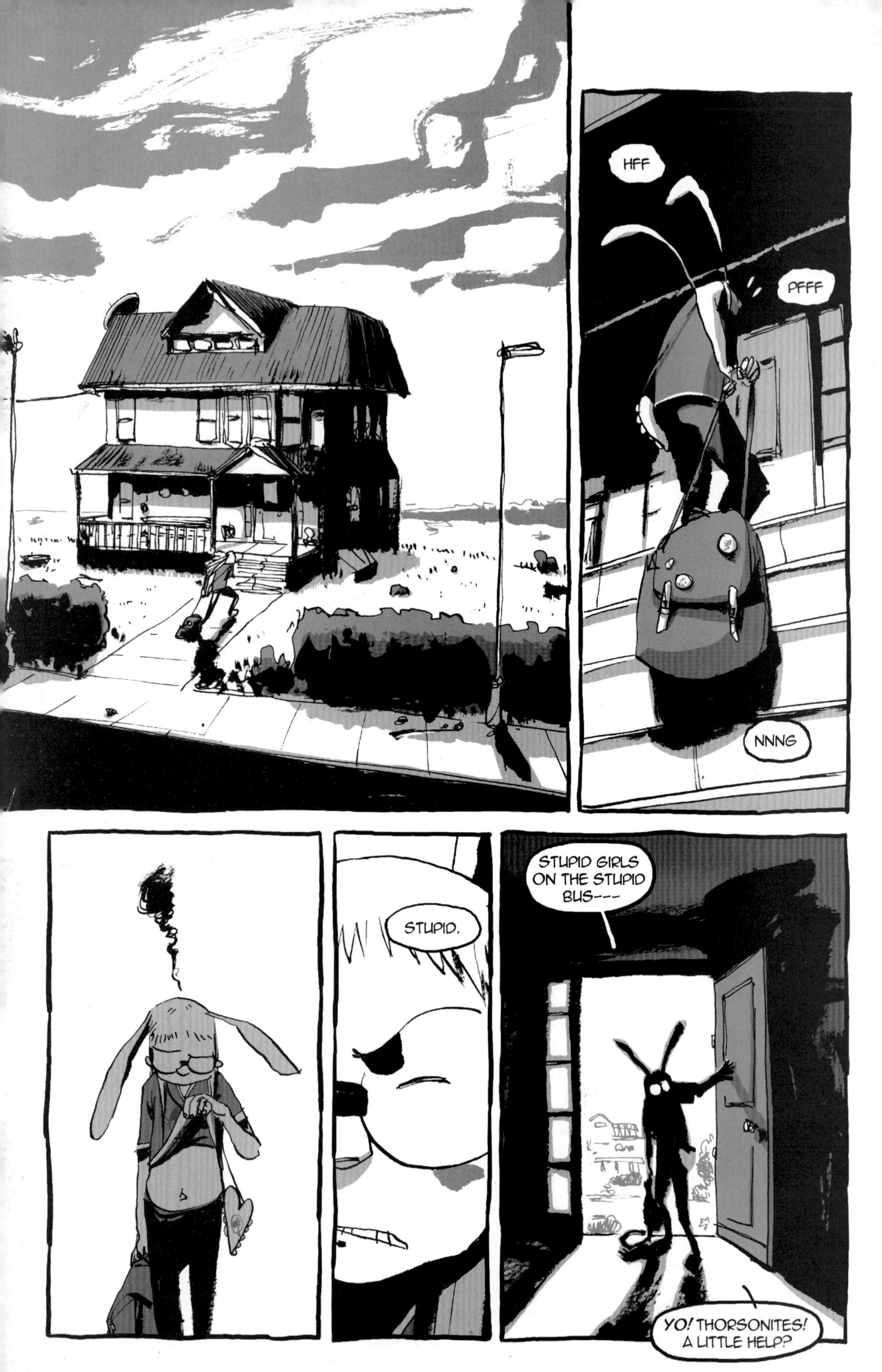
HFF
PFFF
NNNG
STUPID.
STUPID GIRLS ON THE STUPID BUS---
YO! THORSONITES! A LITTLE HELP?

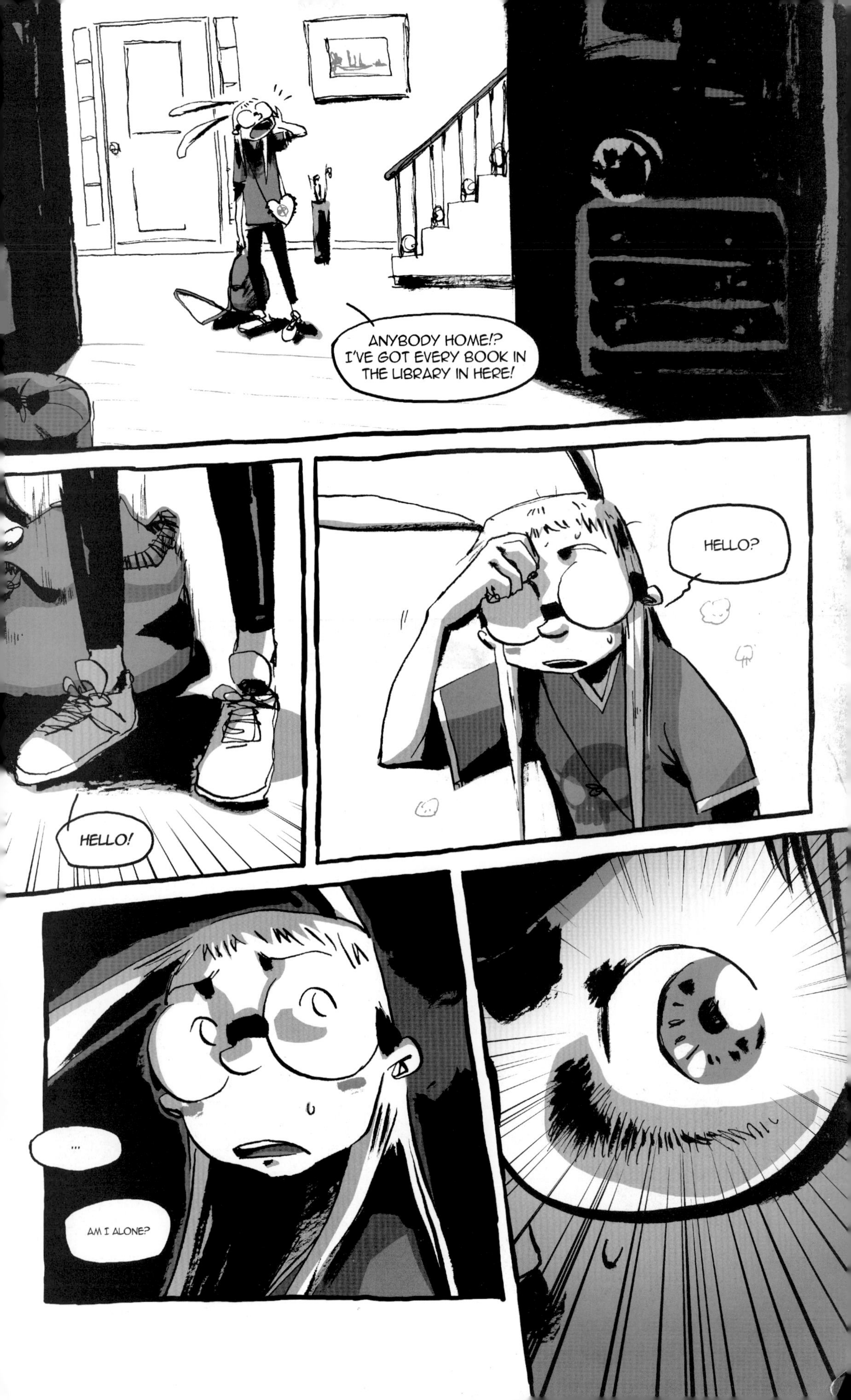
ANYBODY HOME!? I'VE GOT EVERY BOOK IN THE LIBRARY IN HERE!
HELLO!
HELLO?
...
AM I ALONE?

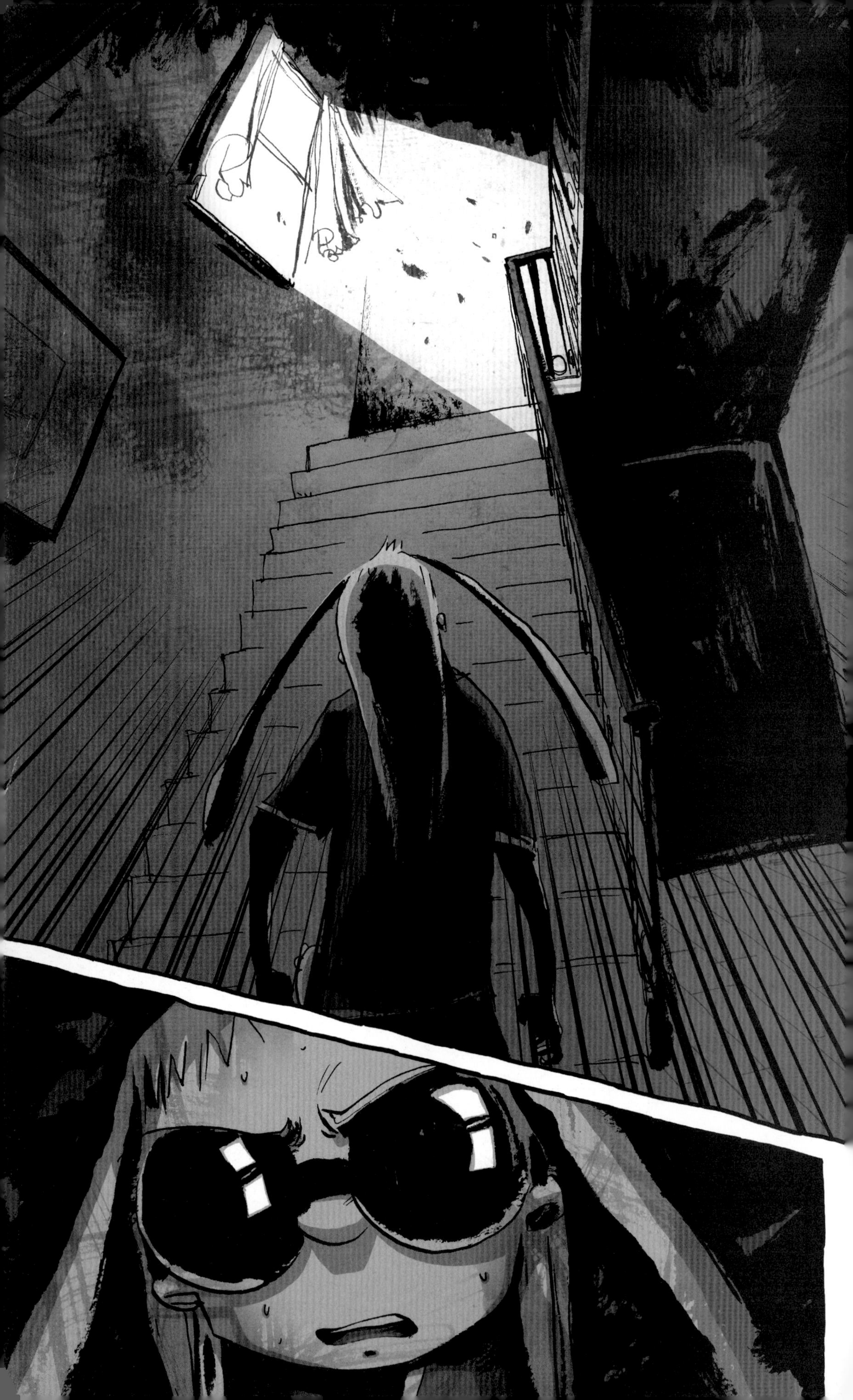

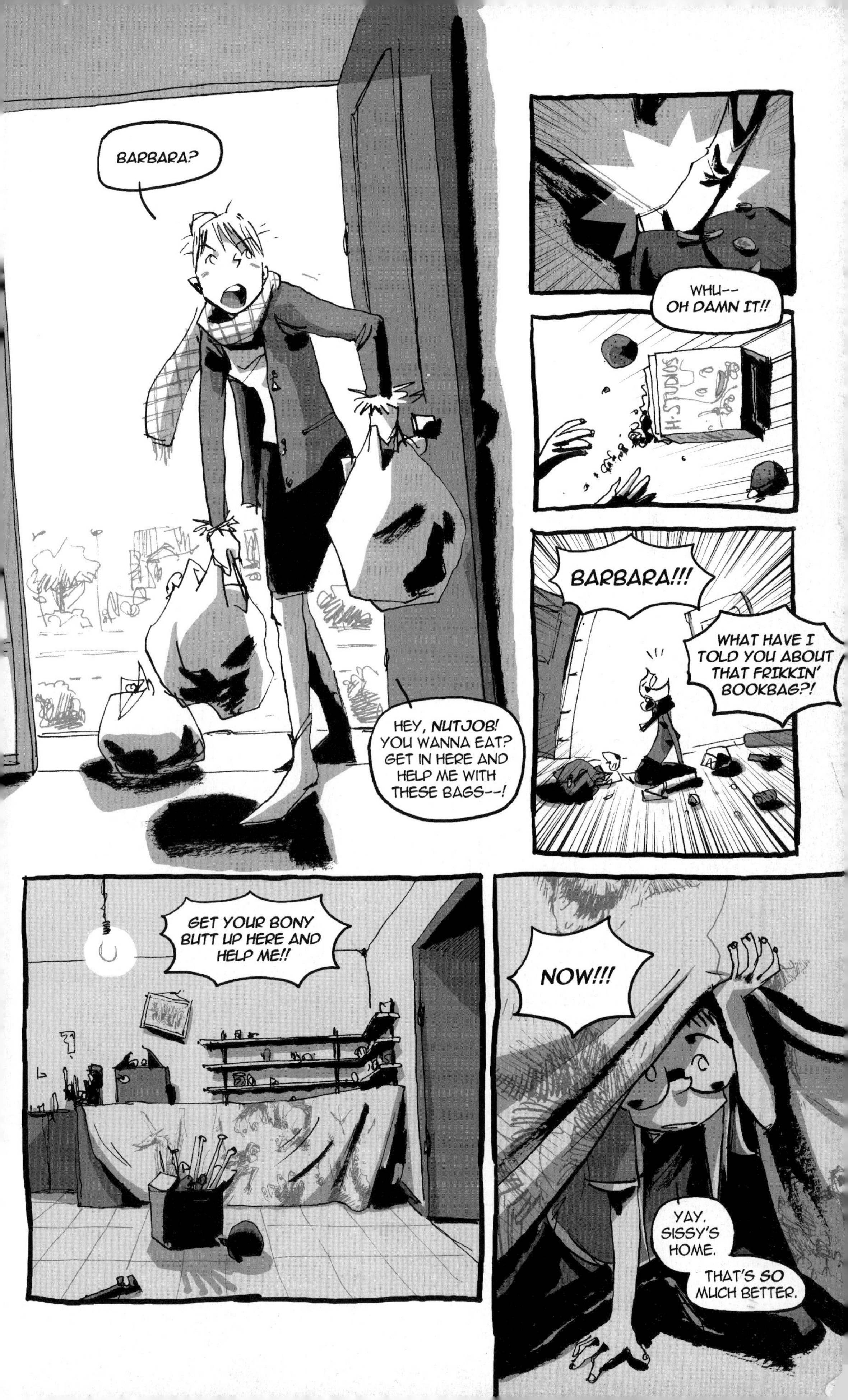
BARBARA?
HEY, NUTJOB! YOU WANNA EAT? GET IN HERE AND HELP ME WITH THESE BAGS--!
WHU-- OH DAMN IT!!
H-STUDIOS
BARBARA!!!
WHAT HAVE I TOLD YOU ABOUT THAT FRIKKIN' BOOKBAG?!
GET YOUR BONY BUTT UP HERE AND HELP ME!!
NOW!!!
YAY. SISSY'S HOME.
THAT'S SO MUCH BETTER.

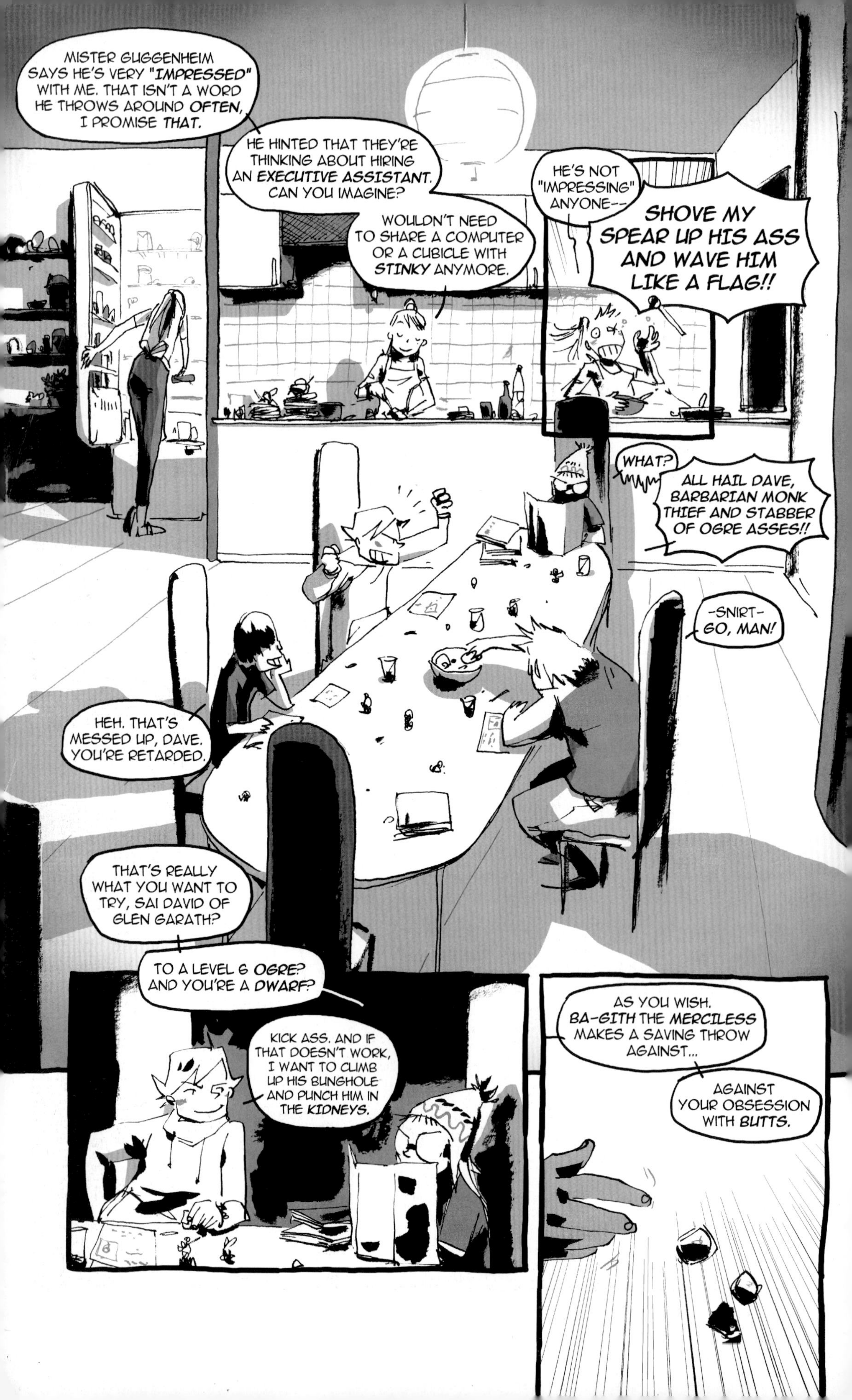

MISTER GUGGENHEIM SAYS HE'S VERY "IMPRESSED" WITH ME. THAT ISN'T A WORD HE THROWS AROUND OFTEN, I PROMISE THAT.
HE HINTED THAT THEY'RE THINKING ABOUT HIRING AN EXECUTIVE ASSISTANT. CAN YOU IMAGINE?
WOULDN'T NEED TO SHARE A COMPUTER OR A CUBICLE WITH STINKY ANYMORE.
HE'S NOT "IMPRESSING" ANYONE--
SHOVE MY SPEAR UP HIS ASS AND WAVE HIM LIKE A FLAG!!
WHAT?
ALL HAIL DAVE, BARBARIAN MONK THIEF AND STABBER OF OGRE ASSES!!
-SNIRT- GO, MAN!
HEH. THAT'S MESSED UP, DAVE. YOU'RE RETARDED.
THAT'S REALLY WHAT YOU WANT TO TRY, SAI DAVID OF GLEN GARATH?
TO A LEVEL 6 OGRE? AND YOU'RE A DWARF?
KICK ASS. AND IF THAT DOESN'T WORK, I WANT TO CLIMB UP HIS BUNGHOLE AND PUNCH HIM IN THE KIDNEYS.
AS YOU WISH. BA-GITH THE MERCILESS MAKES A SAVING THROW AGAINST...
AGAINST YOUR OBSESSION WITH BUTTS.

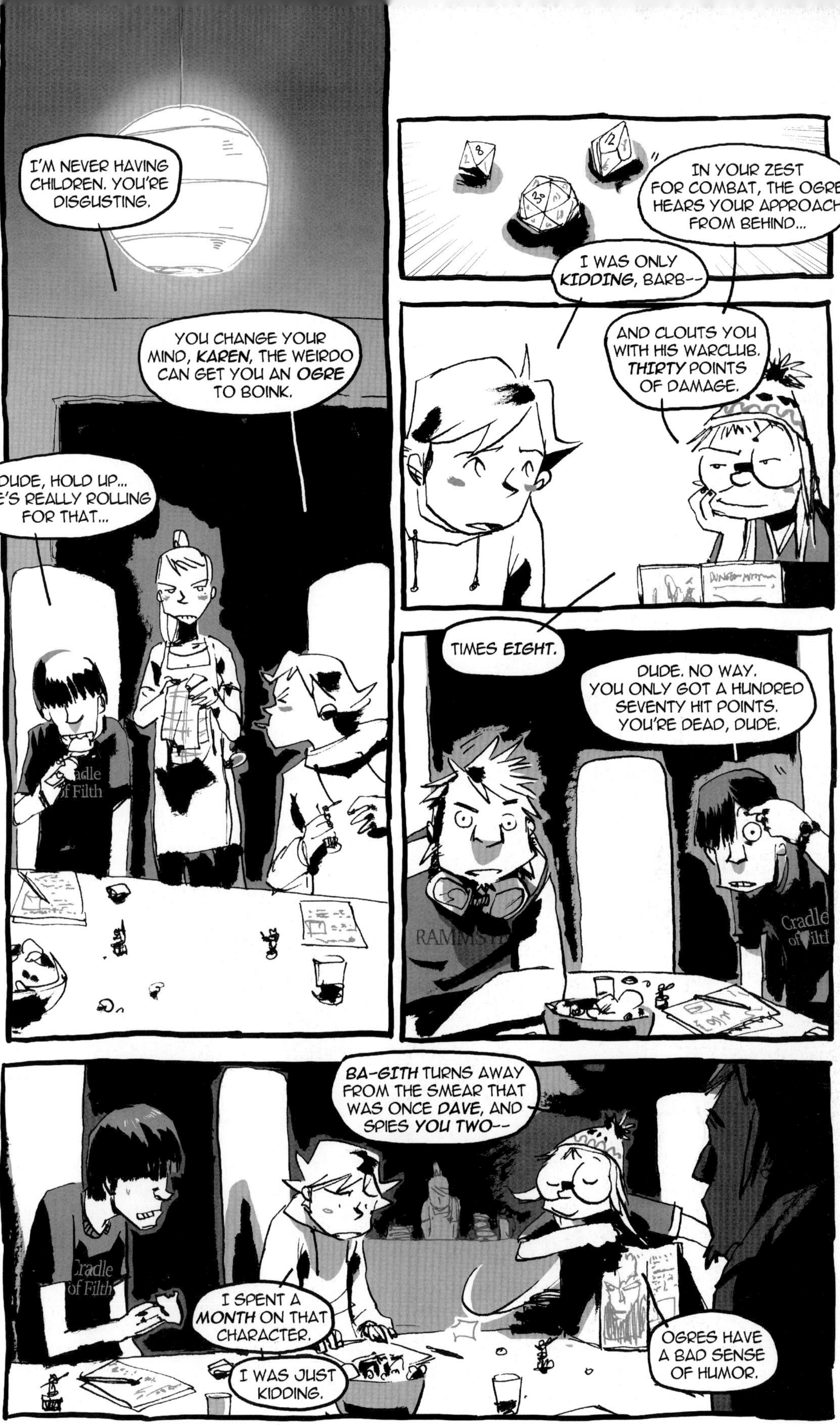
I'M NEVER HAVING CHILDREN. YOU'RE DISGUSTING.
YOU CHANGE YOUR MIND, KAREN, THE WEIRDO CAN GET YOU AN OGRE TO BOINK.
DUDE, HOLD UP... SHE'S REALLY ROLLING FOR THAT...
IN YOUR ZEST FOR COMBAT, THE OGRE HEARS YOUR APPROACH FROM BEHIND...
I WAS ONLY KIDDING, BARB--
AND CLOUTS YOU WITH HIS WARCLUB. THIRTY POINTS OF DAMAGE.
TIMES EIGHT.
DUDE. NO WAY. YOU ONLY GOT A HUNDRED SEVENTY HIT POINTS. YOU'RE DEAD, DUDE.
BA-GITH TURNS AWAY FROM THE SMEAR THAT WAS ONCE DAVE, AND SPIES YOU TWO--
I SPENT A MONTH ON THAT CHARACTER.
I WAS JUST KIDDING.
OGRES HAVE A BAD SENSE OF HUMOR.

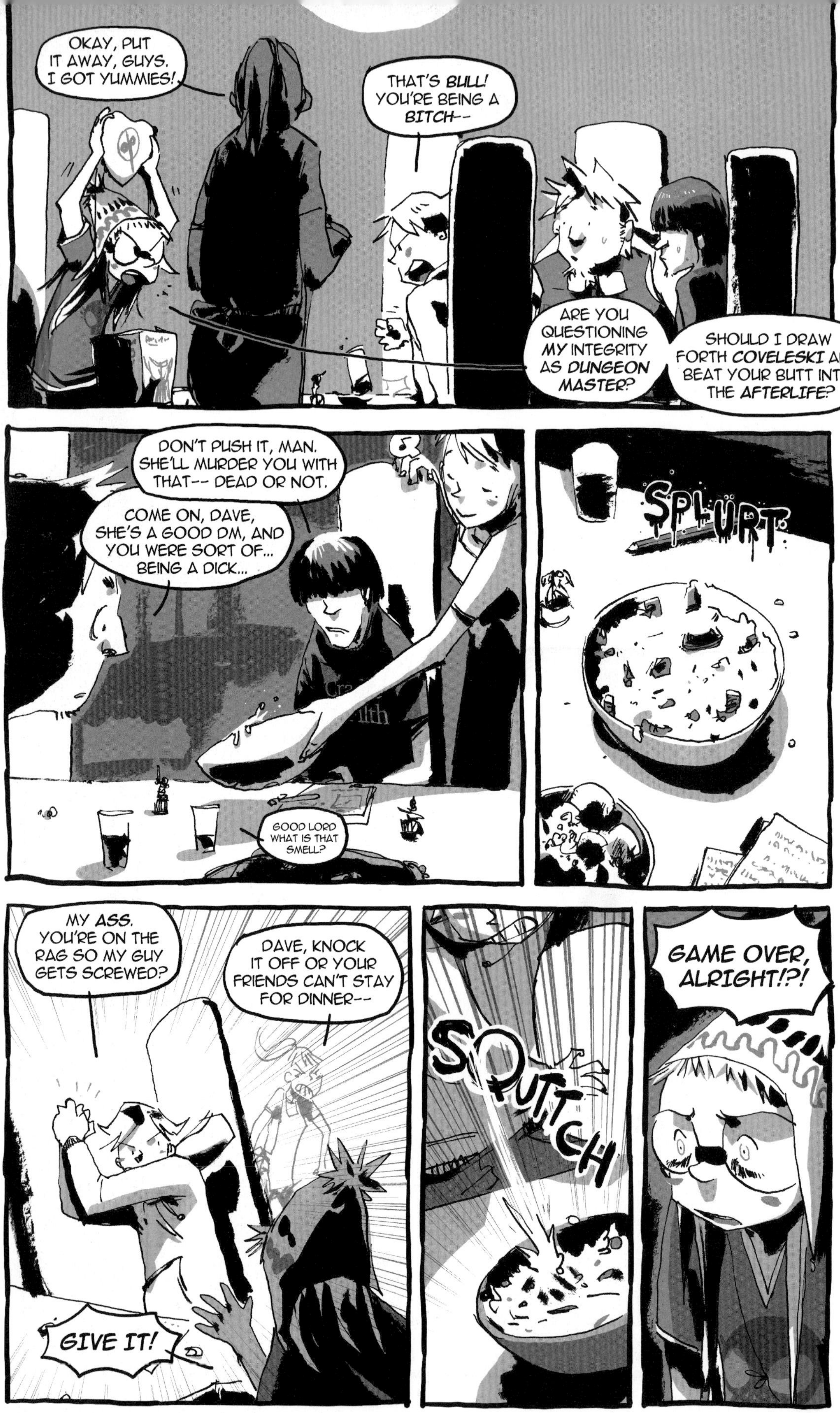
OKAY, PUT IT AWAY, GUYS. I GOT YUMMIES!
THAT'S BULL! YOU'RE BEING A BITCH--
ARE YOU QUESTIONING MY INTEGRITY AS DUNGEON MASTER?
SHOULD I DRAW FORTH COVELESKI AND BEAT YOUR BUTT INTO THE AFTERLIFE?
DON'T PUSH IT, MAN. SHE'LL MURDER YOU WITH THAT-- DEAD OR NOT.
COME ON, DAVE, SHE'S A GOOD DM, AND YOU WERE SORT OF... BEING A DICK...
GOOD LORD WHAT IS THAT SMELL?
SPLÜRT
MY ASS. YOU'RE ON THE RAG SO MY GUY GETS SCREWED?
DAVE, KNOCK IT OFF OR YOUR FRIENDS CAN'T STAY FOR DINNER--
GIVE IT!
SPUTTCH
GAME OVER, ALRIGHT!?!

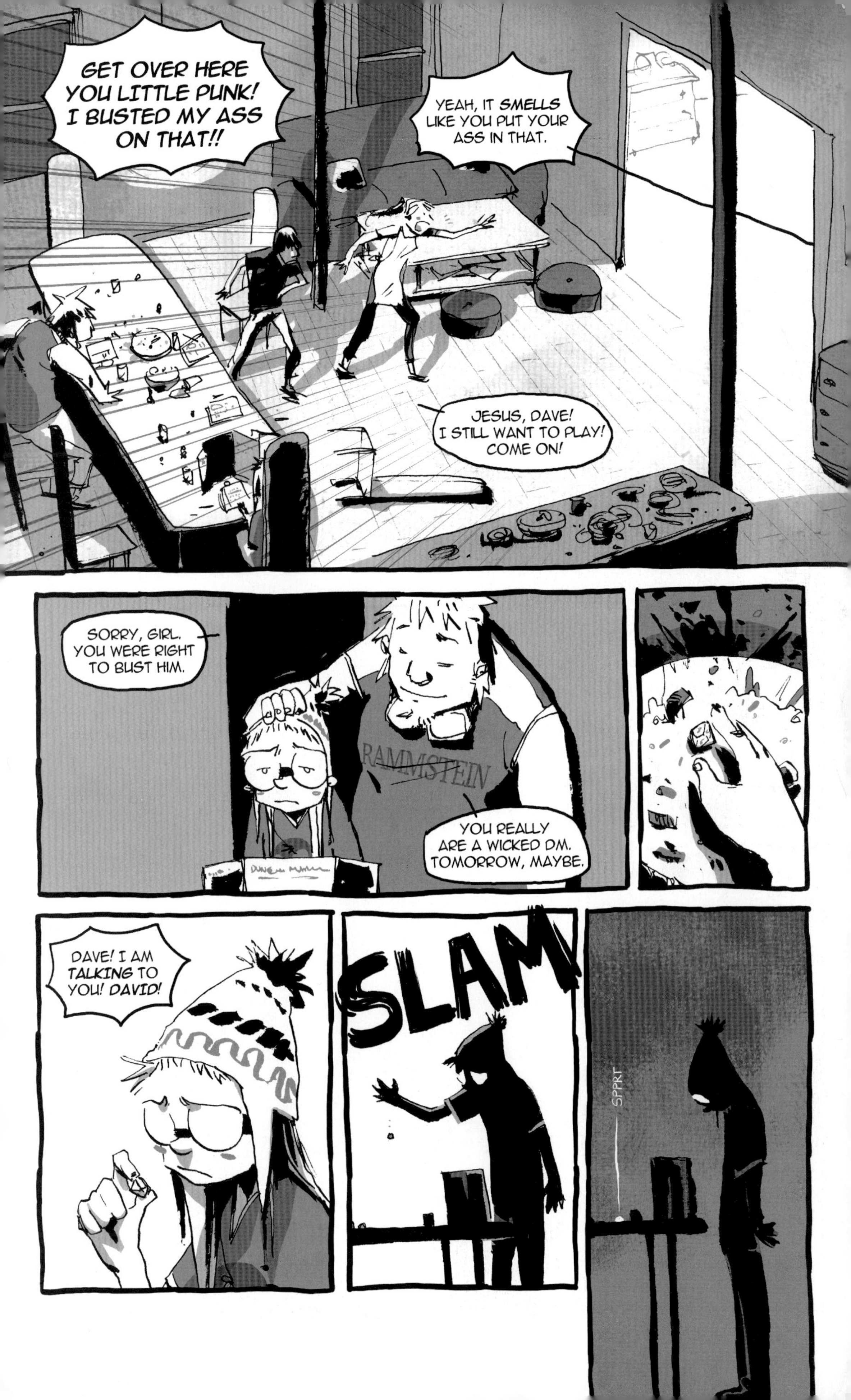
GET OVER HERE YOU LITTLE PUNK! I BUSTED MY ASS ON THAT!!
YEAH, IT SMELLS LIKE YOU PUT YOUR ASS IN THAT.
JESUS, DAVE! I STILL WANT TO PLAY! COME ON!
SORRY, GIRL. YOU WERE RIGHT TO BUST HIM.
RAMMSTEIN
YOU REALLY ARE A WICKED DM. TOMORROW, MAYBE.
DAVE! I AM TALKING TO YOU! DAVID!
SLAM
SPPRT

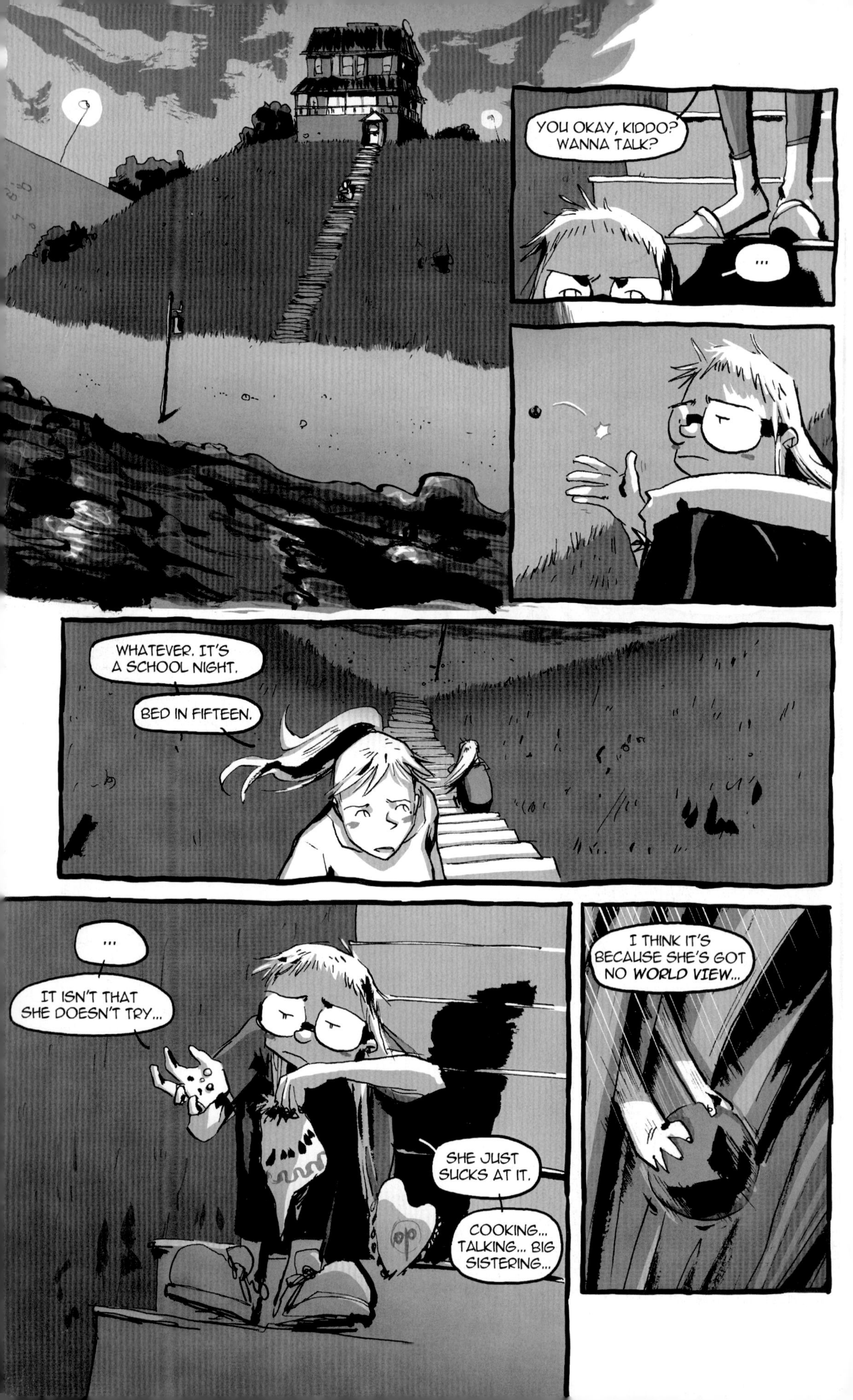
YOU OKAY, KIDDO? WANNA TALK?
...
WHATEVER. IT'S A SCHOOL NIGHT.
BED IN FIFTEEN.
...
IT ISN'T THAT SHE DOESN'T TRY...
SHE JUST SUCKS AT IT.
COOKING... TALKING... BIG SISTERING...
I THINK IT'S BECAUSE SHE'S GOT NO *WORLD VIEW*...

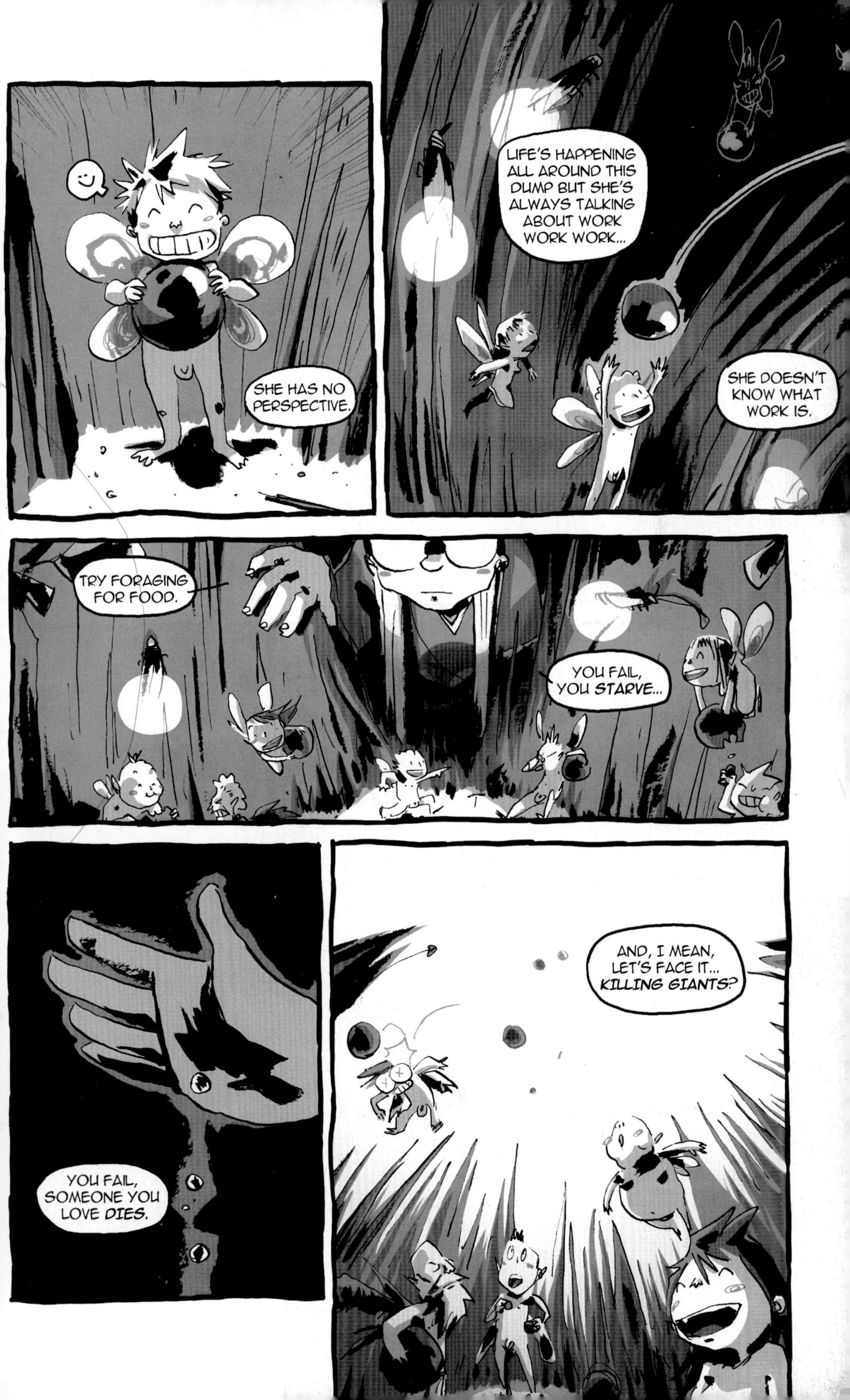
SHE HAS NO PERSPECTIVE.
LIFE'S HAPPENING ALL AROUND THIS DUMP BUT SHE'S ALWAYS TALKING ABOUT WORK WORK WORK...
SHE DOESN'T KNOW WHAT WORK IS.
TRY FORAGING FOR FOOD.
YOU FAIL, YOU STARVE...
YOU FAIL, SOMEONE YOU LOVE DIES.
AND, I MEAN, LET'S FACE IT... KILLING GIANTS?

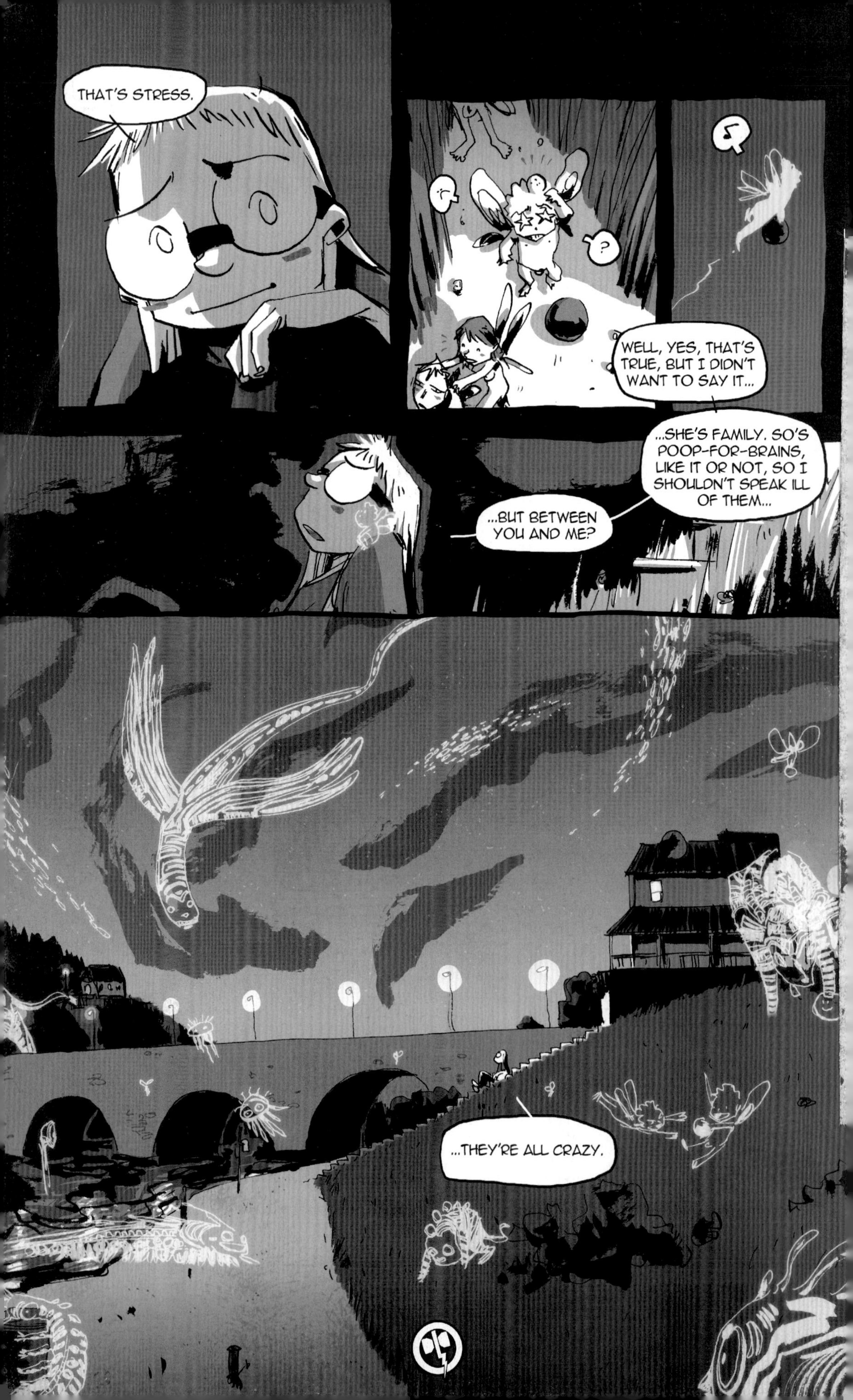

THAT'S STRESS.
WELL, YES, THAT'S TRUE, BUT I DIDN'T WANT TO SAY IT...
...SHE'S FAMILY. SO'S POOP-FOR-BRAINS, LIKE IT OR NOT, SO I SHOULDN'T SPEAK ILL OF THEM...
...BUT BETWEEN YOU AND ME?
...THEY'RE ALL CRAZY.

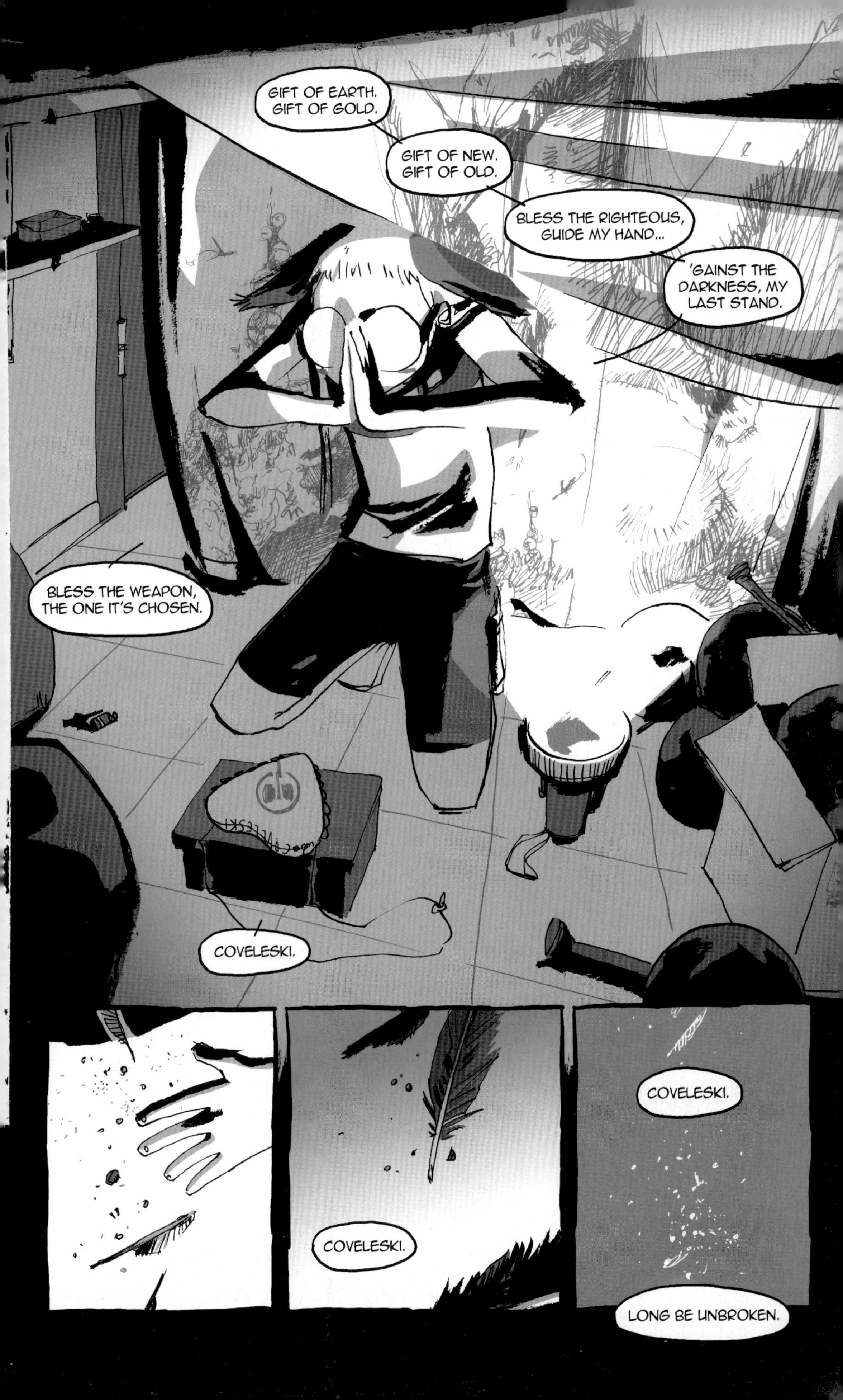
GIFT OF EARTH. GIFT OF GOLD.
GIFT OF NEW. GIFT OF OLD.
BLESS THE RIGHTEOUS, GUIDE MY HAND...
'GAINST THE DARKNESS, MY LAST STAND.
BLESS THE WEAPON, THE ONE IT'S CHOSEN.
COVELESKI.
COVELESKI.
COVELESKI.
LONG BE UNBROKEN.

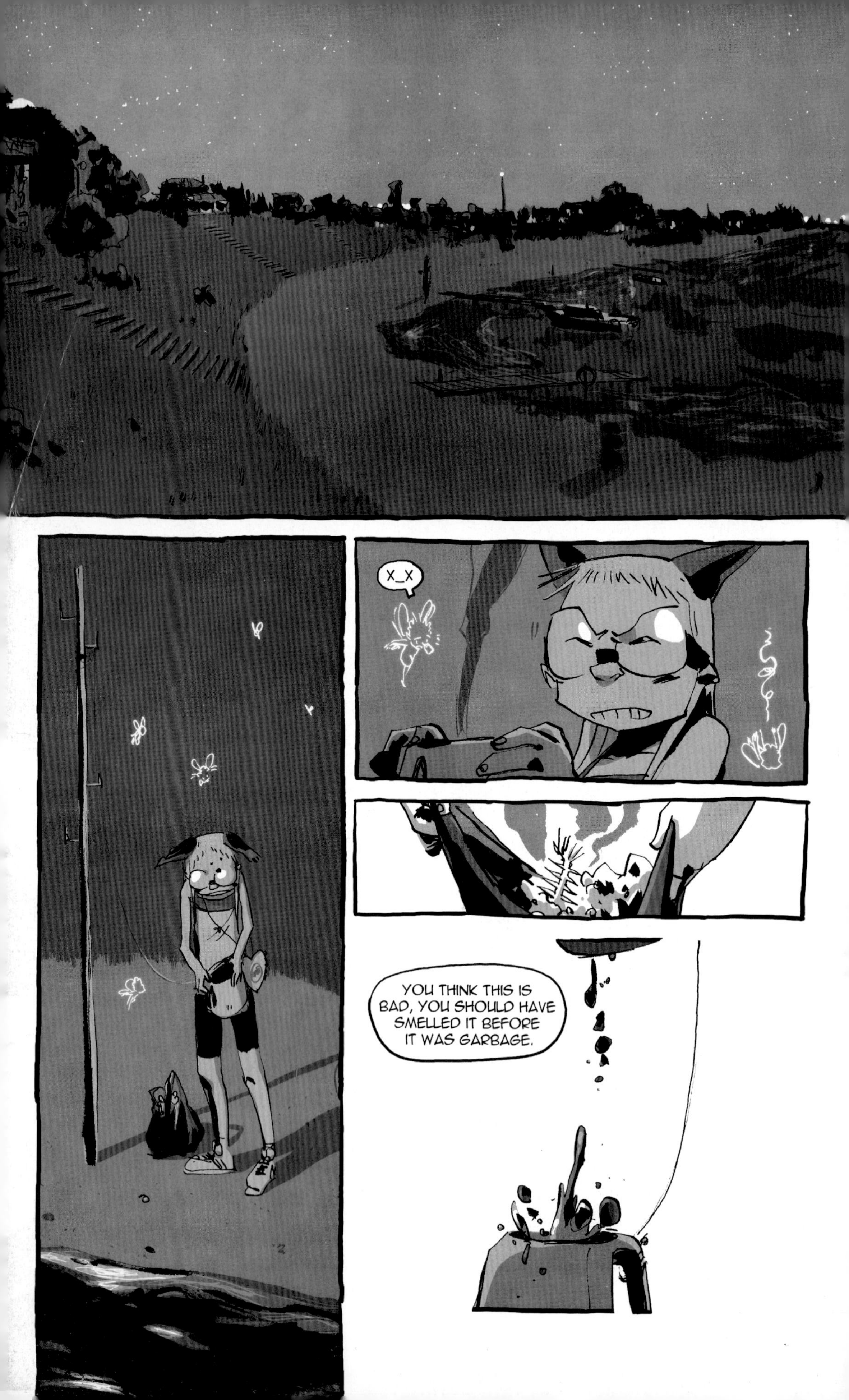
X_X
YOU THINK THIS IS BAD, YOU SHOULD HAVE SMELLED IT BEFORE IT WAS GARBAGE.

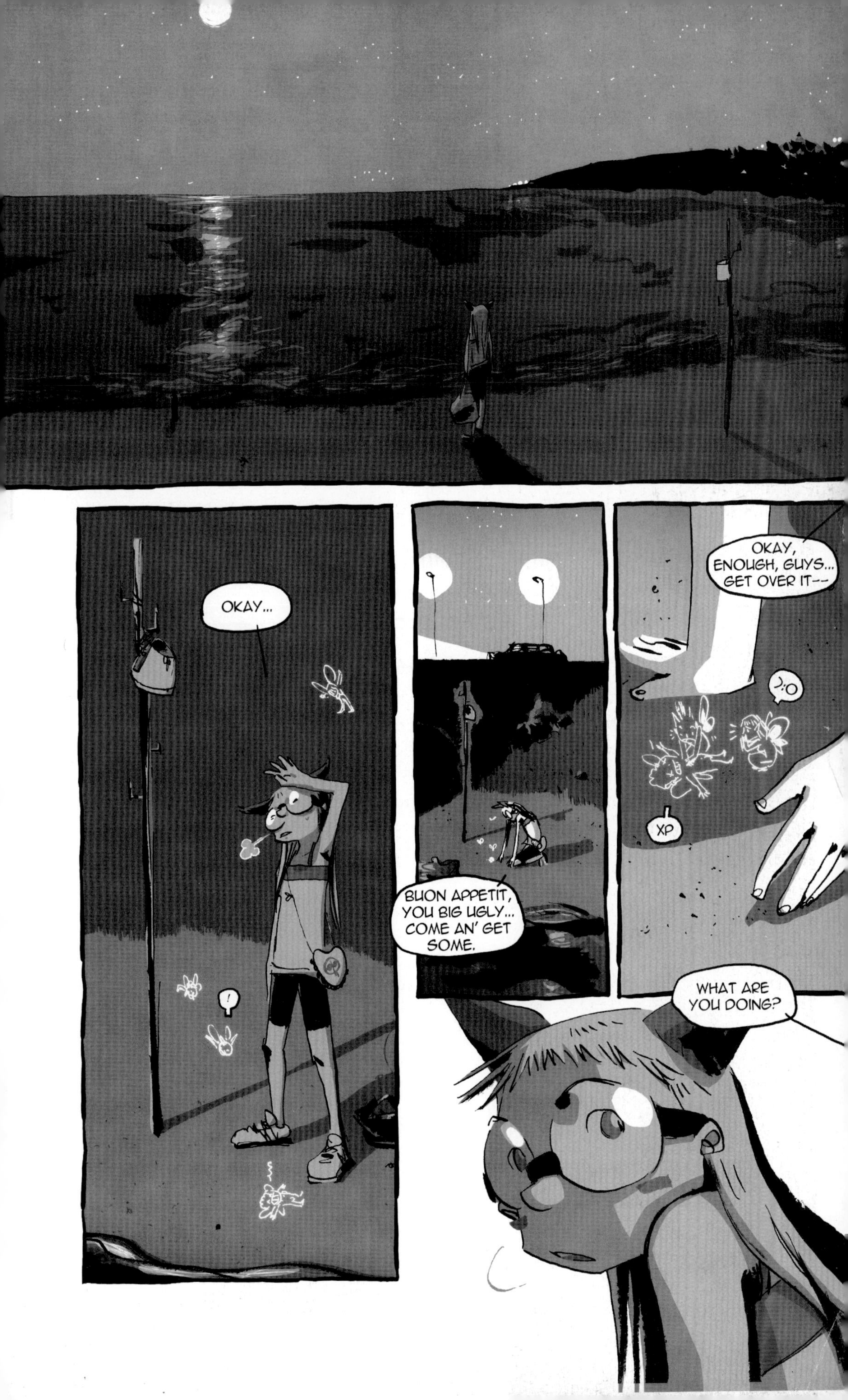
OKAY...
!
BUON APPETIT, YOU BIG UGLY... COME AN' GET SOME.
OKAY, ENOUGH, GUYS... GET OVER IT--
>:O
XP
WHAT ARE YOU DOING?

IKG CHAPTER 2: THE SPARK

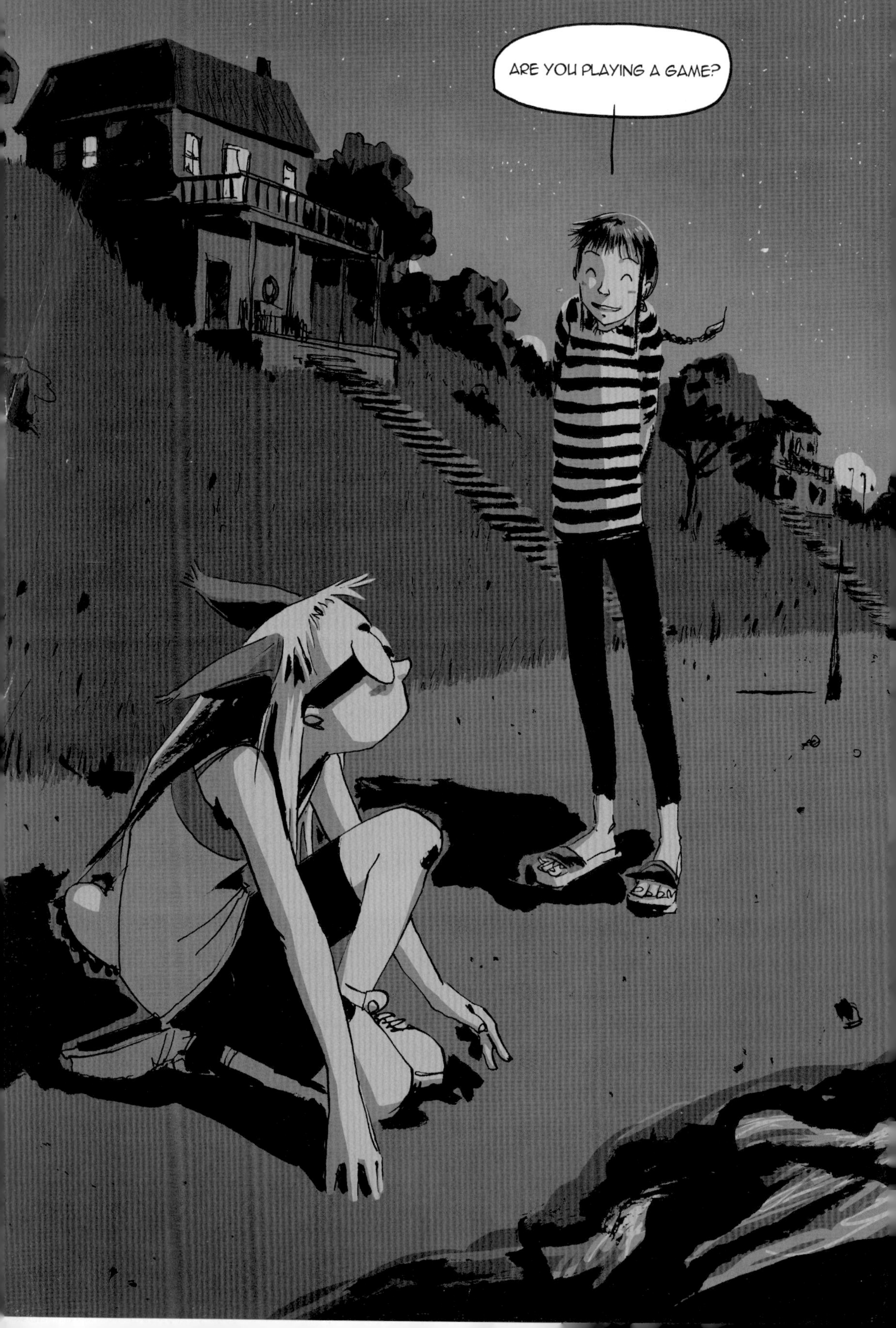
ARE YOU PLAYING A GAME?

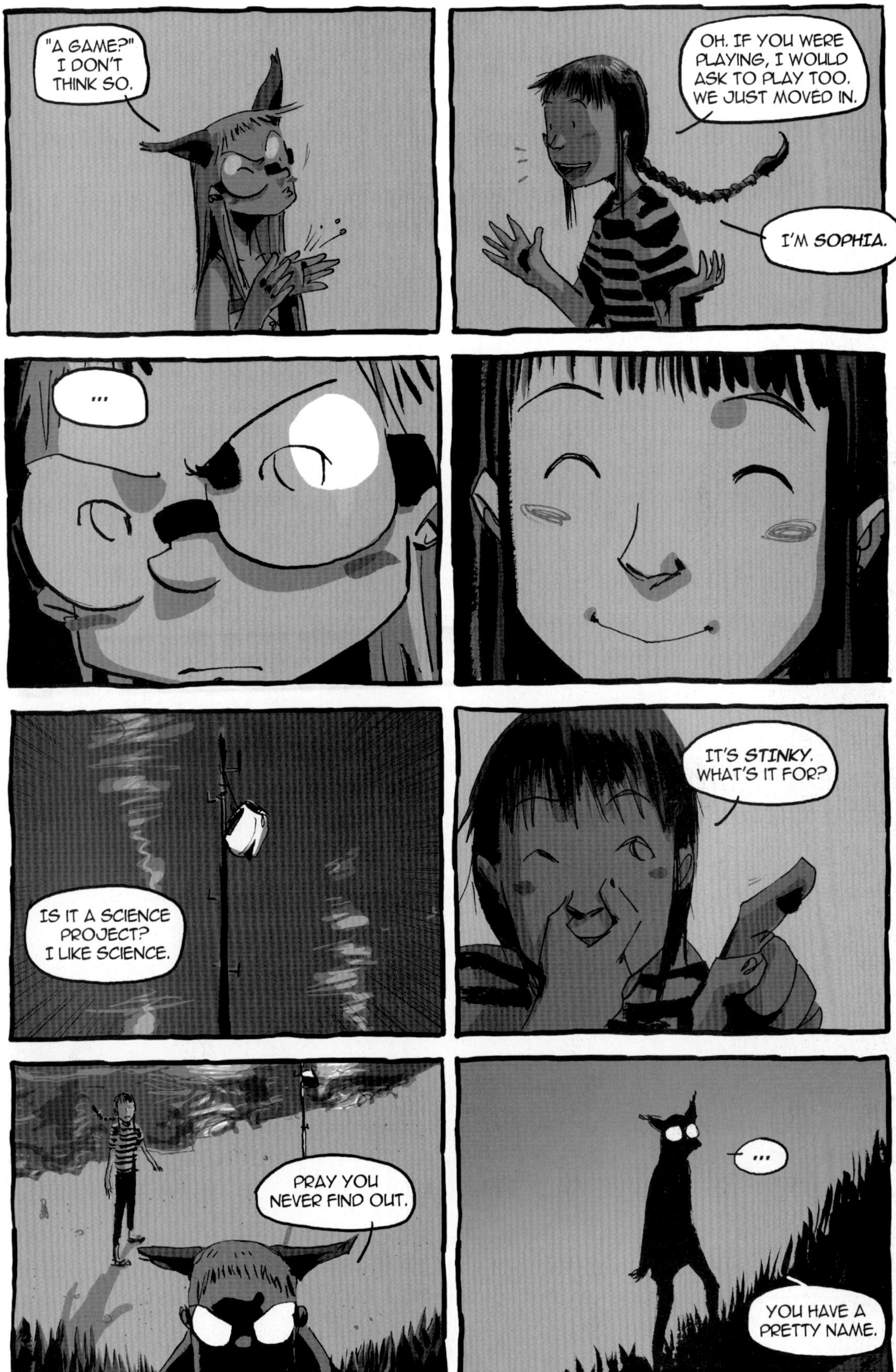
"A GAME?" I DON'T THINK SO.
OH. IF YOU WERE PLAYING, I WOULD ASK TO PLAY TOO. WE JUST MOVED IN.
I'M SOPHIA.
...
IS IT A SCIENCE PROJECT? I LIKE SCIENCE.
IT'S STINKY. WHAT'S IT FOR?
PRAY YOU NEVER FIND OUT.
...
YOU HAVE A PRETTY NAME.

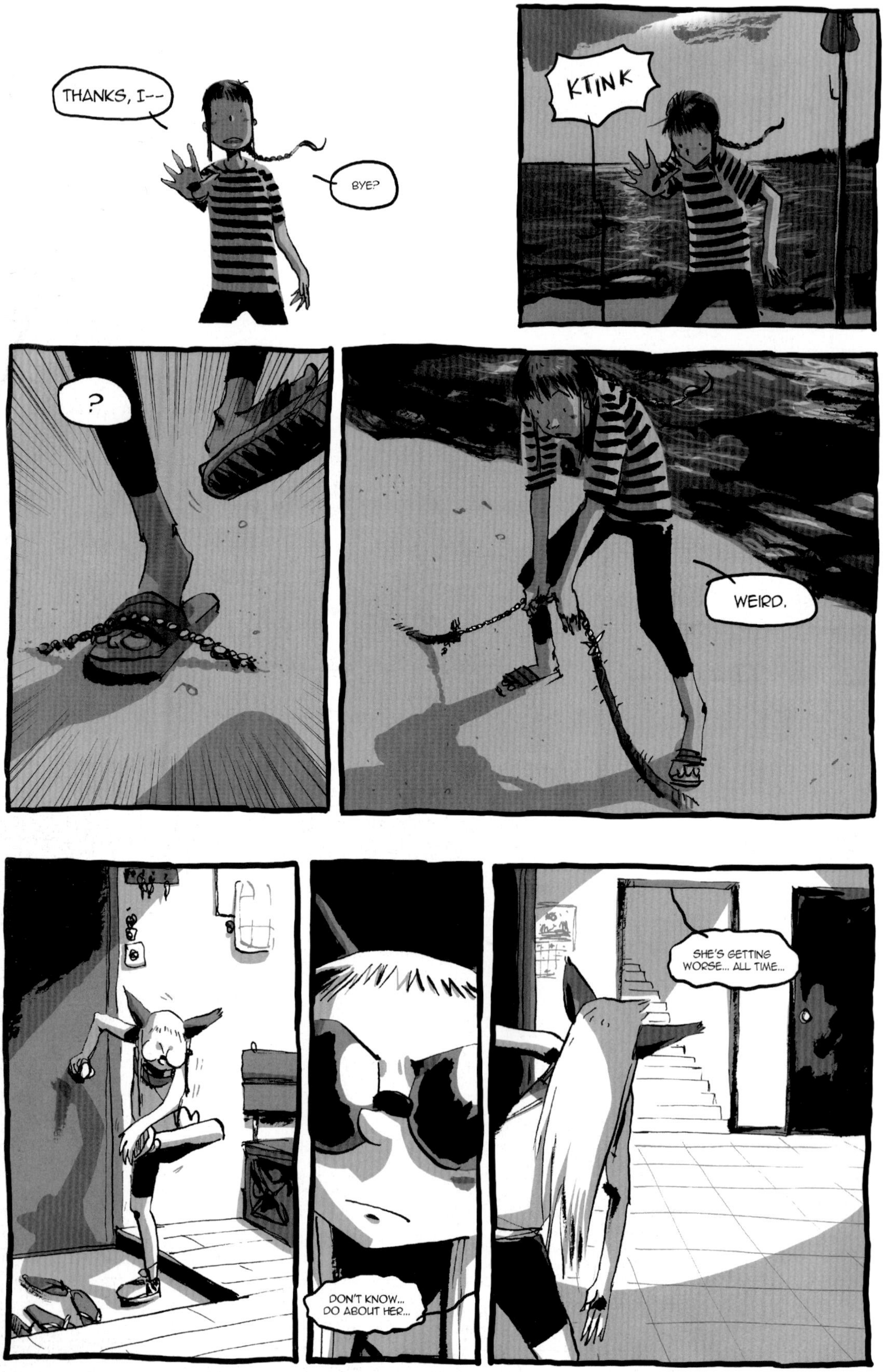
THANKS, I--
BYE?
KTINK
?
WEIRD.
DON'T KNOW... DO ABOUT HER...
SHE'S GETTING WORSE... ALL TIME...

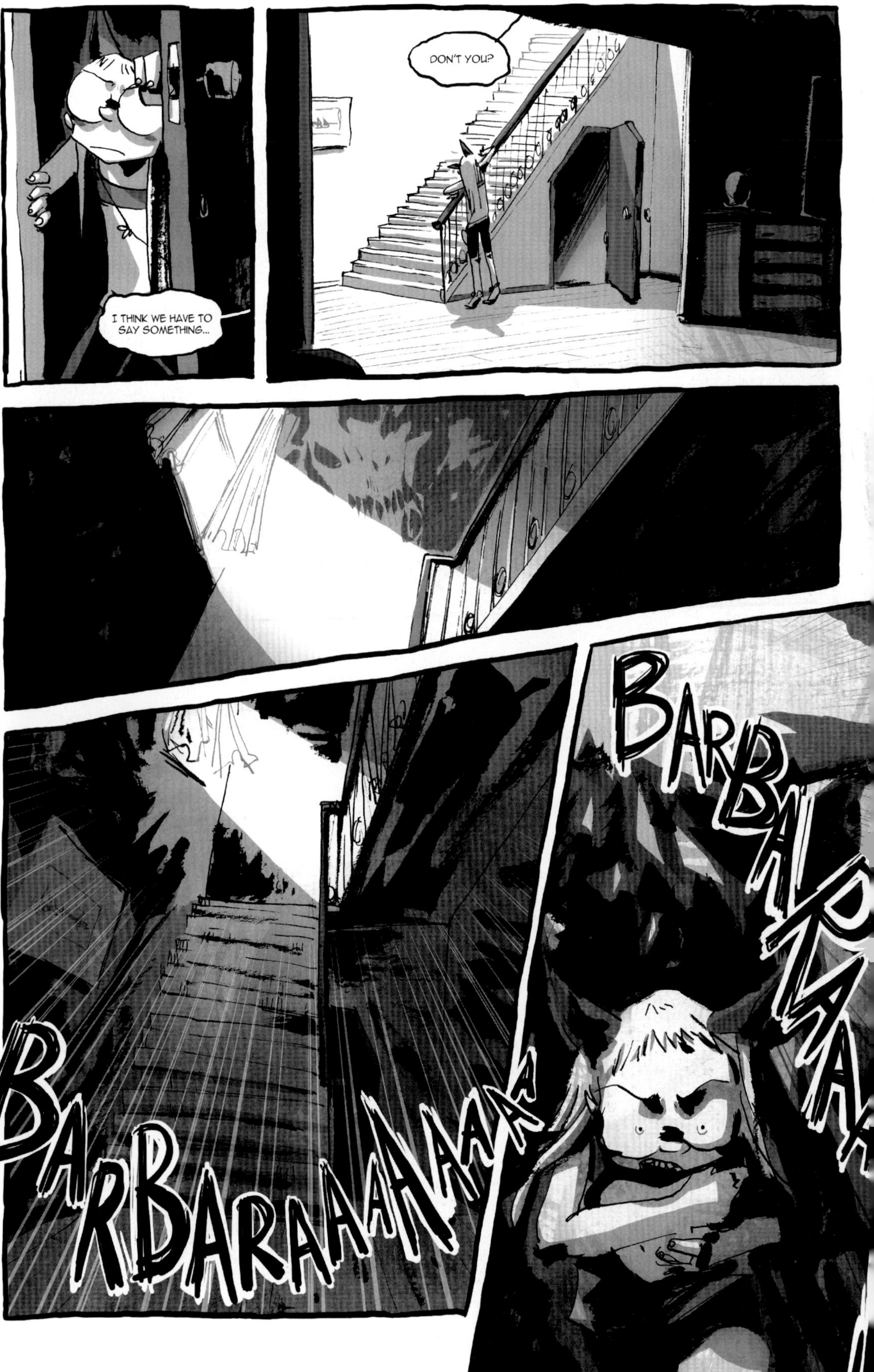
I THINK WE HAVE TO SAY SOMETHING...
DON'T YOU?
BARBARAAAAAAA
BARBARAAAA

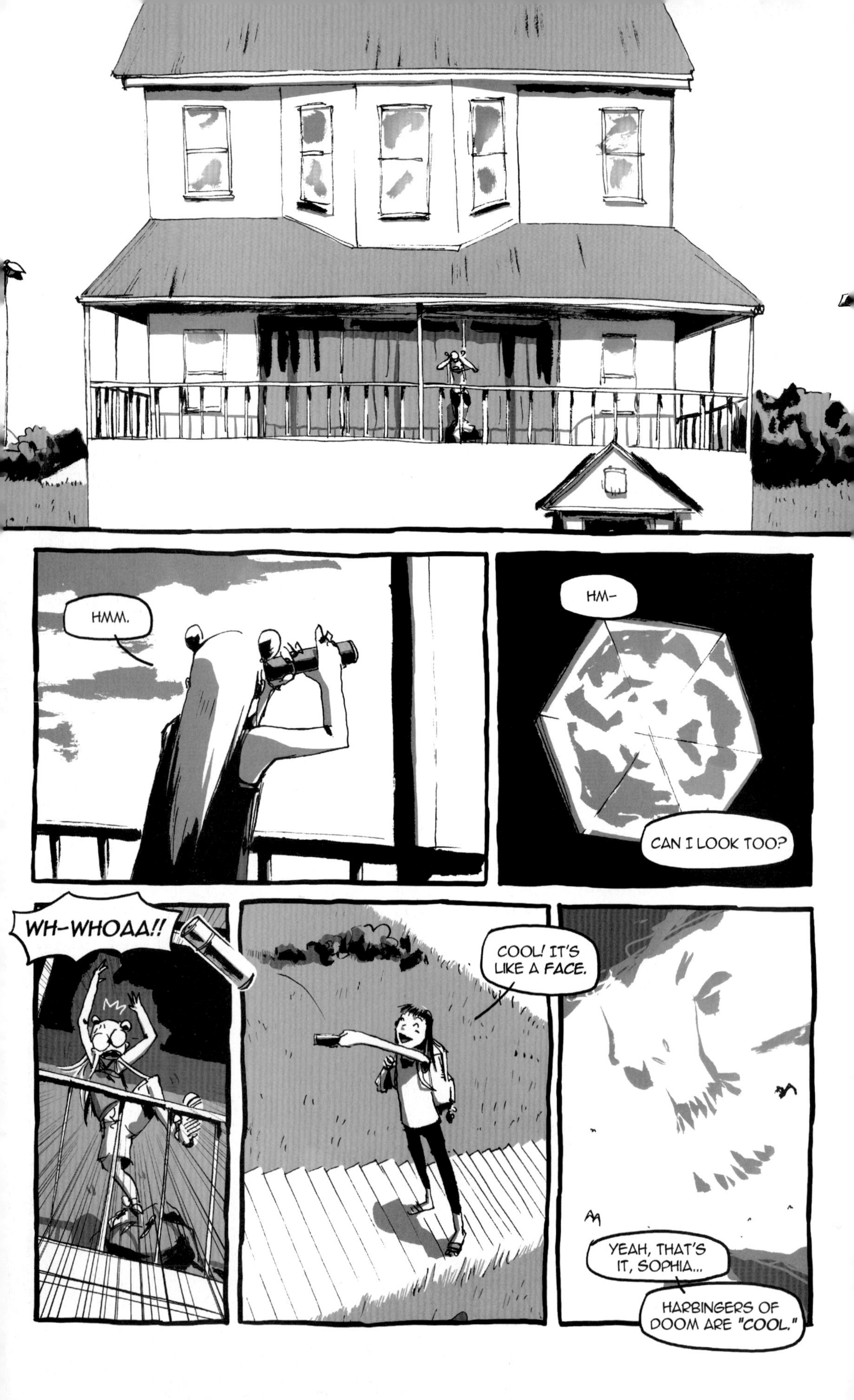

HMM.
HM-
CAN I LOOK TOO?
WH-WHOAA!!
COOL! IT'S LIKE A FACE.
YEAH, THAT'S IT, SOPHIA...
HARBINGERS OF DOOM ARE "COOL."

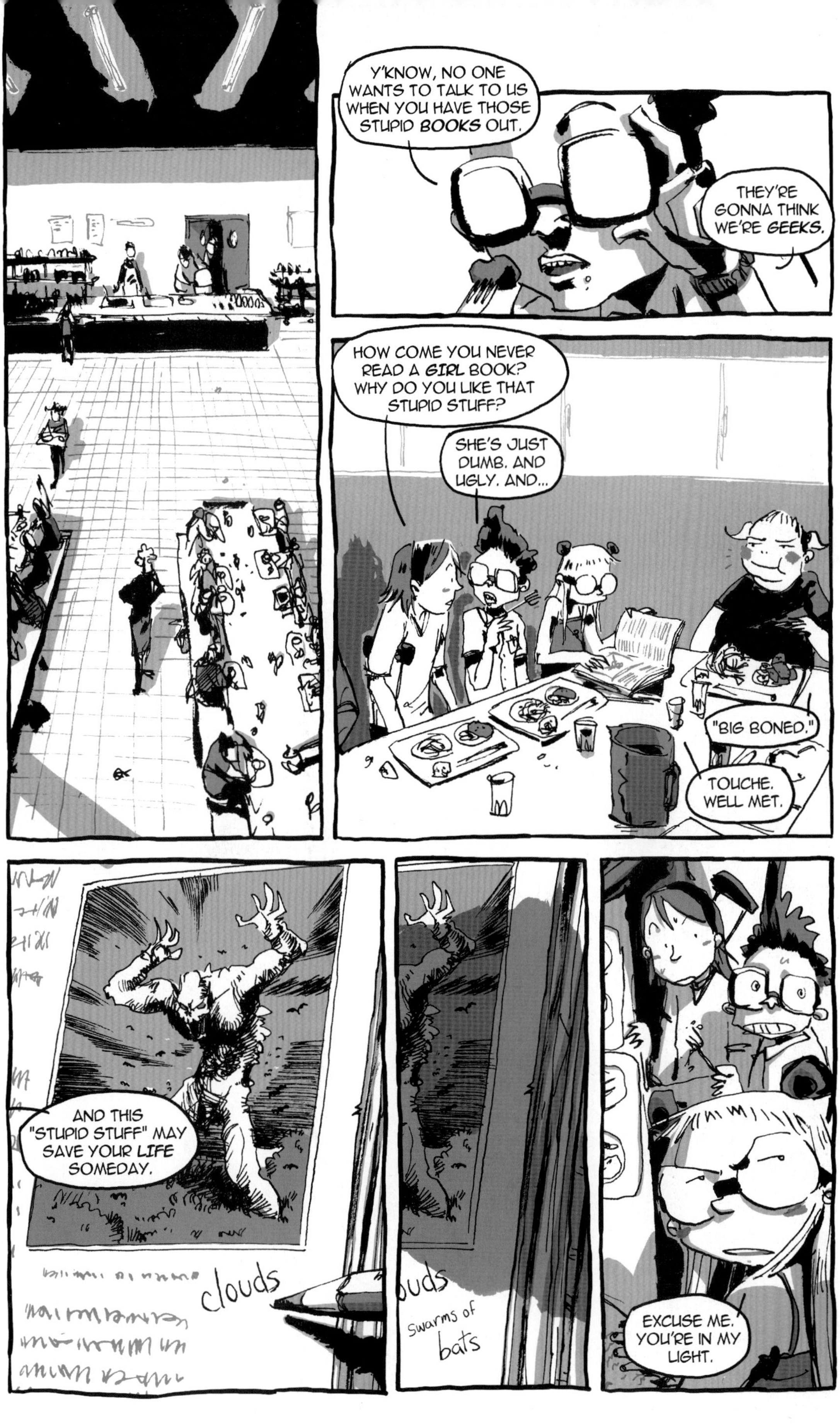
Y'KNOW, NO ONE WANTS TO TALK TO US WHEN YOU HAVE THOSE STUPID BOOKS OUT.
THEY'RE GONNA THINK WE'RE GEEKS.
HOW COME YOU NEVER READ A GIRL BOOK? WHY DO YOU LIKE THAT STUPID STUFF?
SHE'S JUST DUMB. AND UGLY. AND...
"BIG BONED."
TOUCHE. WELL MET.
AND THIS "STUPID STUFF" MAY SAVE YOUR LIFE SOMEDAY.
clouds
swarms of bats
EXCUSE ME. YOU'RE IN MY LIGHT.

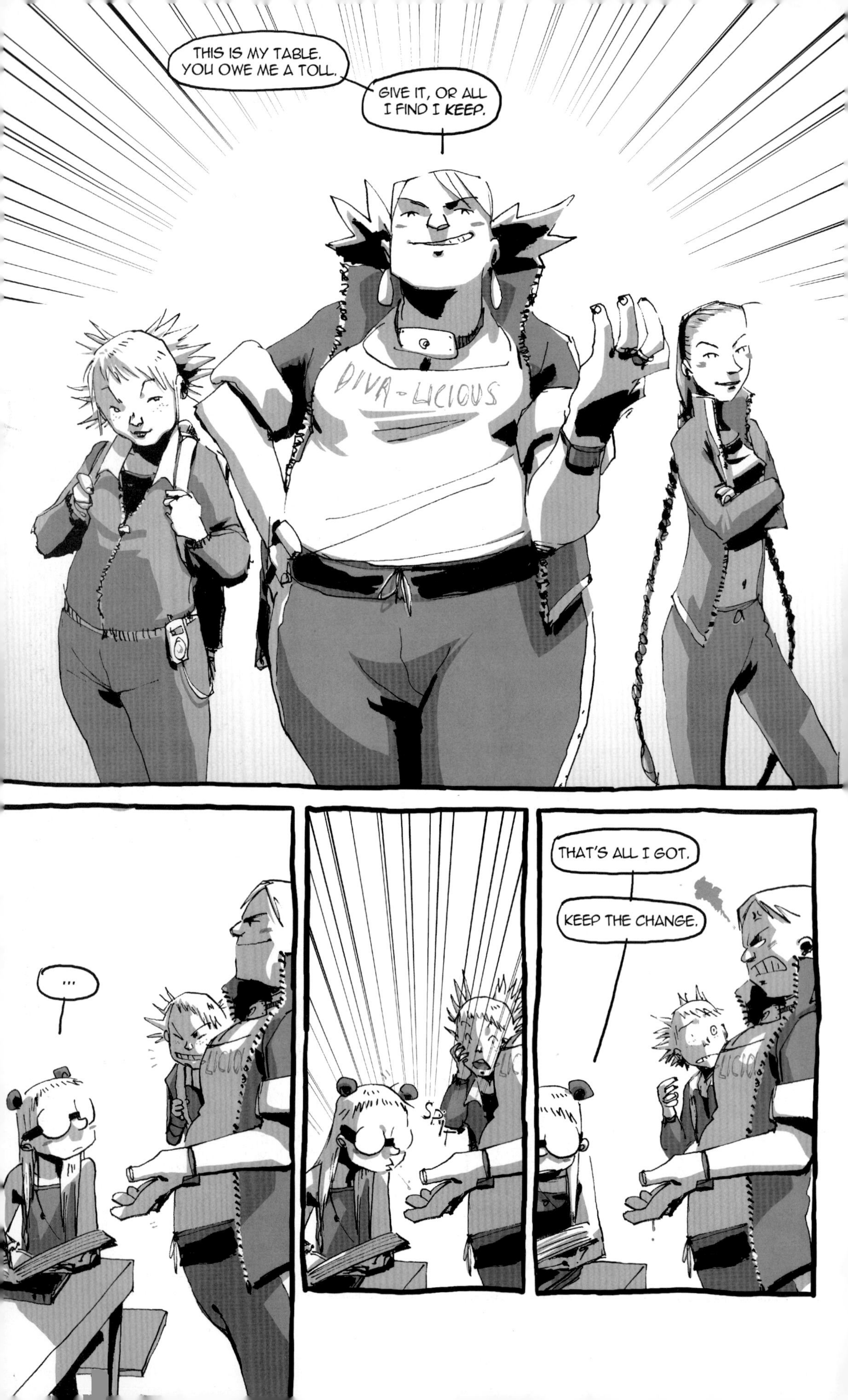
THIS IS MY TABLE. YOU OWE ME A TOLL.
GIVE IT, OR ALL I FIND I KEEP.
DIVA-LICIOUS
...
SPIT
THAT'S ALL I GOT.
KEEP THE CHANGE.

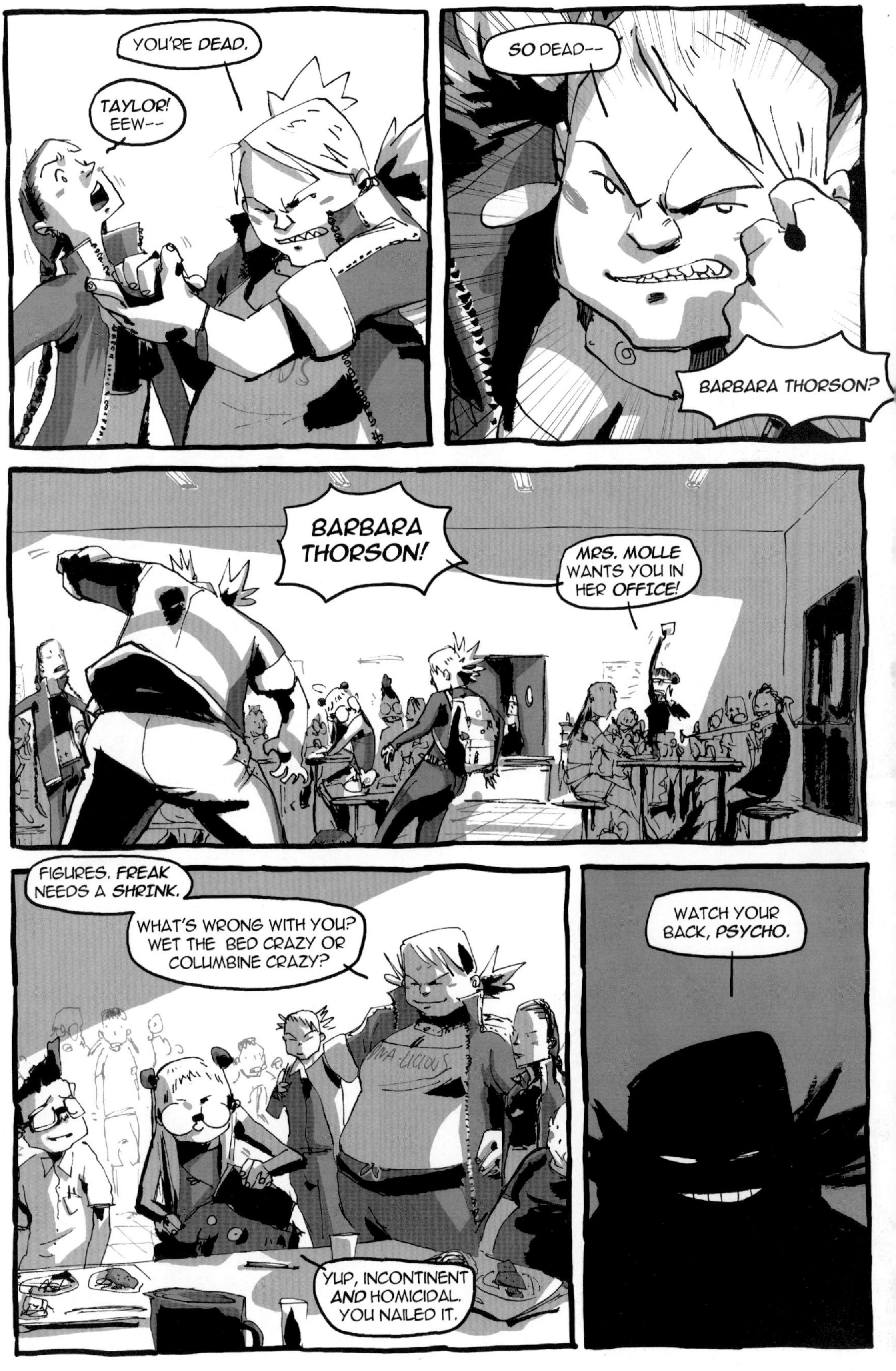
YOU'RE DEAD.
TAYLOR! EEW--
SO DEAD--
BARBARA THORSON?
BARBARA THORSON!
MRS. MOLLE WANTS YOU IN HER OFFICE!
FIGURES. FREAK NEEDS A SHRINK.
WHAT'S WRONG WITH YOU? WET THE BED CRAZY OR COLUMBINE CRAZY?
YUP, INCONTINENT AND HOMICIDAL. YOU NAILED IT.
WATCH YOUR BACK, PSYCHO.

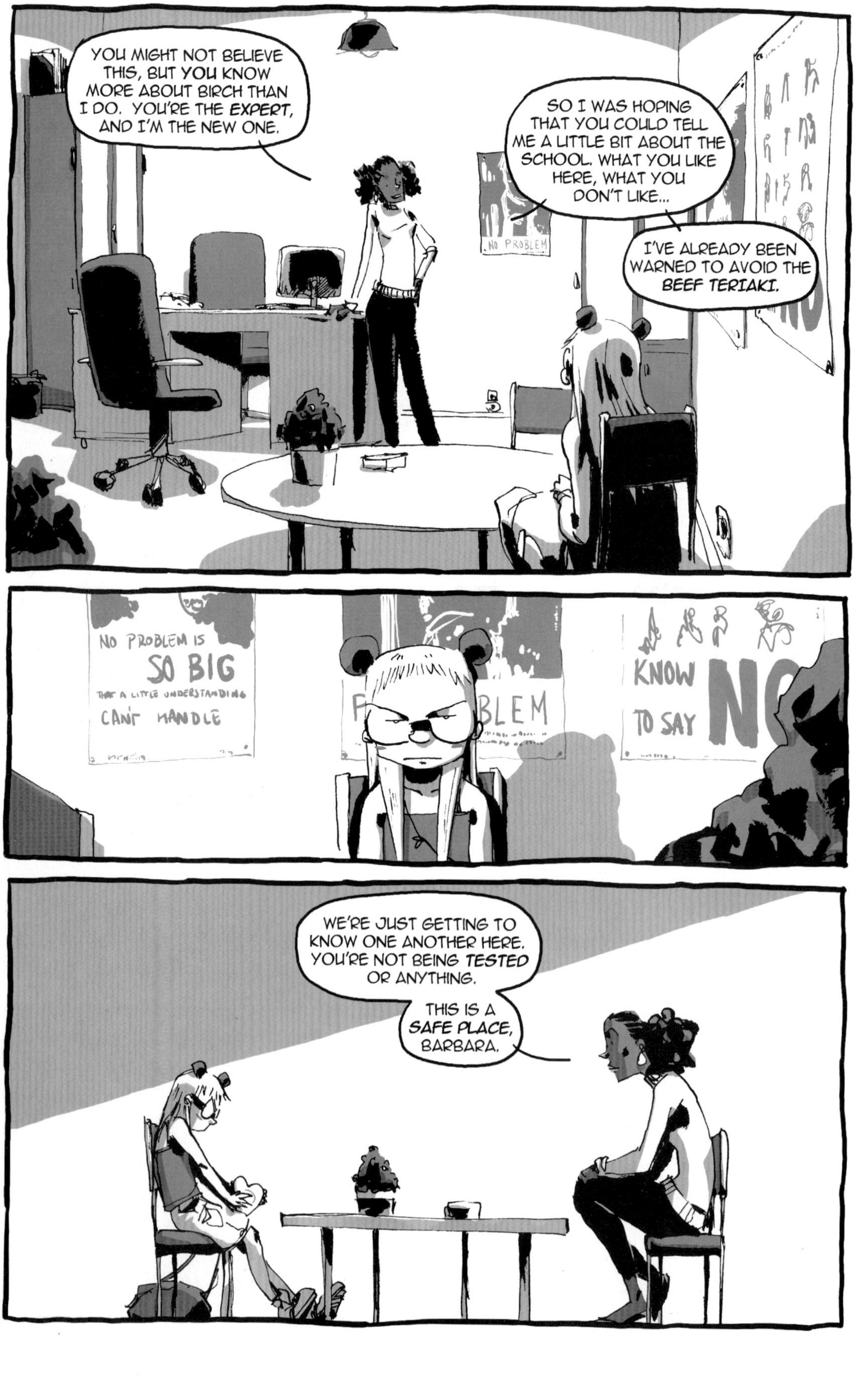

YOU MIGHT NOT BELIEVE THIS, BUT YOU KNOW MORE ABOUT BIRCH THAN I DO. YOU'RE THE *EXPERT*, AND I'M THE NEW ONE.
SO I WAS HOPING THAT YOU COULD TELL ME A LITTLE BIT ABOUT THE SCHOOL. WHAT YOU LIKE HERE, WHAT YOU DON'T LIKE...
NO PROBLEM
I'VE ALREADY BEEN WARNED TO AVOID THE ***BEEF TERIAKI.***
NO PROBLEM IS SO BIG THAT A LITTLE UNDERSTANDING CAN'T HANDLE
KNOW
TO SAY
WE'RE JUST GETTING TO KNOW ONE ANOTHER HERE. YOU'RE NOT BEING *TESTED* OR ANYTHING.
THIS IS A ***SAFE PLACE,*** BARBARA.

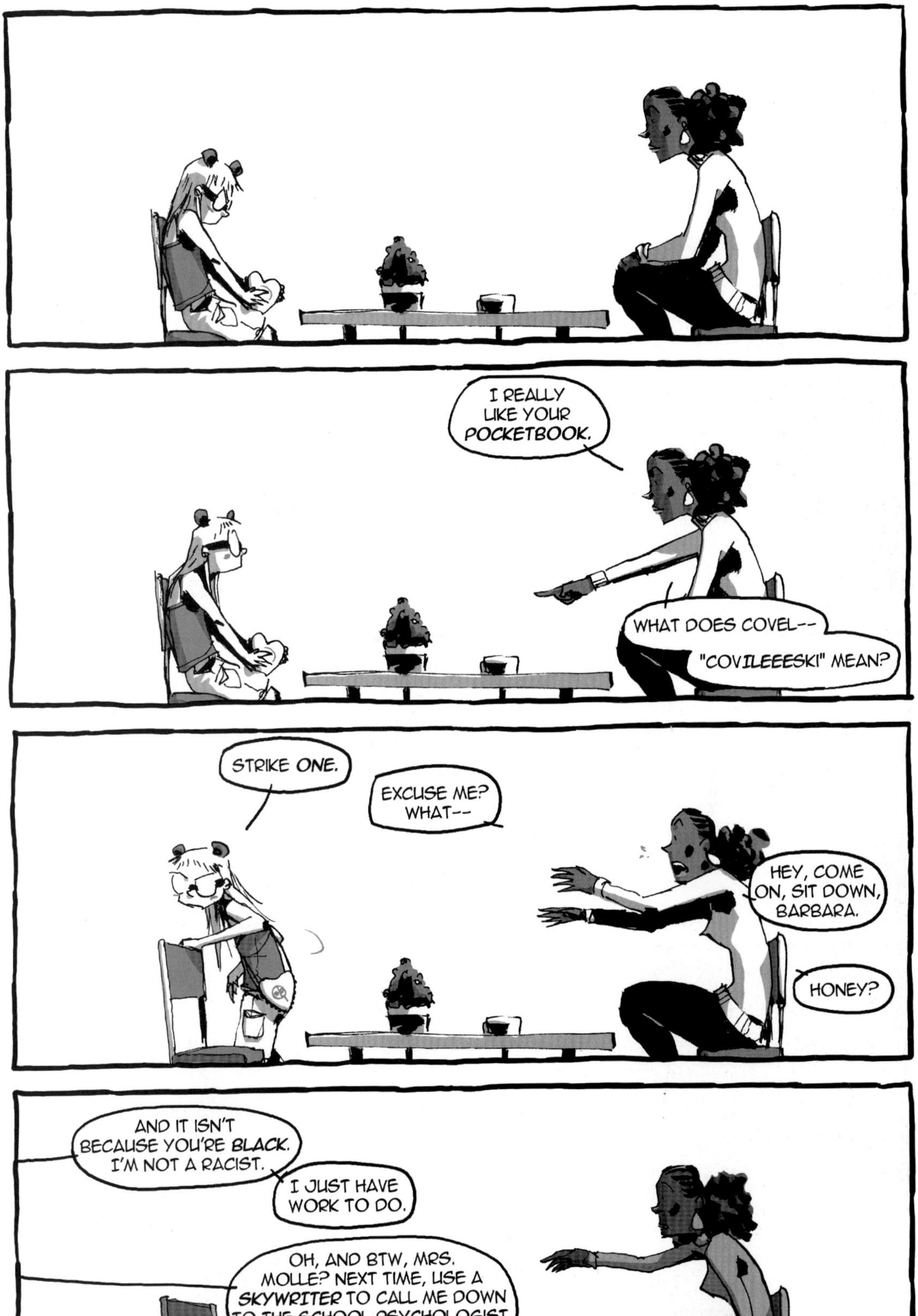
I REALLY LIKE YOUR POCKETBOOK.
WHAT DOES COVEL--
"COVILEEESKI" MEAN?
STRIKE ONE.
EXCUSE ME? WHAT--
HEY, COME ON, SIT DOWN, BARBARA.
HONEY?
AND IT ISN'T BECAUSE YOU'RE BLACK. I'M NOT A RACIST.
I JUST HAVE WORK TO DO.
OH, AND BTW, MRS. MOLLE? NEXT TIME, USE A SKYWRITER TO CALL ME DOWN TO THE SCHOOL PSYCHOLOGIST. LESS EMBARRASSING.

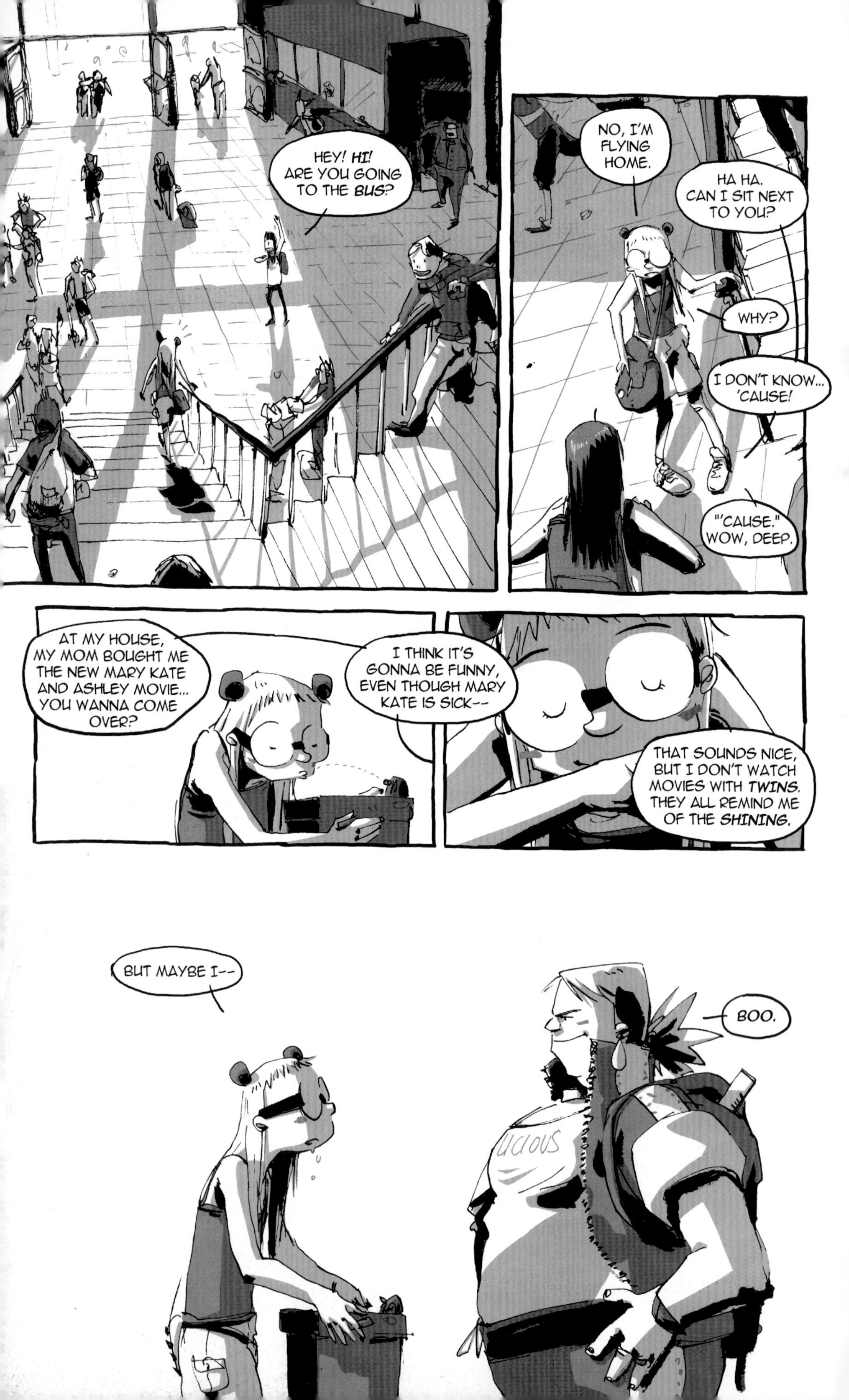
HEY! HI! ARE YOU GOING TO THE BUS?
NO, I'M FLYING HOME.
HA HA. CAN I SIT NEXT TO YOU?
WHY?
I DON'T KNOW... 'CAUSE!
"'CAUSE." WOW, DEEP.
AT MY HOUSE, MY MOM BOUGHT ME THE NEW MARY KATE AND ASHLEY MOVIE... YOU WANNA COME OVER?
I THINK IT'S GONNA BE FUNNY, EVEN THOUGH MARY KATE IS SICK--
THAT SOUNDS NICE, BUT I DON'T WATCH MOVIES WITH TWINS. THEY ALL REMIND ME OF THE SHINING.
BUT MAYBE I--
BOO.

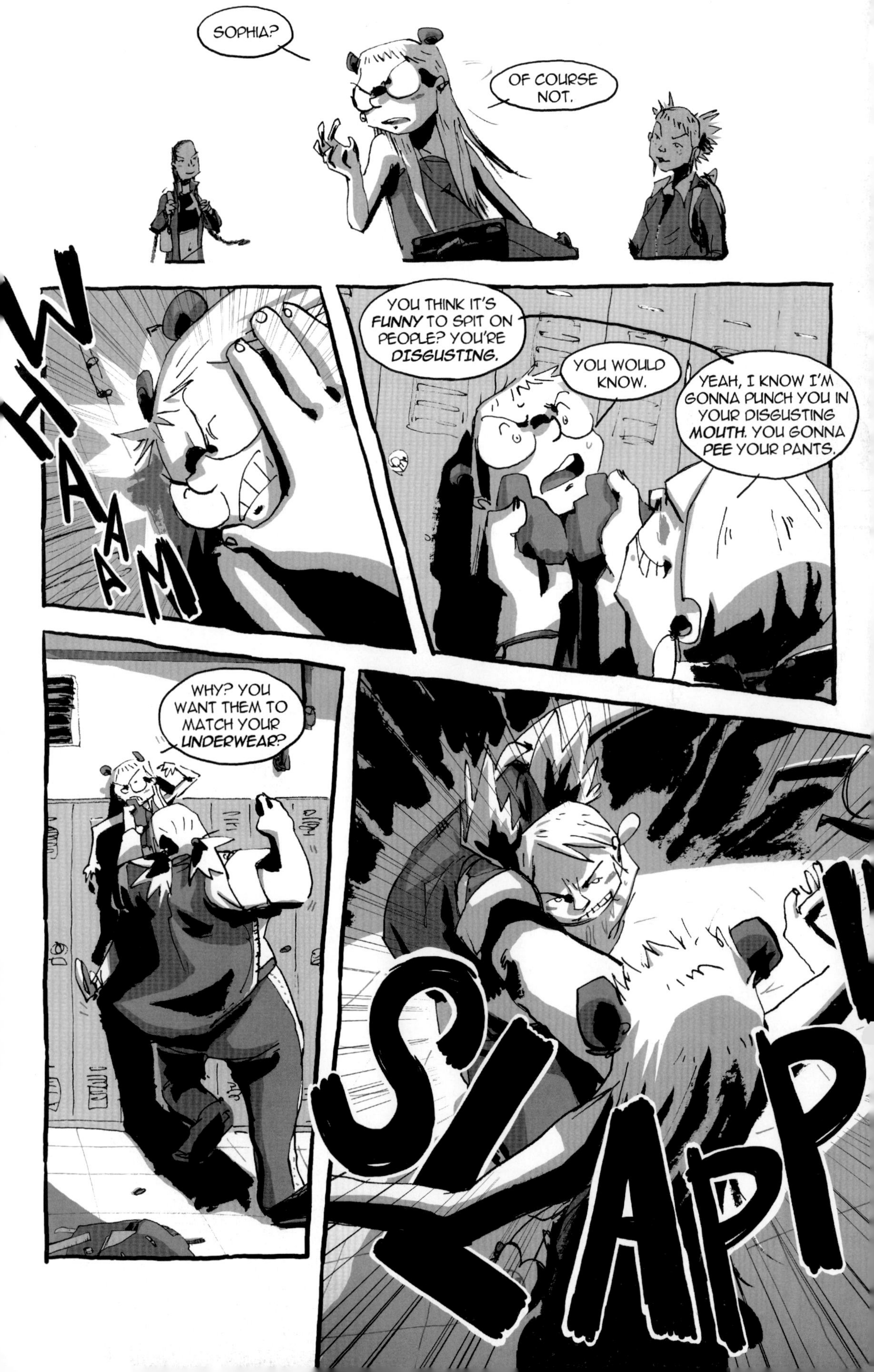
SOPHIA?
OF COURSE NOT.
WHAAAAM
YOU THINK IT'S FUNNY TO SPIT ON PEOPLE? YOU'RE DISGUSTING.
YOU WOULD KNOW.
YEAH, I KNOW I'M GONNA PUNCH YOU IN YOUR DISGUSTING MOUTH. YOU GONNA PEE YOUR PANTS.
WHY? YOU WANT THEM TO MATCH YOUR UNDERWEAR?
SLAPP

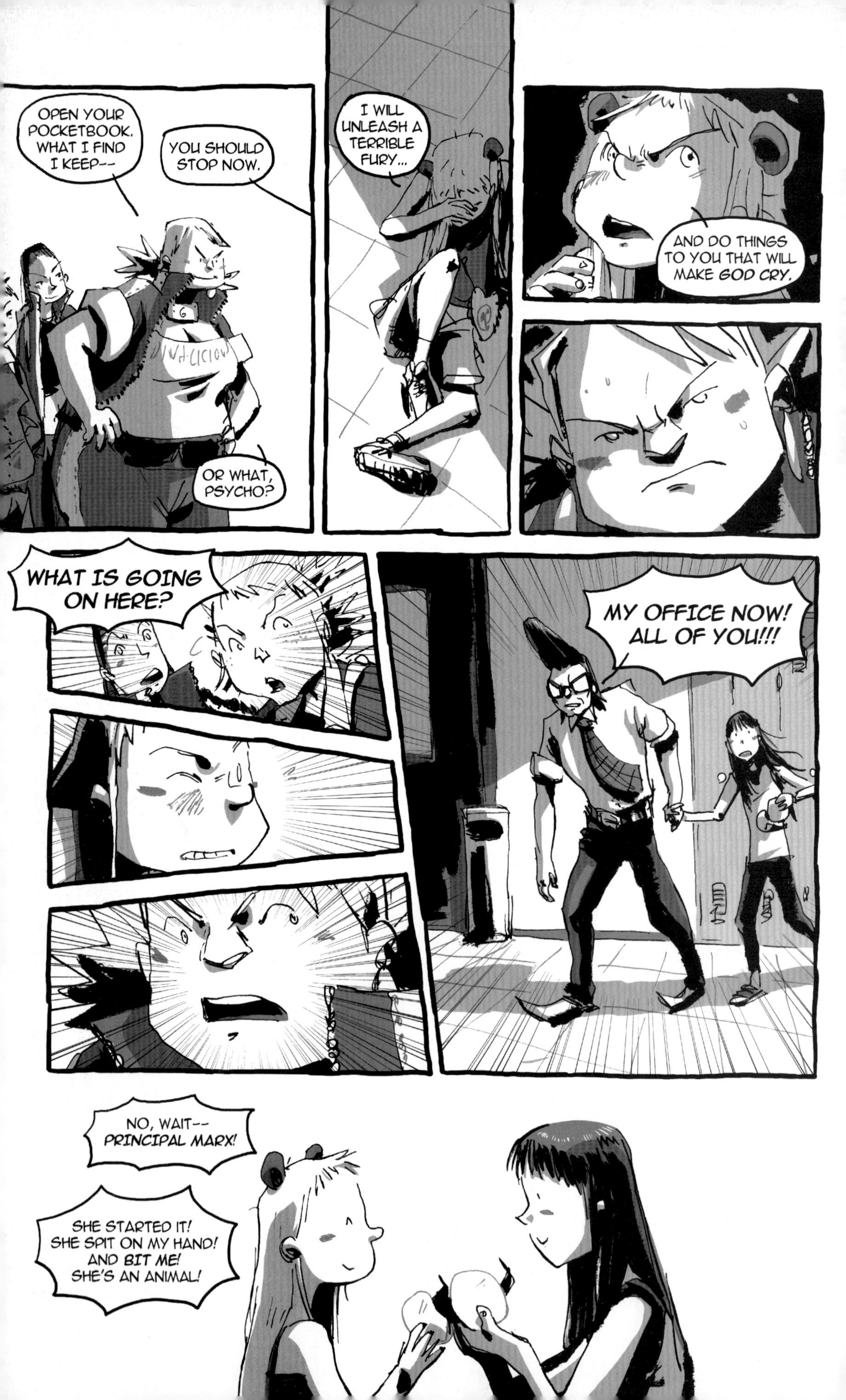
OPEN YOUR POCKETBOOK. WHAT I FIND I KEEP--
YOU SHOULD STOP NOW.
OR WHAT, PSYCHO?
I WILL UNLEASH A TERRIBLE FURY...
AND DO THINGS TO YOU THAT WILL MAKE GOD CRY.
WHAT IS GOING ON HERE?
MY OFFICE NOW! ALL OF YOU!!!
NO, WAIT-- PRINCIPAL MARX!
SHE STARTED IT! SHE SPIT ON MY HAND! AND BIT ME! SHE'S AN ANIMAL!

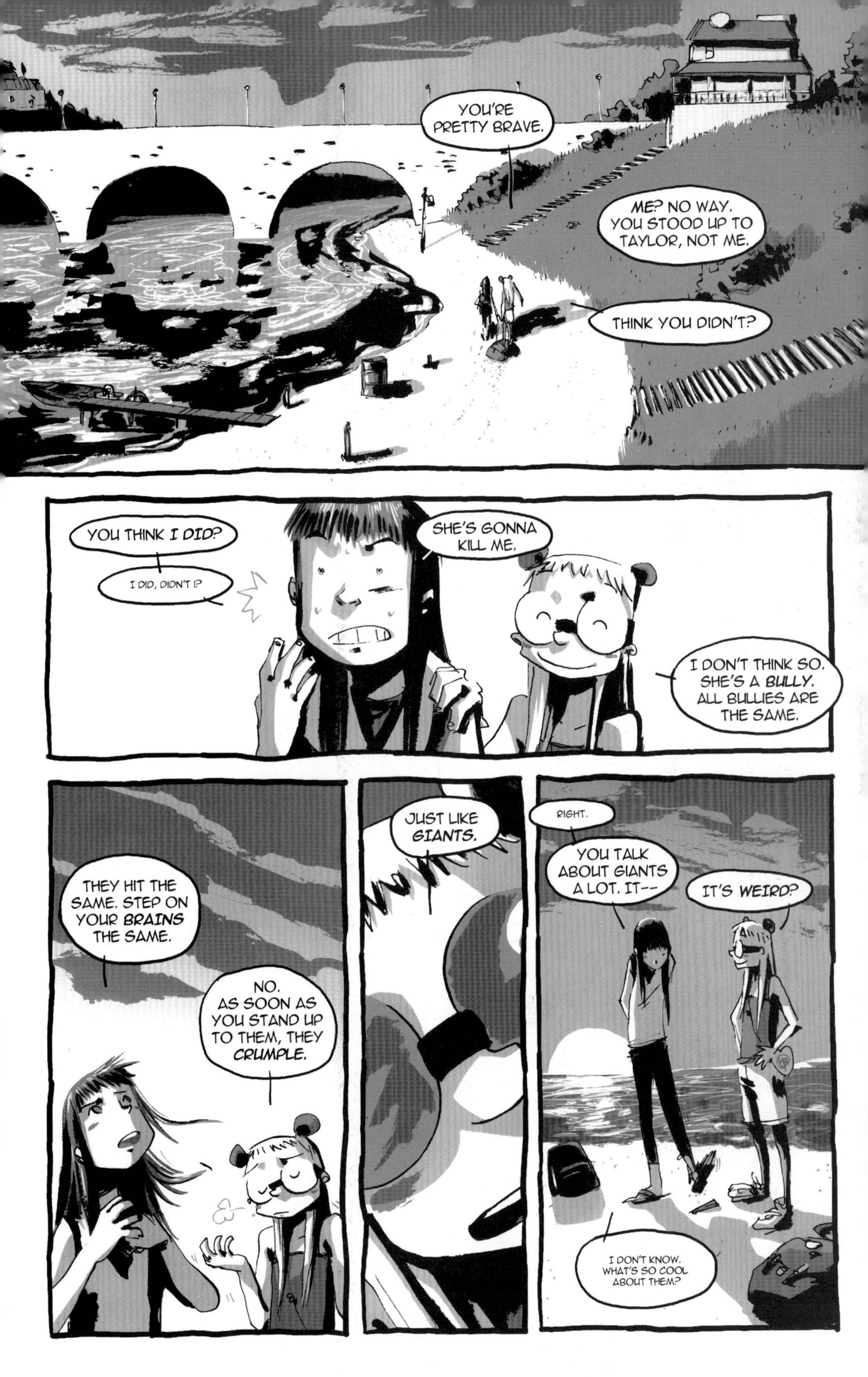
YOU'RE PRETTY BRAVE.
ME? NO WAY. YOU STOOD UP TO TAYLOR, NOT ME.
THINK YOU DIDN'T?
YOU THINK I DID?
I DID, DIDN'T I?
SHE'S GONNA KILL ME.
I DON'T THINK SO. SHE'S A BULLY. ALL BULLIES ARE THE SAME.
THEY HIT THE SAME. STEP ON YOUR BRAINS THE SAME.
NO. AS SOON AS YOU STAND UP TO THEM, THEY CRUMPLE.
JUST LIKE GIANTS.
RIGHT.
YOU TALK ABOUT GIANTS A LOT. IT--
IT'S WEIRD?
I DON'T KNOW. WHAT'S SO COOL ABOUT THEM?

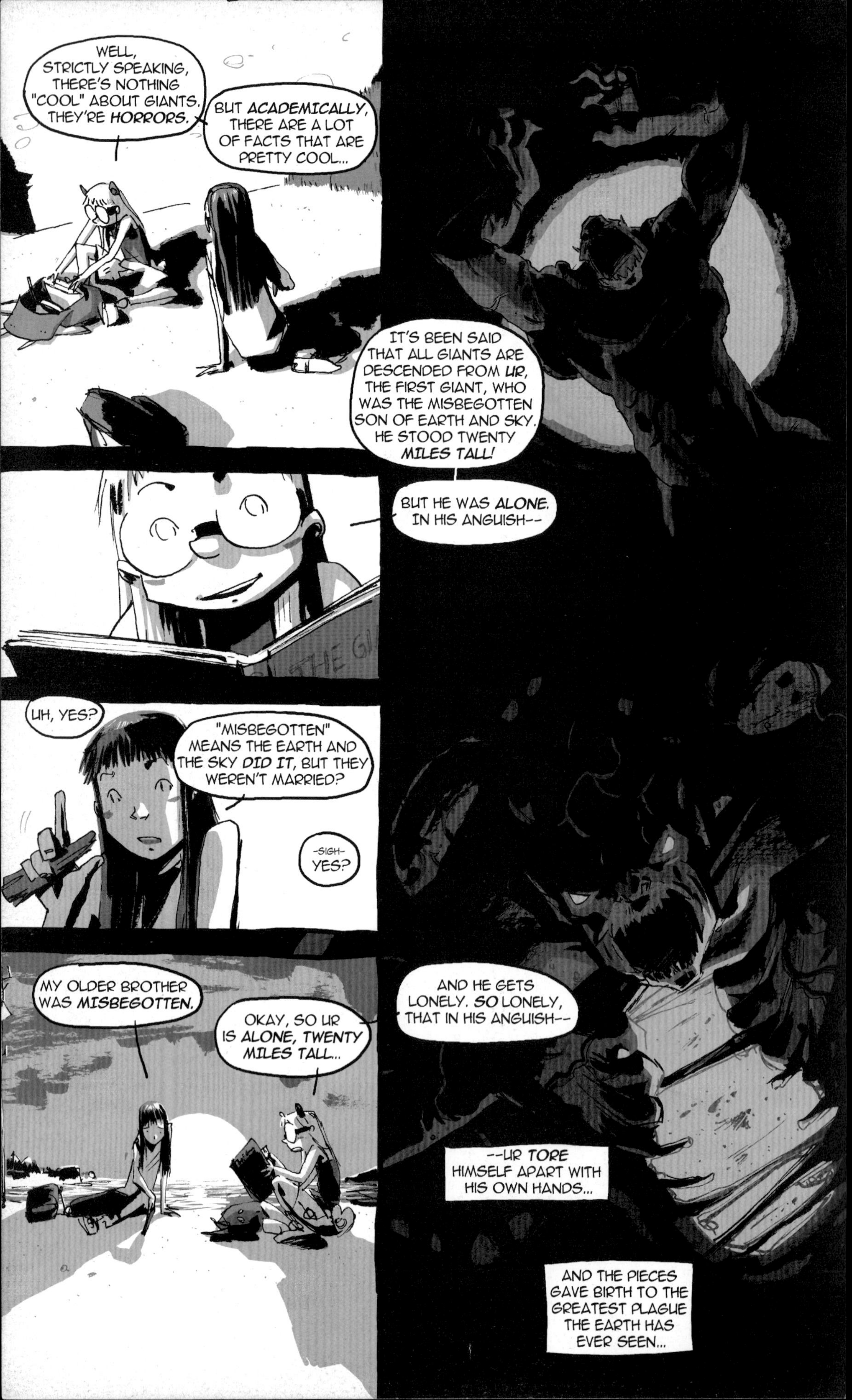
WELL, STRICTLY SPEAKING, THERE'S NOTHING "COOL" ABOUT GIANTS. THEY'RE HORRORS.
BUT ACADEMICALLY, THERE ARE A LOT OF FACTS THAT ARE PRETTY COOL...
IT'S BEEN SAID THAT ALL GIANTS ARE DESCENDED FROM UR, THE FIRST GIANT, WHO WAS THE MISBEGOTTEN SON OF EARTH AND SKY. HE STOOD TWENTY MILES TALL!
BUT HE WAS ALONE. IN HIS ANGUISH--
UH, YES?
"MISBEGOTTEN" MEANS THE EARTH AND THE SKY DID IT, BUT THEY WEREN'T MARRIED?
-SIGH- YES?
MY OLDER BROTHER WAS MISBEGOTTEN.
OKAY, SO UR IS ALONE, TWENTY MILES TALL...
AND HE GETS LONELY. SO LONELY, THAT IN HIS ANGUISH--
--UR TORE HIMSELF APART WITH HIS OWN HANDS...
AND THE PIECES GAVE BIRTH TO THE GREATEST PLAGUE THE EARTH HAS EVER SEEN...

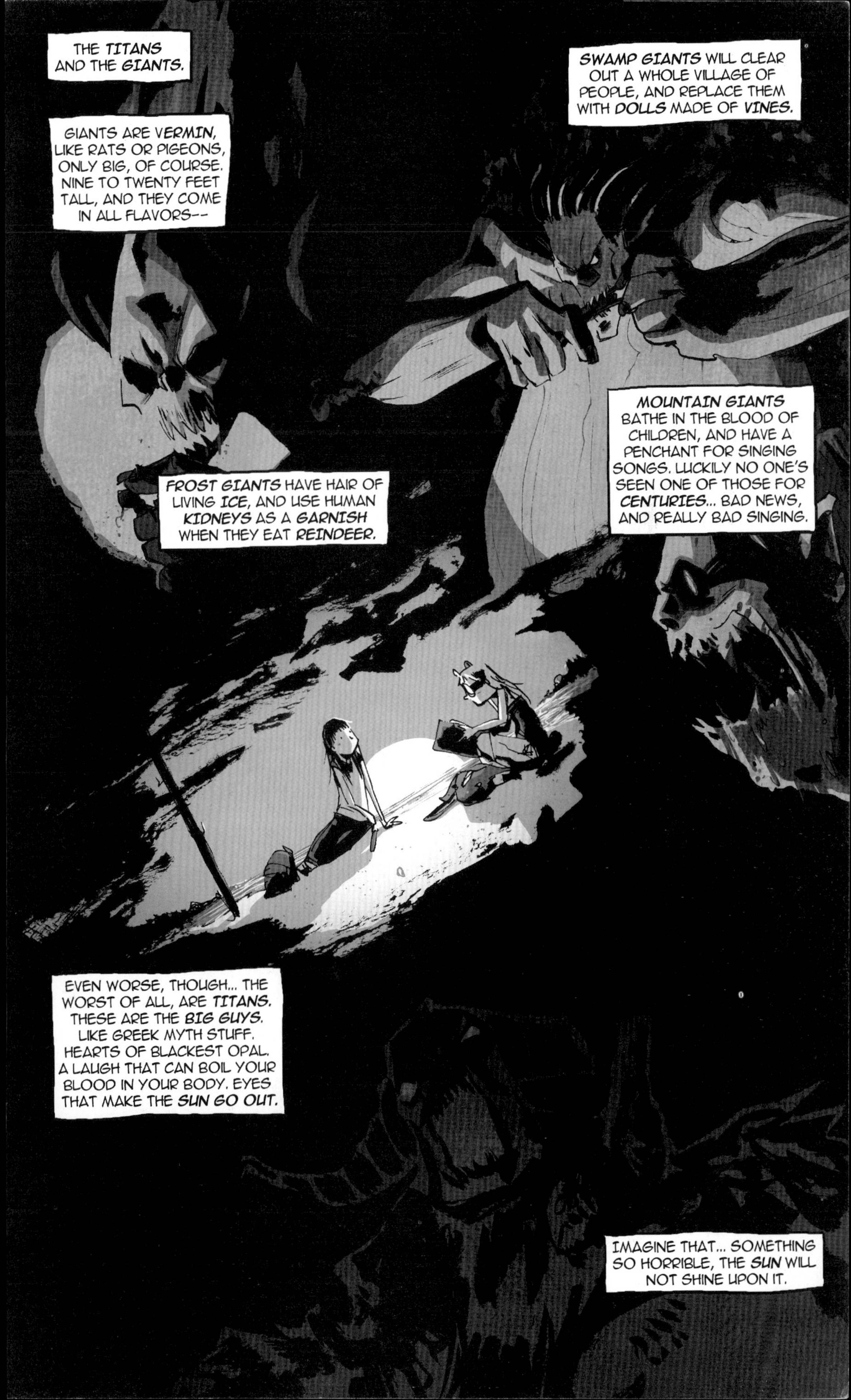
THE TITANS AND THE GIANTS.
GIANTS ARE VERMIN, LIKE RATS OR PIGEONS, ONLY BIG, OF COURSE. NINE TO TWENTY FEET TALL, AND THEY COME IN ALL FLAVORS--
SWAMP GIANTS WILL CLEAR OUT A WHOLE VILLAGE OF PEOPLE, AND REPLACE THEM WITH DOLLS MADE OF VINES.
FROST GIANTS HAVE HAIR OF LIVING ICE, AND USE HUMAN KIDNEYS AS A GARNISH WHEN THEY EAT REINDEER.
MOUNTAIN GIANTS BATHE IN THE BLOOD OF CHILDREN, AND HAVE A PENCHANT FOR SINGING SONGS. LUCKILY NO ONE'S SEEN ONE OF THOSE FOR CENTURIES... BAD NEWS, AND REALLY BAD SINGING.
EVEN WORSE, THOUGH... THE WORST OF ALL, ARE TITANS. THESE ARE THE BIG GUYS. LIKE GREEK MYTH STUFF. HEARTS OF BLACKEST OPAL. A LAUGH THAT CAN BOIL YOUR BLOOD IN YOUR BODY. EYES THAT MAKE THE SUN GO OUT.
IMAGINE THAT... SOMETHING SO HORRIBLE, THE SUN WILL NOT SHINE UPON IT.

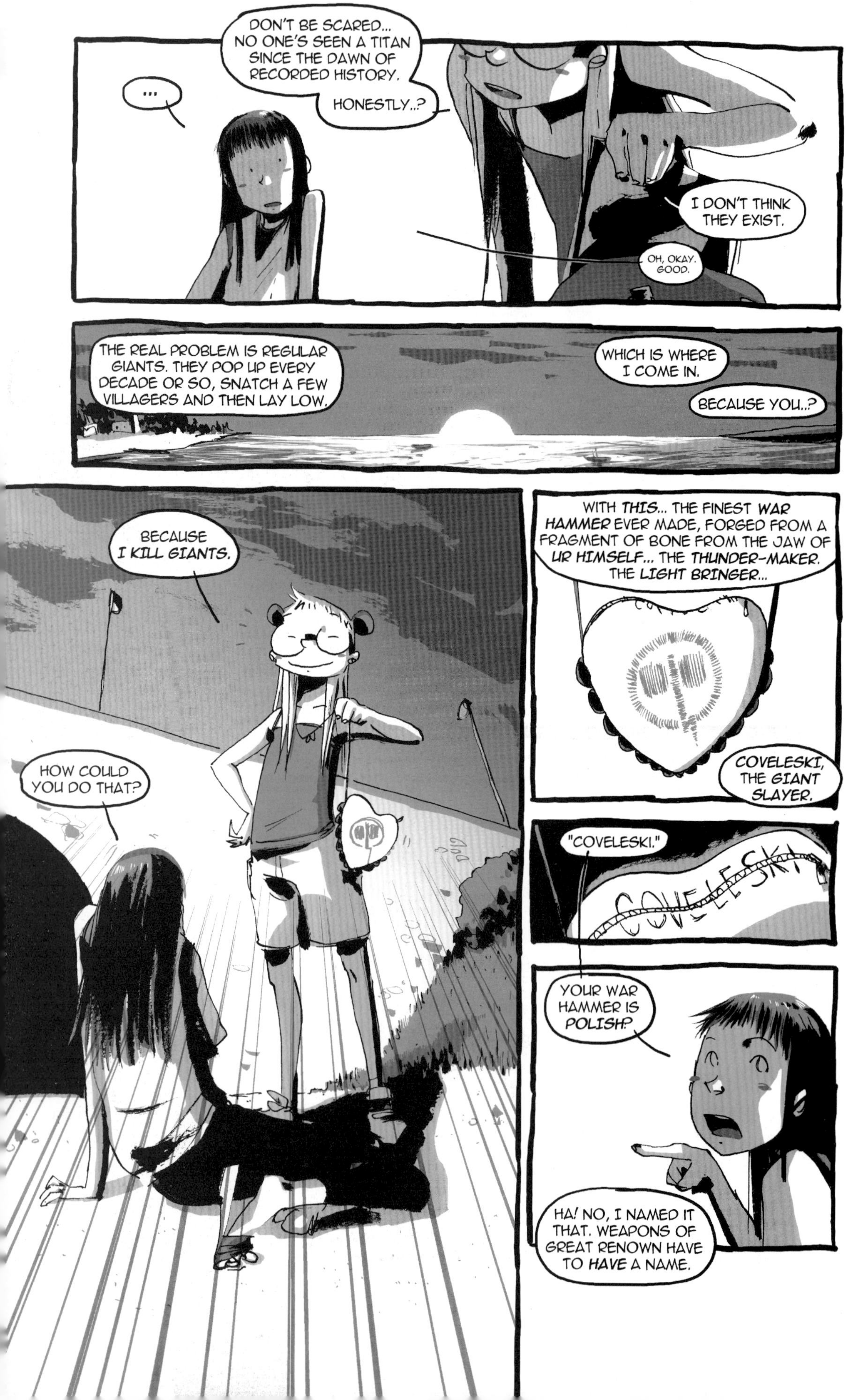
DON'T BE SCARED... NO ONE'S SEEN A TITAN SINCE THE DAWN OF RECORDED HISTORY.
...
HONESTLY..?
I DON'T THINK THEY EXIST.
OH, OKAY. GOOD.
THE REAL PROBLEM IS REGULAR GIANTS. THEY POP UP EVERY DECADE OR SO, SNATCH A FEW VILLAGERS AND THEN LAY LOW.
WHICH IS WHERE I COME IN.
BECAUSE YOU..?
BECAUSE I KILL GIANTS.
HOW COULD YOU DO THAT?
WITH THIS... THE FINEST WAR HAMMER EVER MADE, FORGED FROM A FRAGMENT OF BONE FROM THE JAW OF UR HIMSELF... THE THUNDER-MAKER. THE LIGHT BRINGER...
COVELESKI, THE GIANT SLAYER.
"COVELESKI."
COVELESKI
YOUR WAR HAMMER IS POLISH?
HA! NO, I NAMED IT THAT. WEAPONS OF GREAT RENOWN HAVE TO HAVE A NAME.

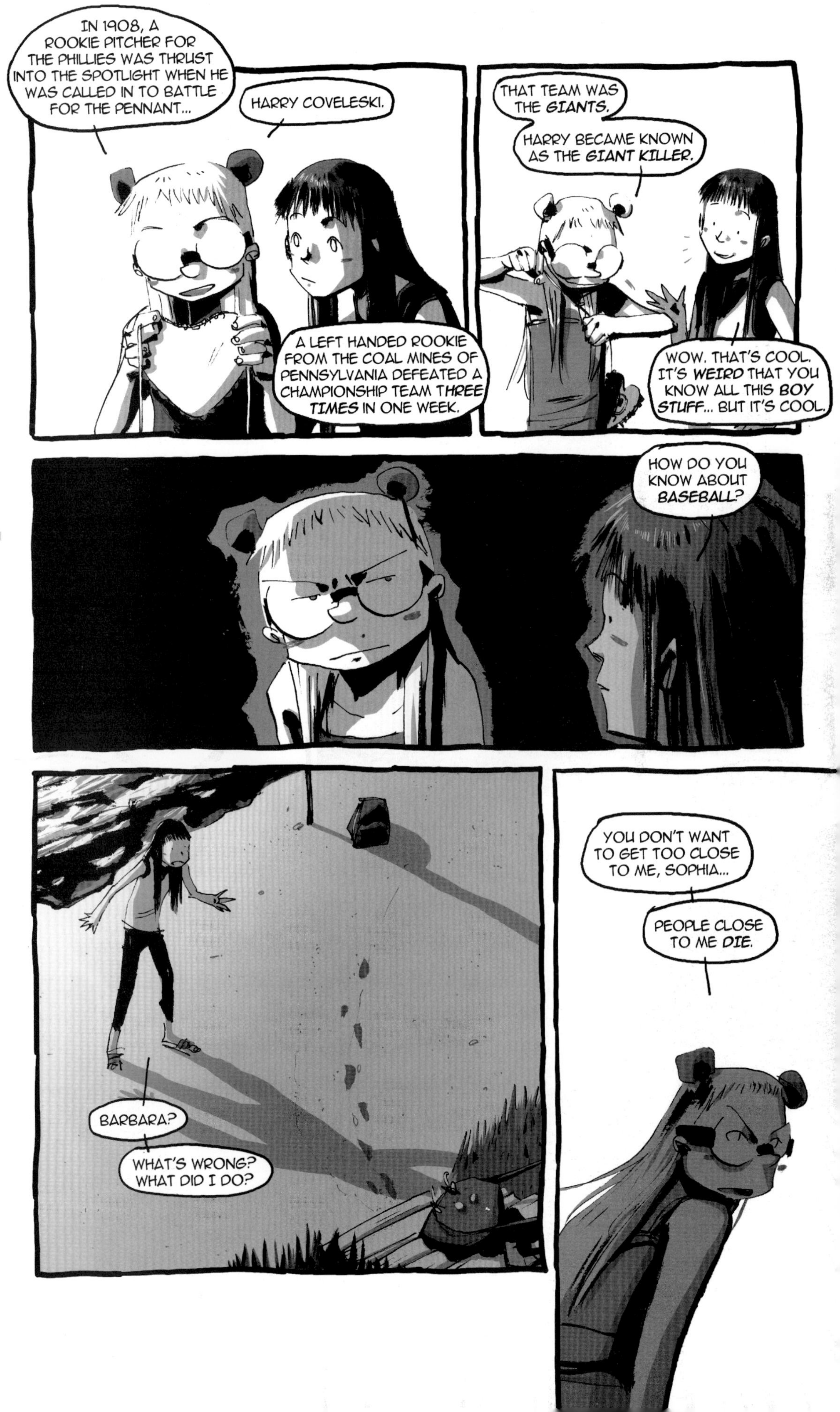
IN 1908, A ROOKIE PITCHER FOR THE PHILLIES WAS THRUST INTO THE SPOTLIGHT WHEN HE WAS CALLED IN TO BATTLE FOR THE PENNANT...
HARRY COVELESKI.
A LEFT HANDED ROOKIE FROM THE COAL MINES OF PENNSYLVANIA DEFEATED A CHAMPIONSHIP TEAM THREE TIMES IN ONE WEEK.
THAT TEAM WAS THE GIANTS.
HARRY BECAME KNOWN AS THE GIANT KILLER.
WOW. THAT'S COOL. IT'S WEIRD THAT YOU KNOW ALL THIS BOY STUFF... BUT IT'S COOL.
HOW DO YOU KNOW ABOUT BASEBALL?
BARBARA?
WHAT'S WRONG? WHAT DID I DO?
YOU DON'T WANT TO GET TOO CLOSE TO ME, SOPHIA...
PEOPLE CLOSE TO ME DIE.

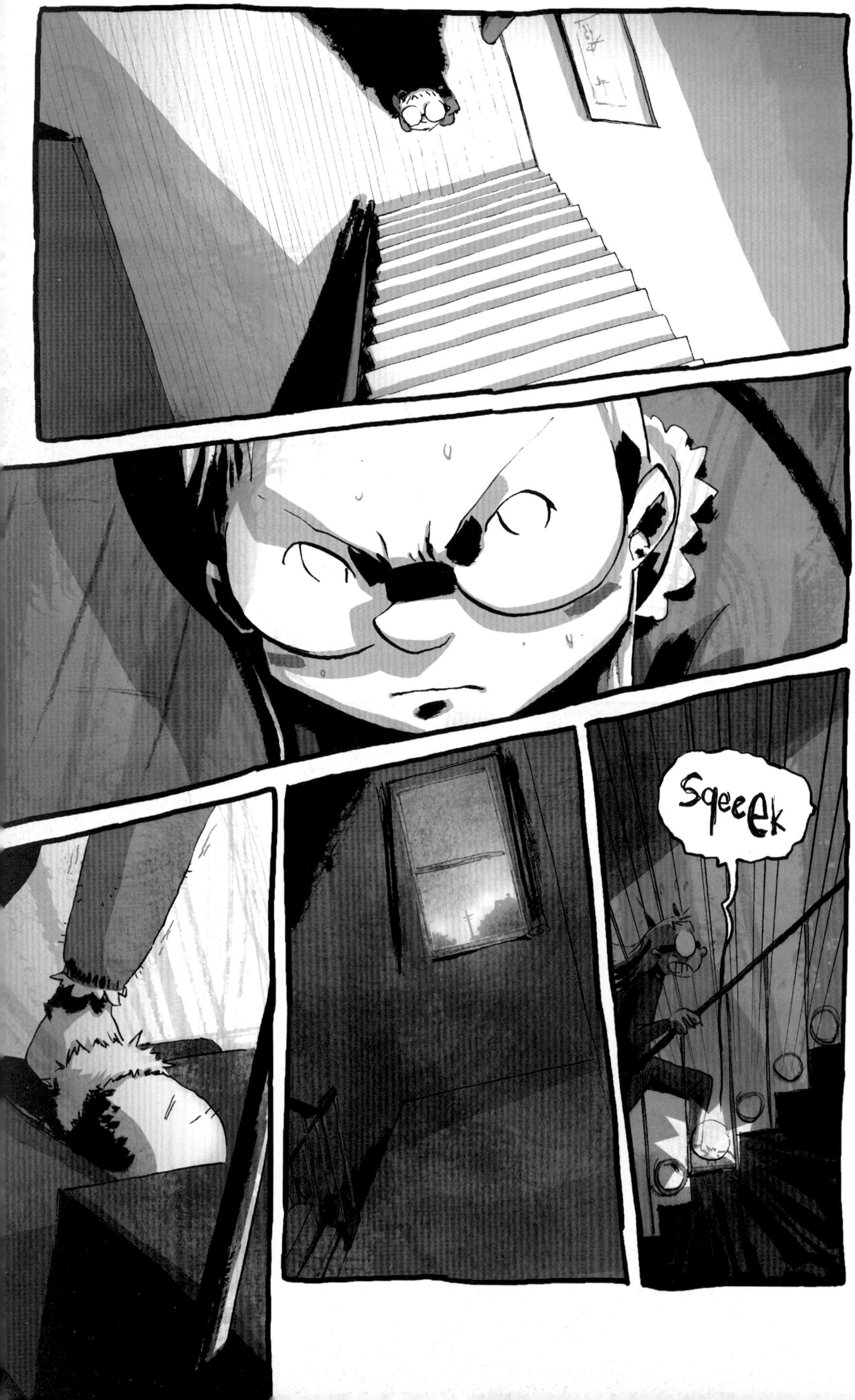
Sqeeek

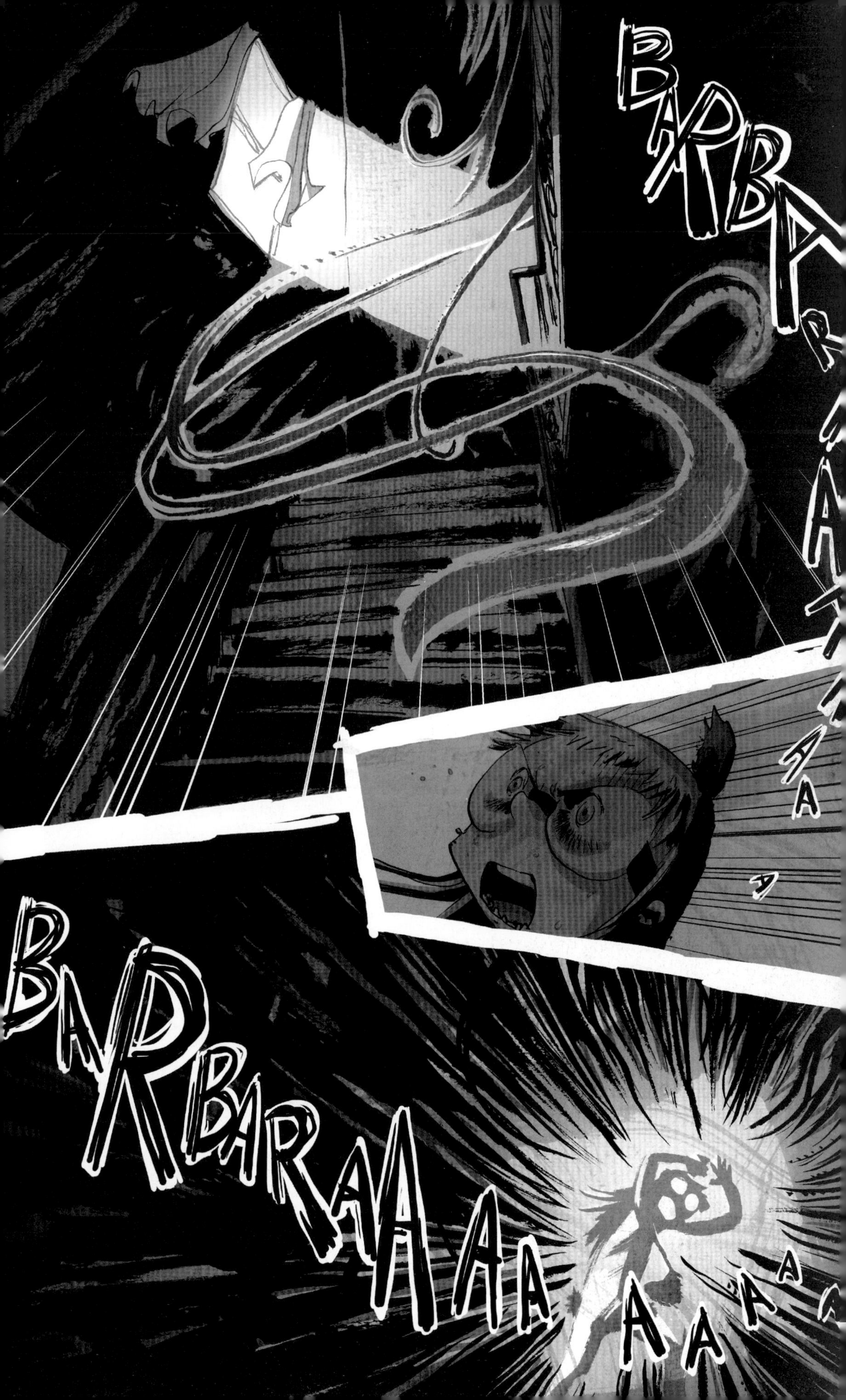

BARBARA
BARBARAAAAA

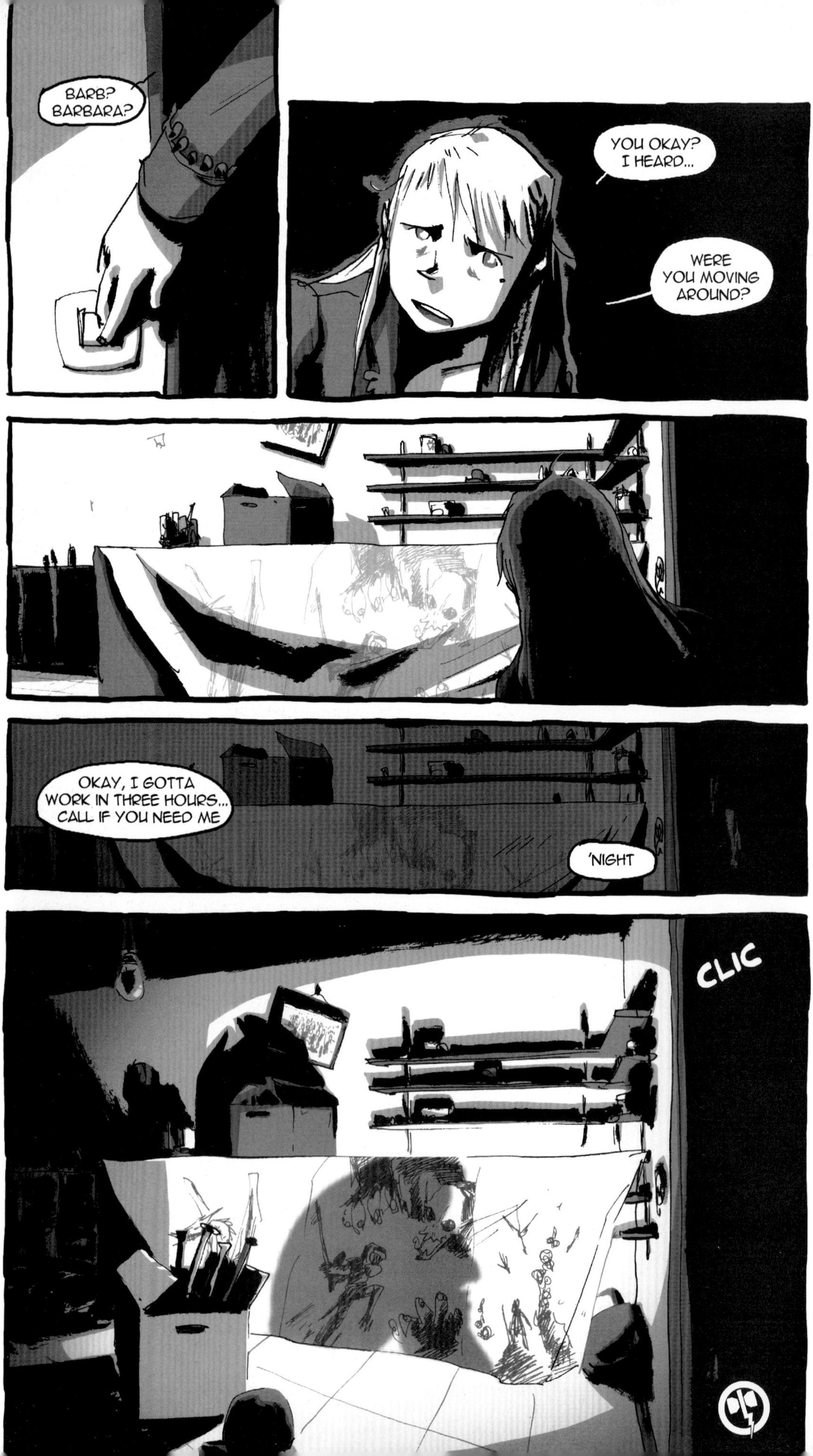
BARB? BARBARA?
YOU OKAY? I HEARD...
WERE YOU MOVING AROUND?
OKAY, I GOTTA WORK IN THREE HOURS... CALL IF YOU NEED ME
'NIGHT
CLIC

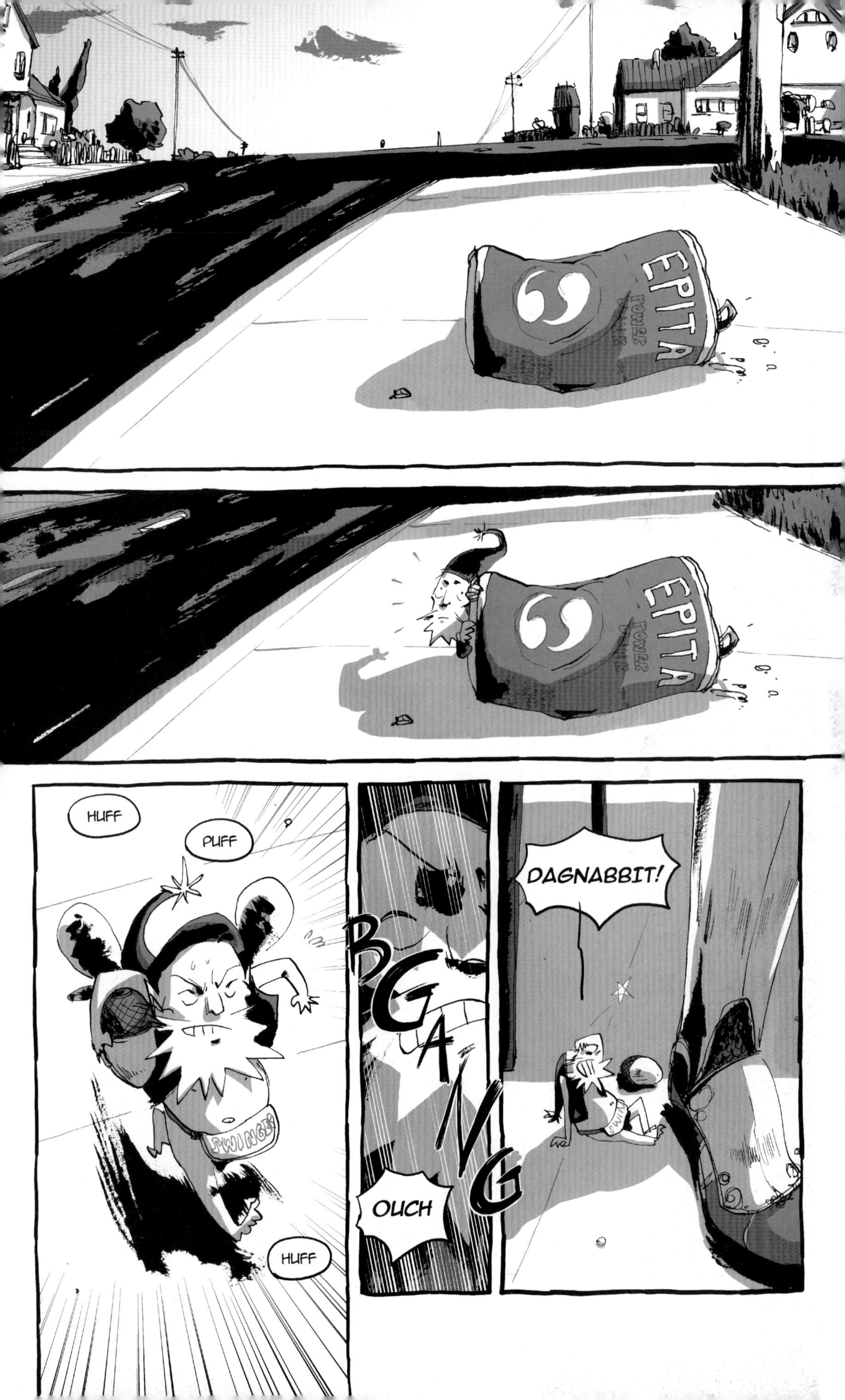
EPITA
POWER DRINK
HUFF
PUFF
HUFF
BGANG
OUCH
DAGNABBIT!

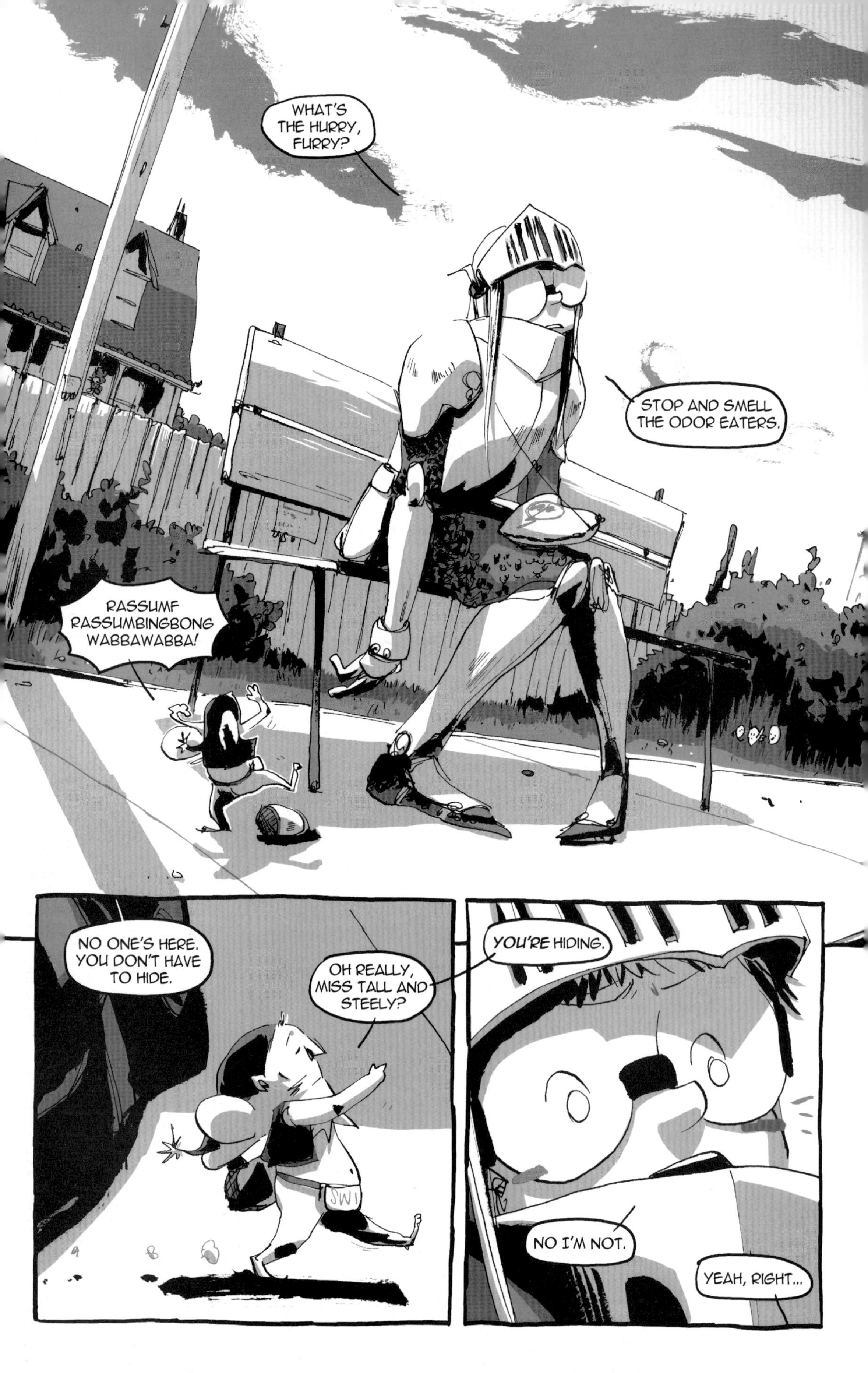
WHAT'S THE HURRY, FURRY?
STOP AND SMELL THE ODOR EATERS.
RASSUMF RASSUMBINGBONG WABBAWABBA!
NO ONE'S HERE. YOU DON'T HAVE TO HIDE.
OH REALLY, MISS TALL AND STEELY?
YOU'RE HIDING.
NO I'M NOT.
YEAH, RIGHT...

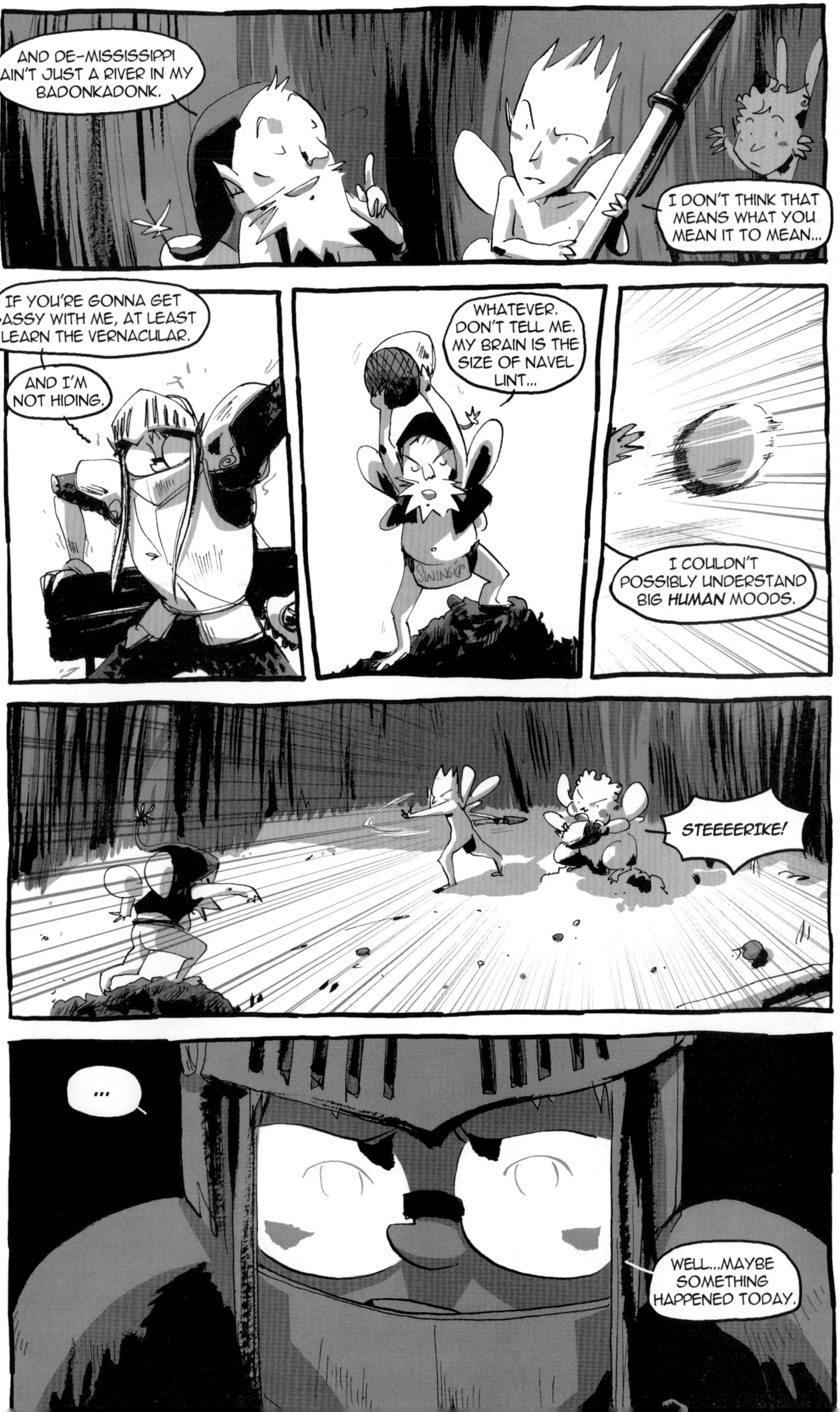
AND DE-MISSISSIPPI AIN'T JUST A RIVER IN MY BADONKADONK.
I DON'T THINK THAT MEANS WHAT YOU MEAN IT TO MEAN...
IF YOU'RE GONNA GET SASSY WITH ME, AT LEAST LEARN THE VERNACULAR.
AND I'M NOT HIDING.
WHATEVER. DON'T TELL ME. MY BRAIN IS THE SIZE OF NAVEL LINT...
I COULDN'T POSSIBLY UNDERSTAND BIG HUMAN MOODS.
STEEEERIKE!
...
WELL...MAYBE SOMETHING HAPPENED TODAY.

IKG CHAPTER 3: THE ARMOR

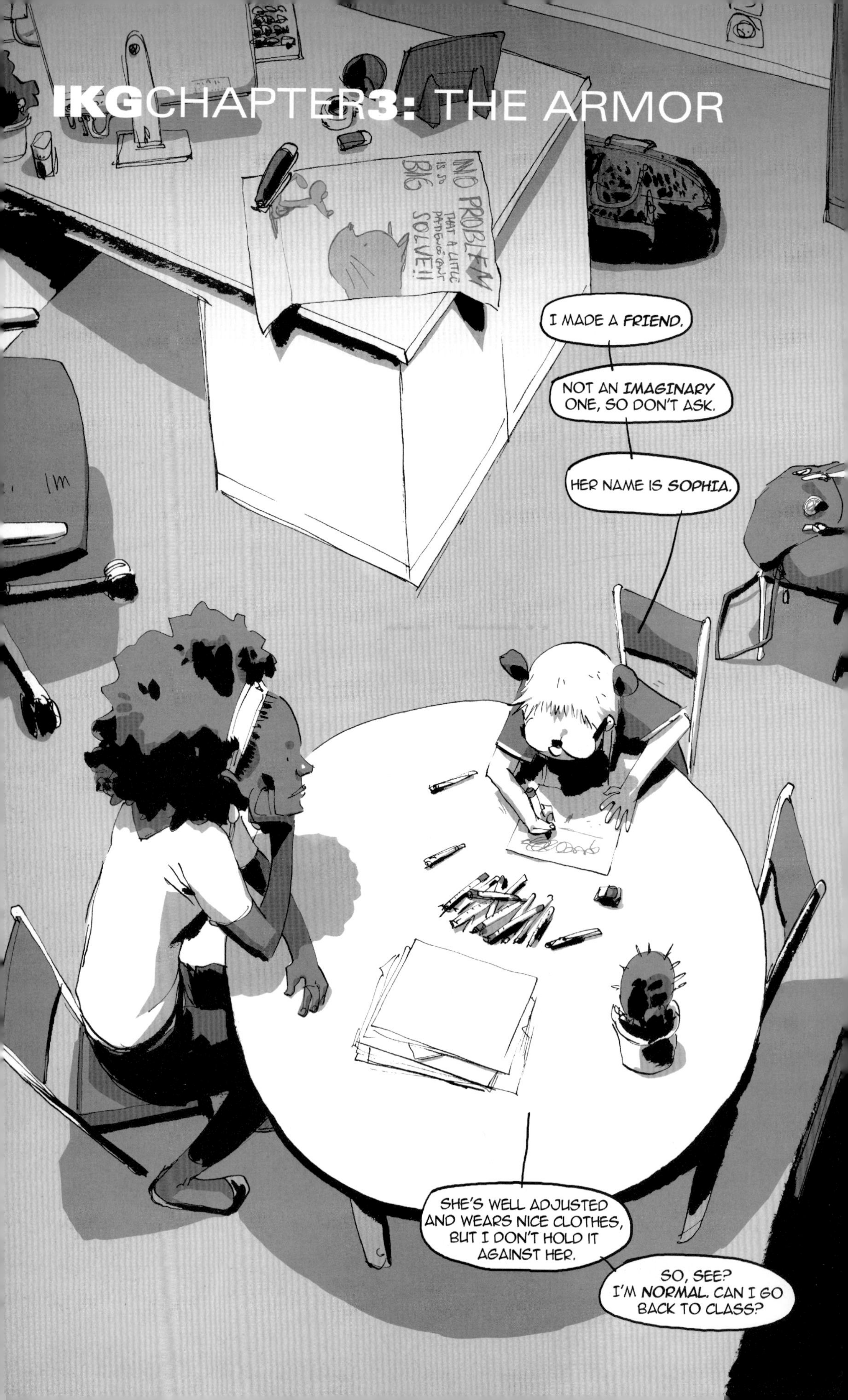
NO PROBLEM
IS SO BIG
THAT A LITTLE
CAN'T
SOLVE!!
I MADE A FRIEND.
NOT AN IMAGINARY ONE, SO DON'T ASK.
HER NAME IS SOPHIA.
SHE'S WELL ADJUSTED AND WEARS NICE CLOTHES, BUT I DON'T HOLD IT AGAINST HER.
SO, SEE? I'M NORMAL. CAN I GO BACK TO CLASS?

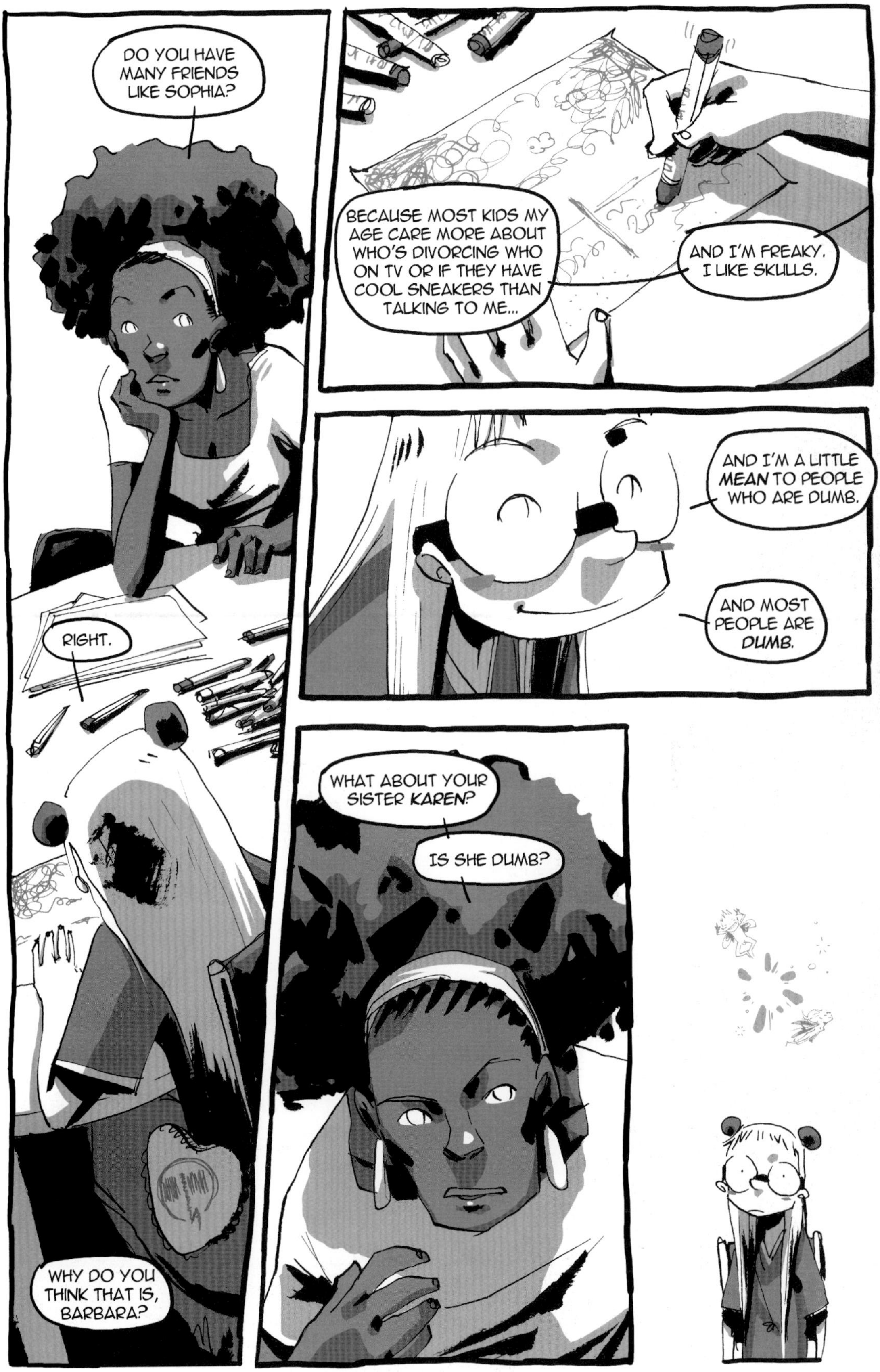
DO YOU HAVE MANY FRIENDS LIKE SOPHIA?
RIGHT.
WHY DO YOU THINK THAT IS, BARBARA?
BECAUSE MOST KIDS MY AGE CARE MORE ABOUT WHO'S DIVORCING WHO ON TV OR IF THEY HAVE COOL SNEAKERS THAN TALKING TO ME...
AND I'M FREAKY. I LIKE SKULLS.
AND I'M A LITTLE *MEAN* TO PEOPLE WHO ARE DUMB.
AND MOST PEOPLE ARE *DUMB*.
WHAT ABOUT YOUR SISTER *KAREN*?
IS SHE DUMB?

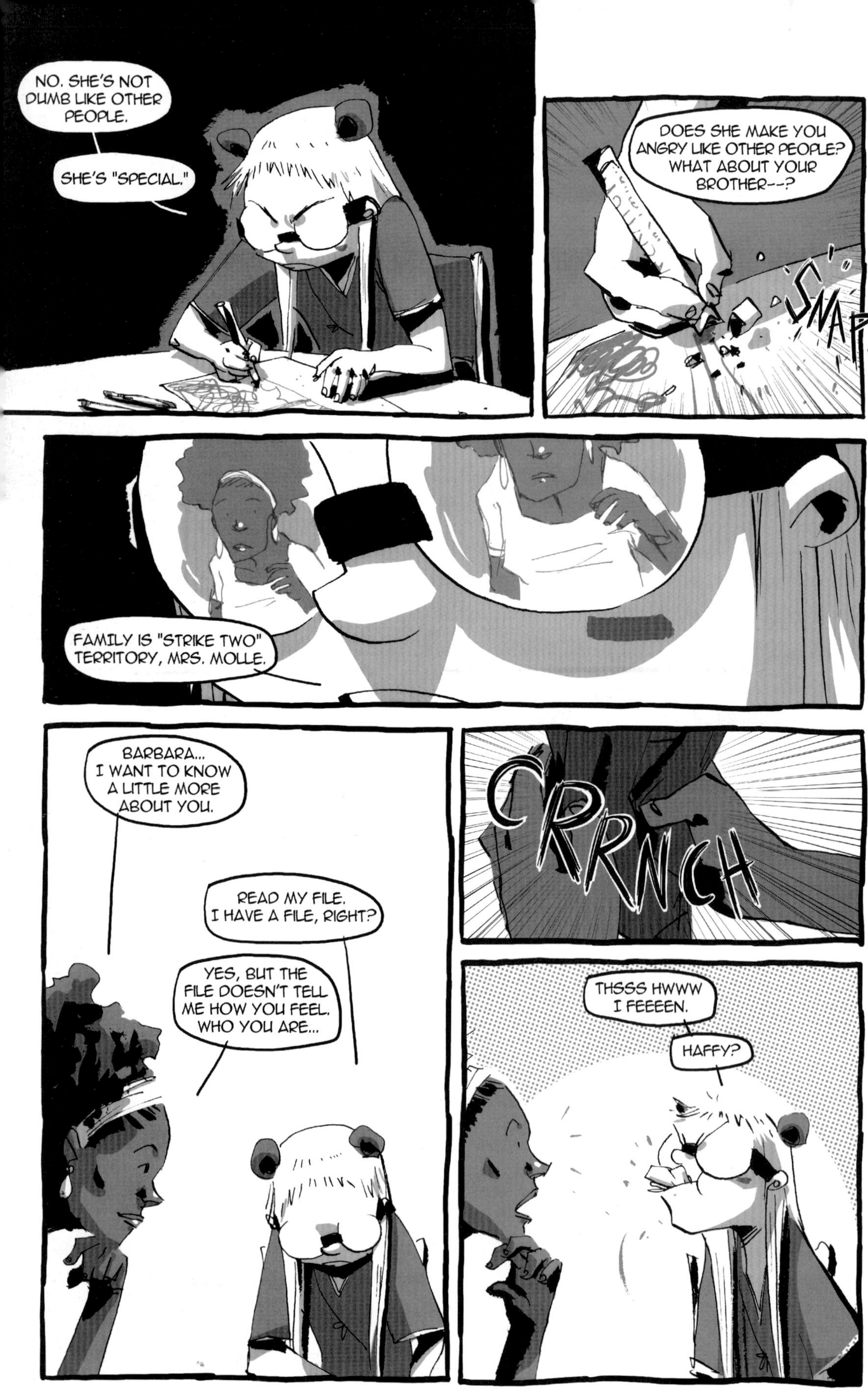
NO. SHE'S NOT DUMB LIKE OTHER PEOPLE.
SHE'S "SPECIAL."
DOES SHE MAKE YOU ANGRY LIKE OTHER PEOPLE? WHAT ABOUT YOUR BROTHER--?
SNAP
FAMILY IS "STRIKE TWO" TERRITORY, MRS. MOLLE.
BARBARA... I WANT TO KNOW A LITTLE MORE ABOUT YOU.
READ MY FILE. I HAVE A FILE, RIGHT?
YES, BUT THE FILE DOESN'T TELL ME HOW YOU FEEL. WHO YOU ARE...
CRRNCH
THSSS HWWW I FEEEEN.
HAFFY?

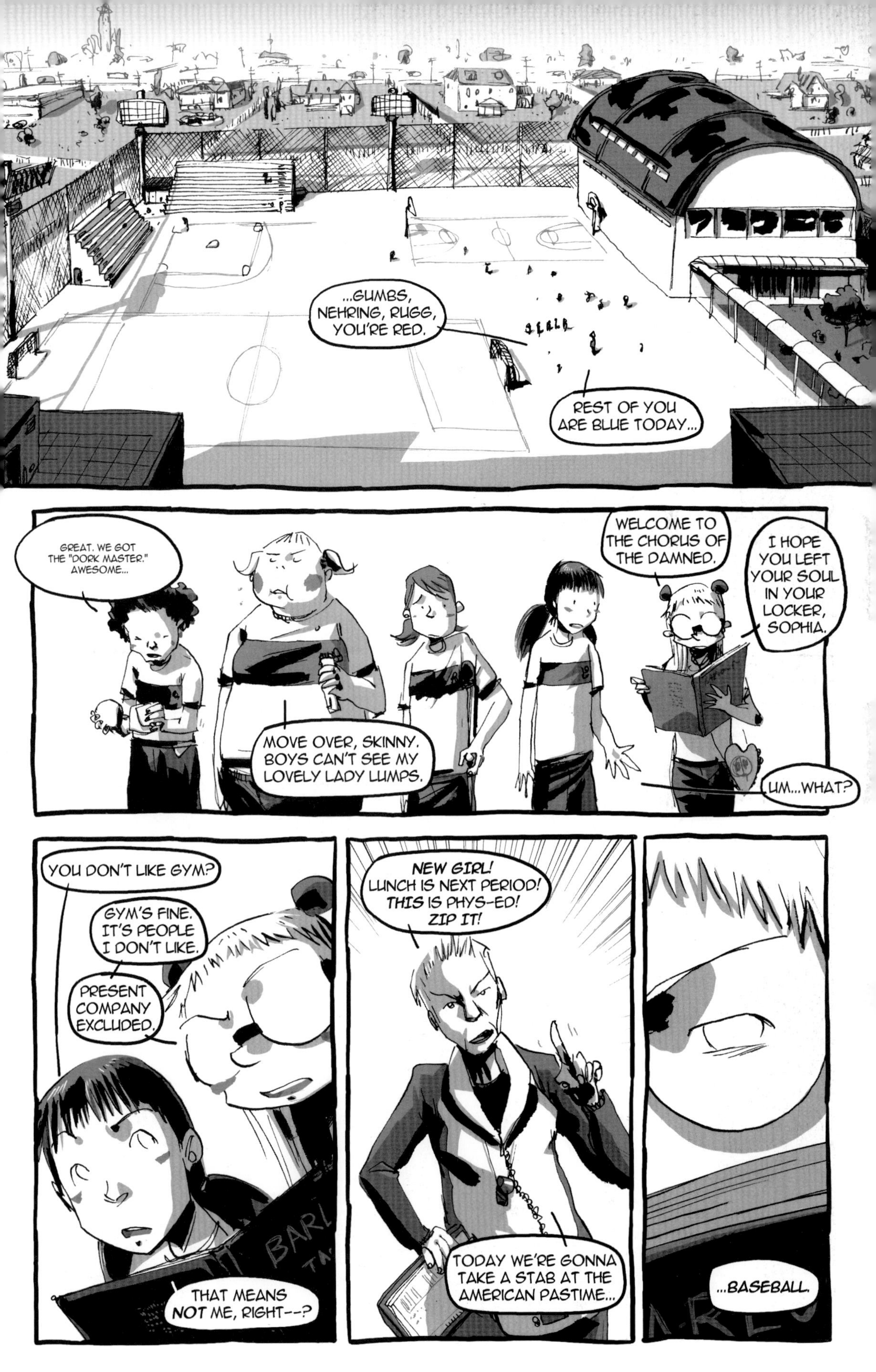
...GUMBS, NEHRING, RUGG, YOU'RE RED.
REST OF YOU ARE BLUE TODAY...
GREAT. WE GOT THE "DORK MASTER." AWESOME...
MOVE OVER, SKINNY. BOYS CAN'T SEE MY LOVELY LADY LUMPS.
WELCOME TO THE CHORUS OF THE DAMNED.
I HOPE YOU LEFT YOUR SOUL IN YOUR LOCKER, SOPHIA.
UM...WHAT?
YOU DON'T LIKE GYM?
GYM'S FINE. IT'S PEOPLE I DON'T LIKE.
PRESENT COMPANY EXCLUDED.
THAT MEANS NOT ME, RIGHT--?
NEW GIRL! LUNCH IS NEXT PERIOD! THIS IS PHYS-ED! ZIP IT!
TODAY WE'RE GONNA TAKE A STAB AT THE AMERICAN PASTIME...
...BASEBALL.

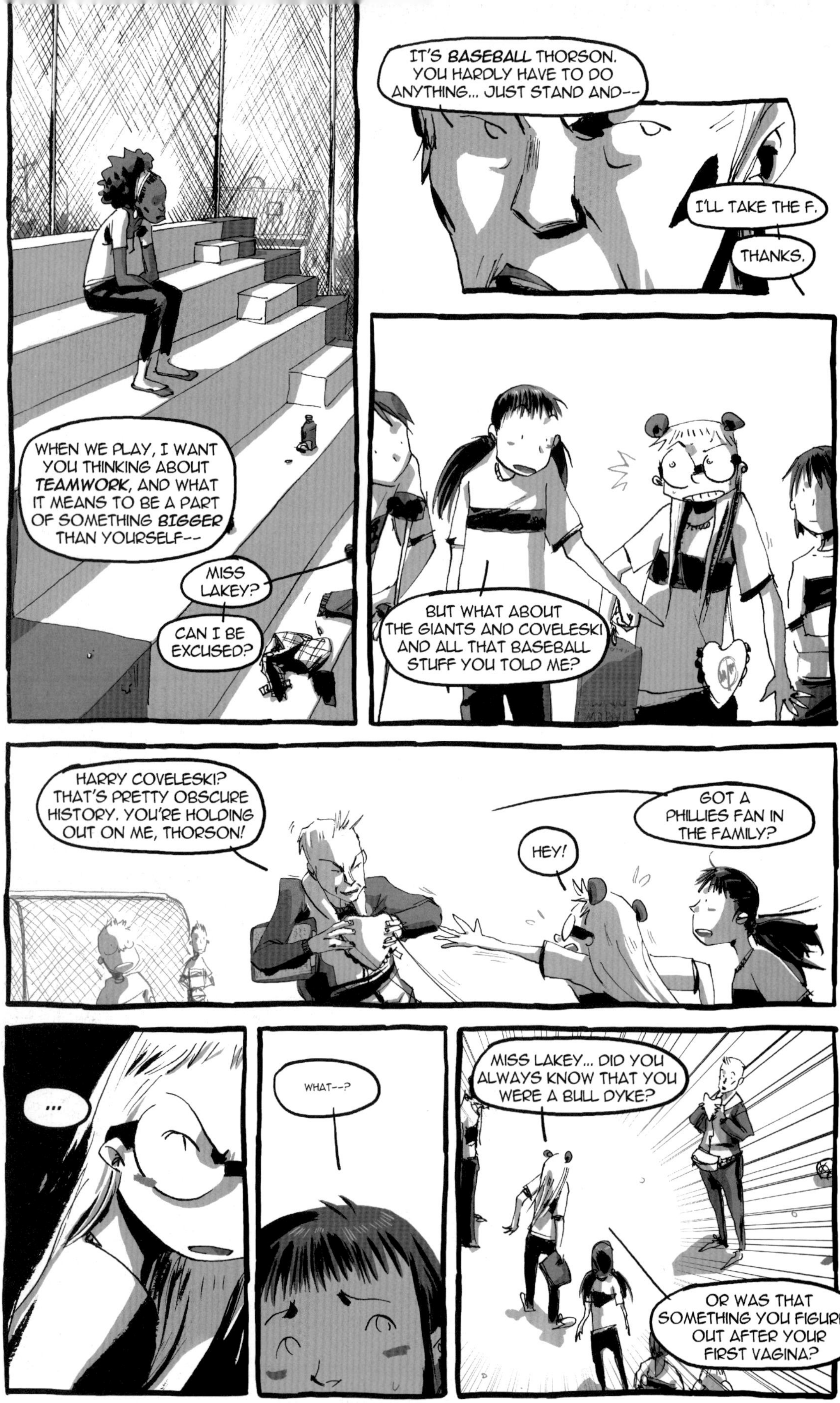
IT'S BASEBALL THORSON. YOU HARDLY HAVE TO DO ANYTHING... JUST STAND AND--
I'LL TAKE THE F.
THANKS.
WHEN WE PLAY, I WANT YOU THINKING ABOUT TEAMWORK, AND WHAT IT MEANS TO BE A PART OF SOMETHING BIGGER THAN YOURSELF--
MISS LAKEY?
CAN I BE EXCUSED?
BUT WHAT ABOUT THE GIANTS AND COVELESKI AND ALL THAT BASEBALL STUFF YOU TOLD ME?
HARRY COVELESKI? THAT'S PRETTY OBSCURE HISTORY. YOU'RE HOLDING OUT ON ME, THORSON!
HEY!
GOT A PHILLIES FAN IN THE FAMILY?
...
WHAT--?
MISS LAKEY... DID YOU ALWAYS KNOW THAT YOU WERE A BULL DYKE?
OR WAS THAT SOMETHING YOU FIGURED OUT AFTER YOUR FIRST VAGINA?

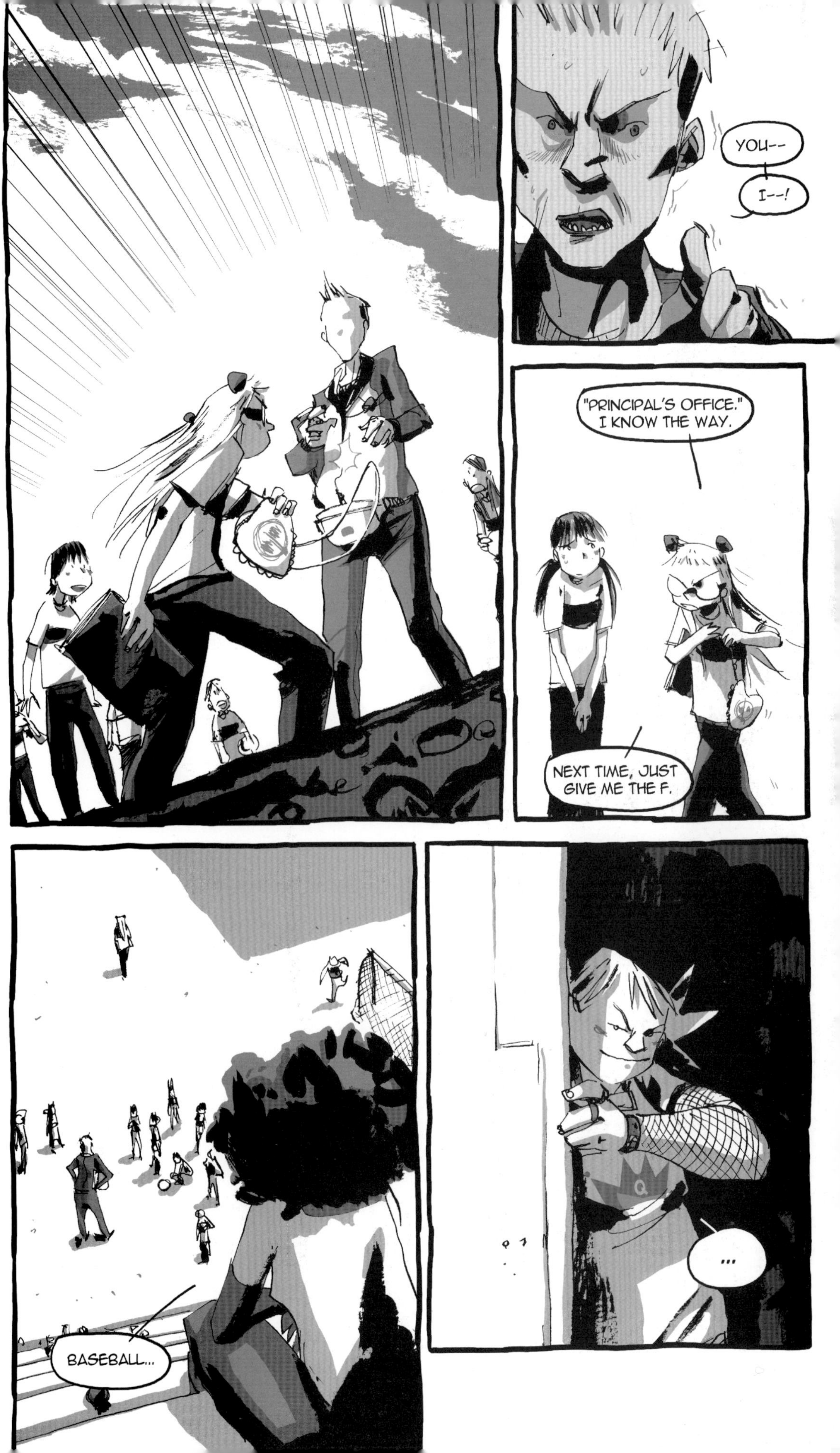
YOU--
I--!
"PRINCIPAL'S OFFICE." I KNOW THE WAY.
NEXT TIME, JUST GIVE ME THE F.
BASEBALL...
...

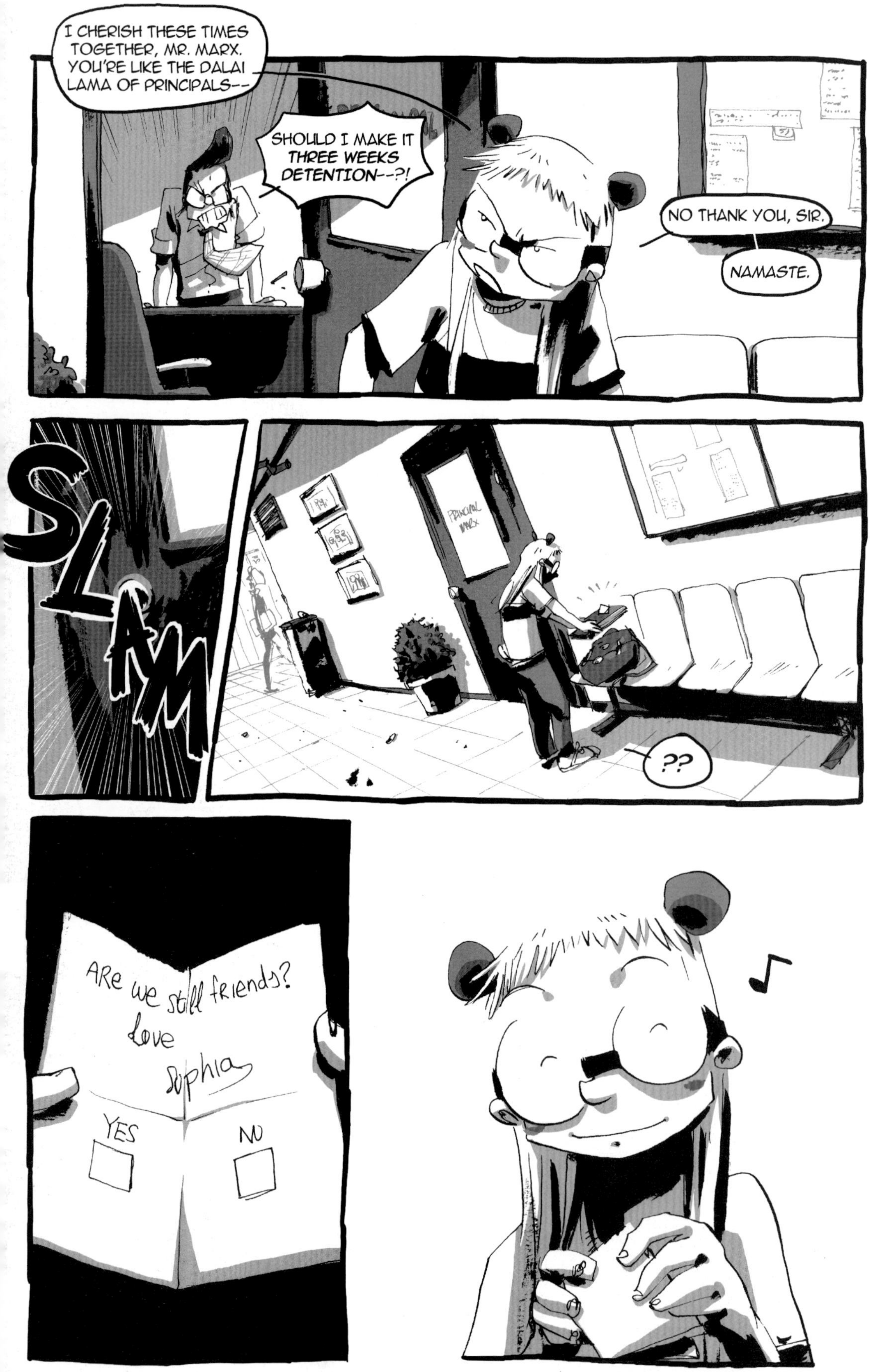
I CHERISH THESE TIMES TOGETHER, MR. MARX. YOU'RE LIKE THE DALAI LAMA OF PRINCIPALS--
SHOULD I MAKE IT THREE WEEKS DETENTION--?!
NO THANK YOU, SIR.
NAMASTE.
SLAM
??
Are we still friends?
love
Sophia
YES
NO
♪

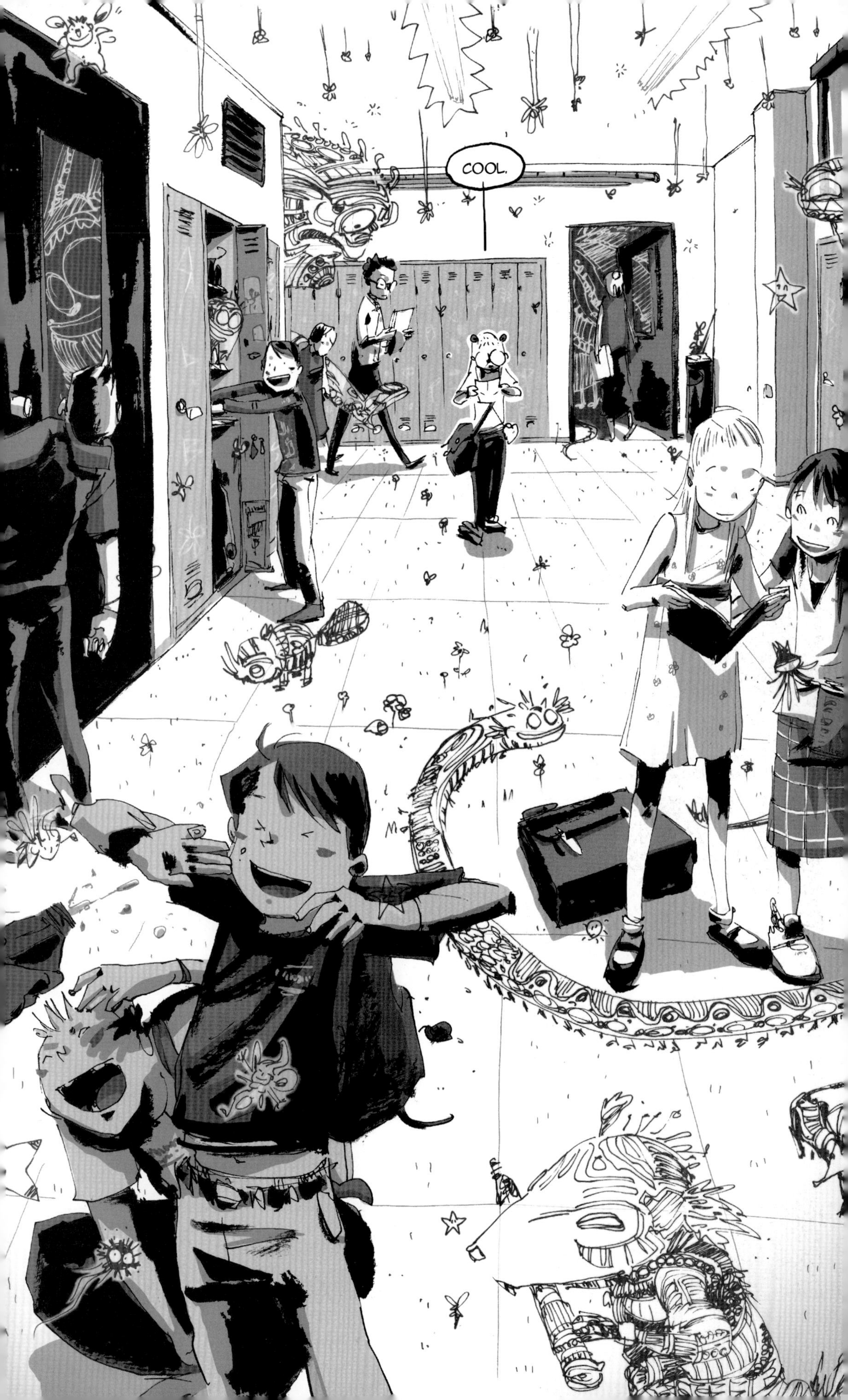
COOL.

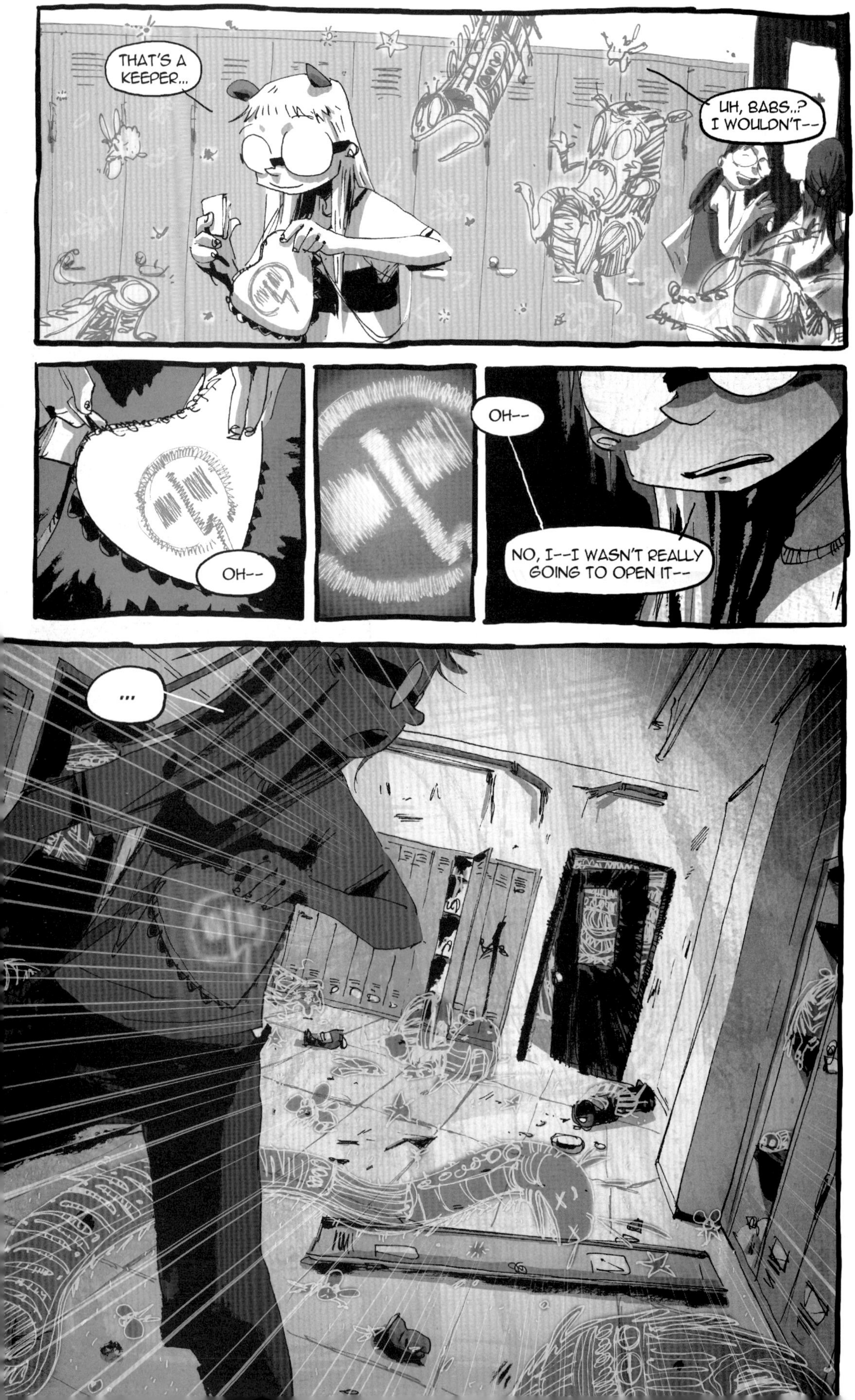
THAT'S A KEEPER...
UH, BABS..? I WOULDN'T--
OH--
OH--
NO, I--I WASN'T REALLY GOING TO OPEN IT--
...

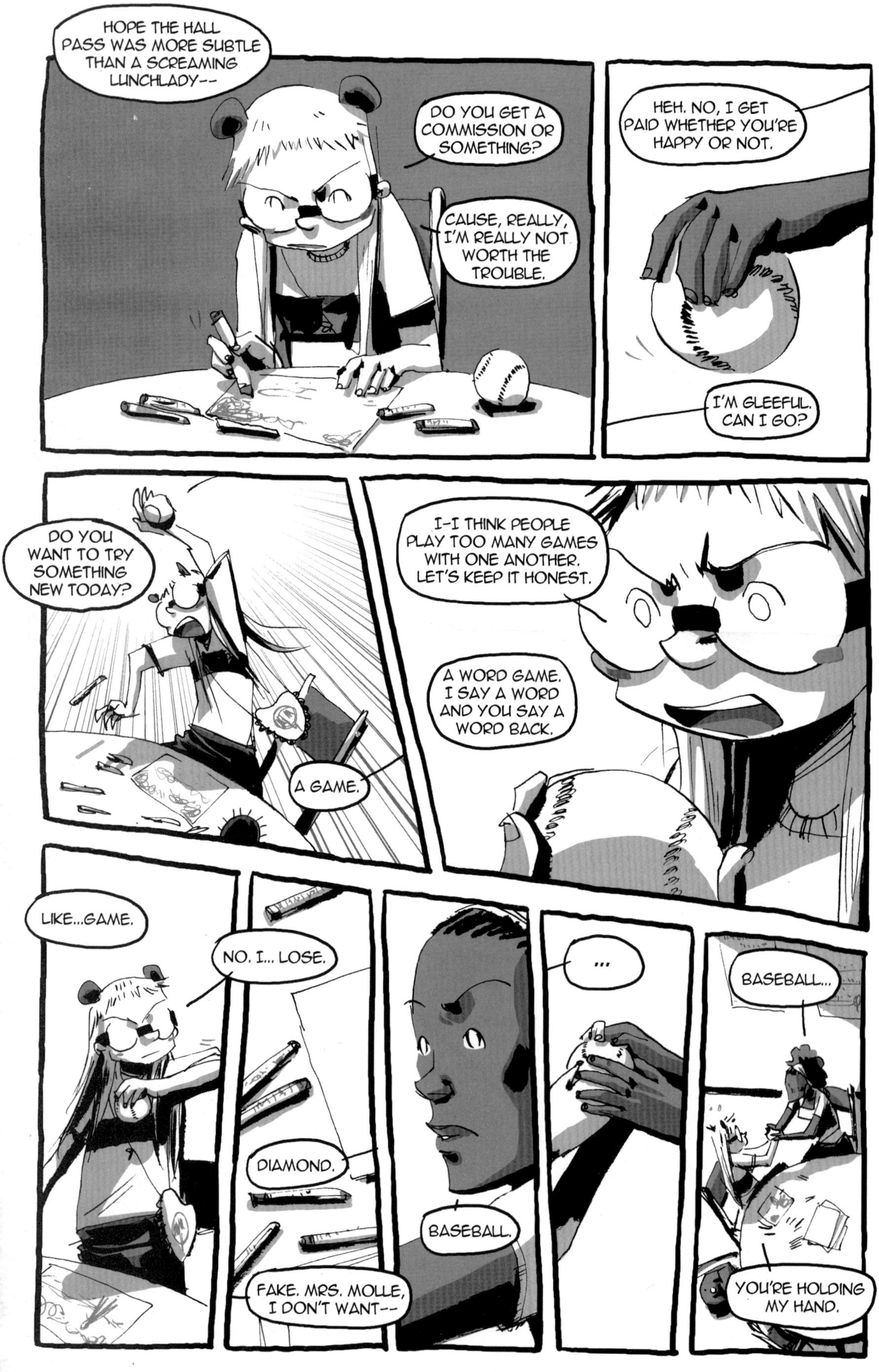
HOPE THE HALL PASS WAS MORE SUBTLE THAN A SCREAMING LUNCHLADY--
DO YOU GET A COMMISSION OR SOMETHING?
CAUSE, REALLY, I'M REALLY NOT WORTH THE TROUBLE.
HEH. NO, I GET PAID WHETHER YOU'RE HAPPY OR NOT.
I'M GLEEFUL. CAN I GO?
DO YOU WANT TO TRY SOMETHING NEW TODAY?
A GAME.
I-I THINK PEOPLE PLAY TOO MANY GAMES WITH ONE ANOTHER. LET'S KEEP IT HONEST.
A WORD GAME. I SAY A WORD AND YOU SAY A WORD BACK.
LIKE...GAME.
NO. I... LOSE.
DIAMOND.
FAKE. MRS. MOLLE, I DON'T WANT--
BASEBALL.
...
BASEBALL...
YOU'RE HOLDING MY HAND.

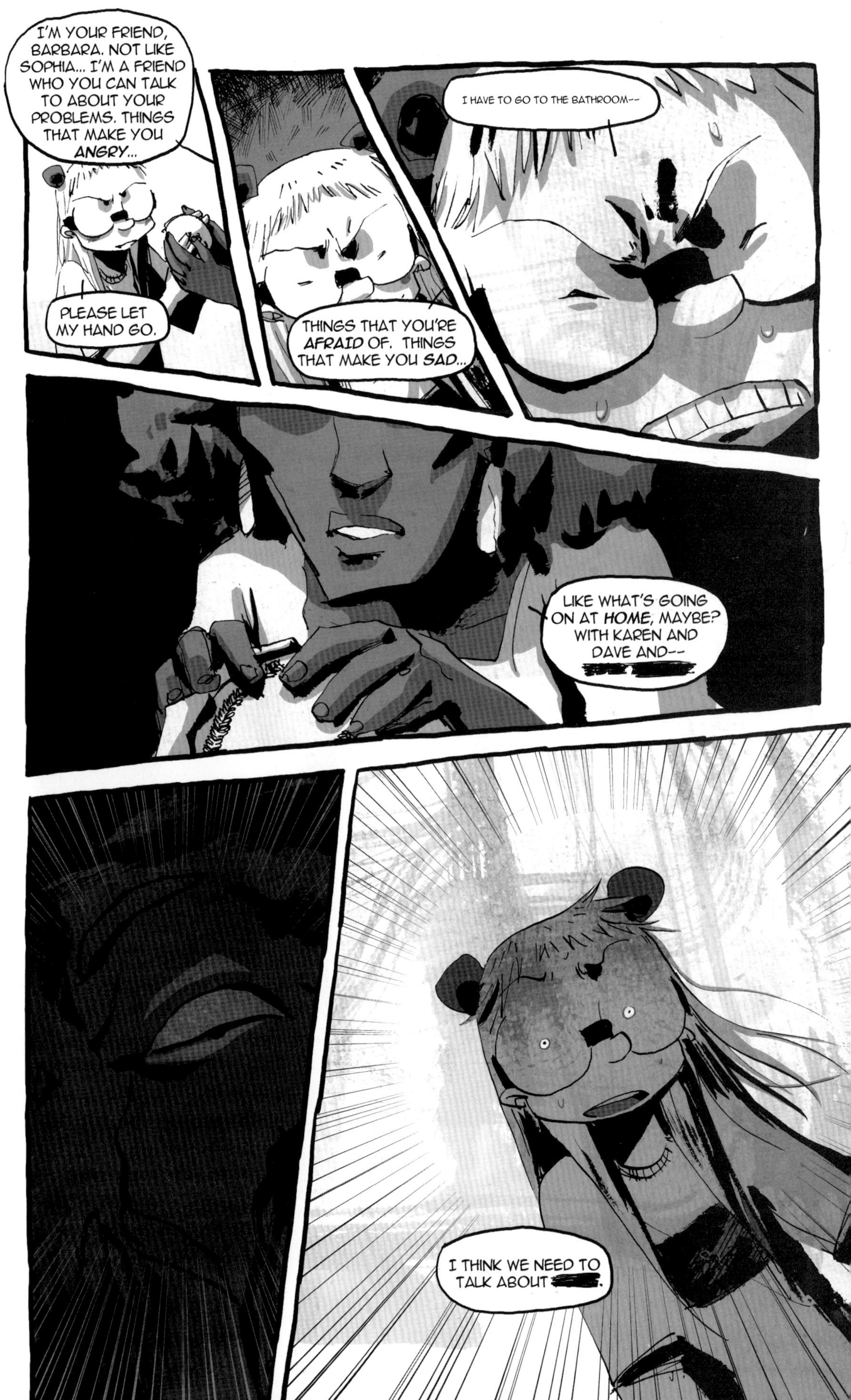
I'M YOUR FRIEND, BARBARA. NOT LIKE SOPHIA... I'M A FRIEND WHO YOU CAN TALK TO ABOUT YOUR PROBLEMS. THINGS THAT MAKE YOU ANGRY...
PLEASE LET MY HAND GO.
THINGS THAT YOU'RE AFRAID OF. THINGS THAT MAKE YOU SAD...
I HAVE TO GO TO THE BATHROOM--
LIKE WHAT'S GOING ON AT HOME, MAYBE? WITH KAREN AND DAVE AND-- [redacted]
I THINK WE NEED TO TALK ABOUT [redacted].

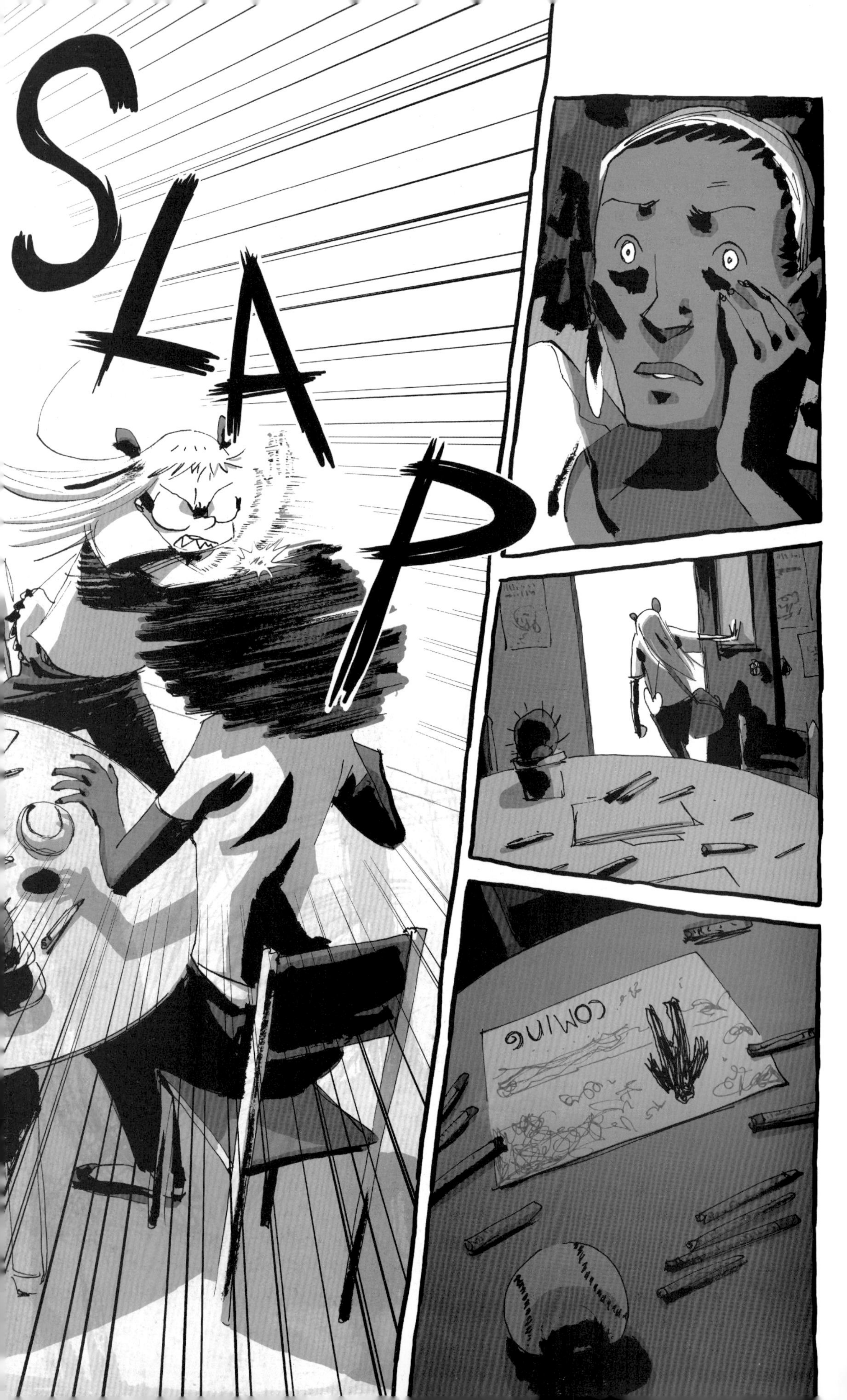
SLAP
COMING

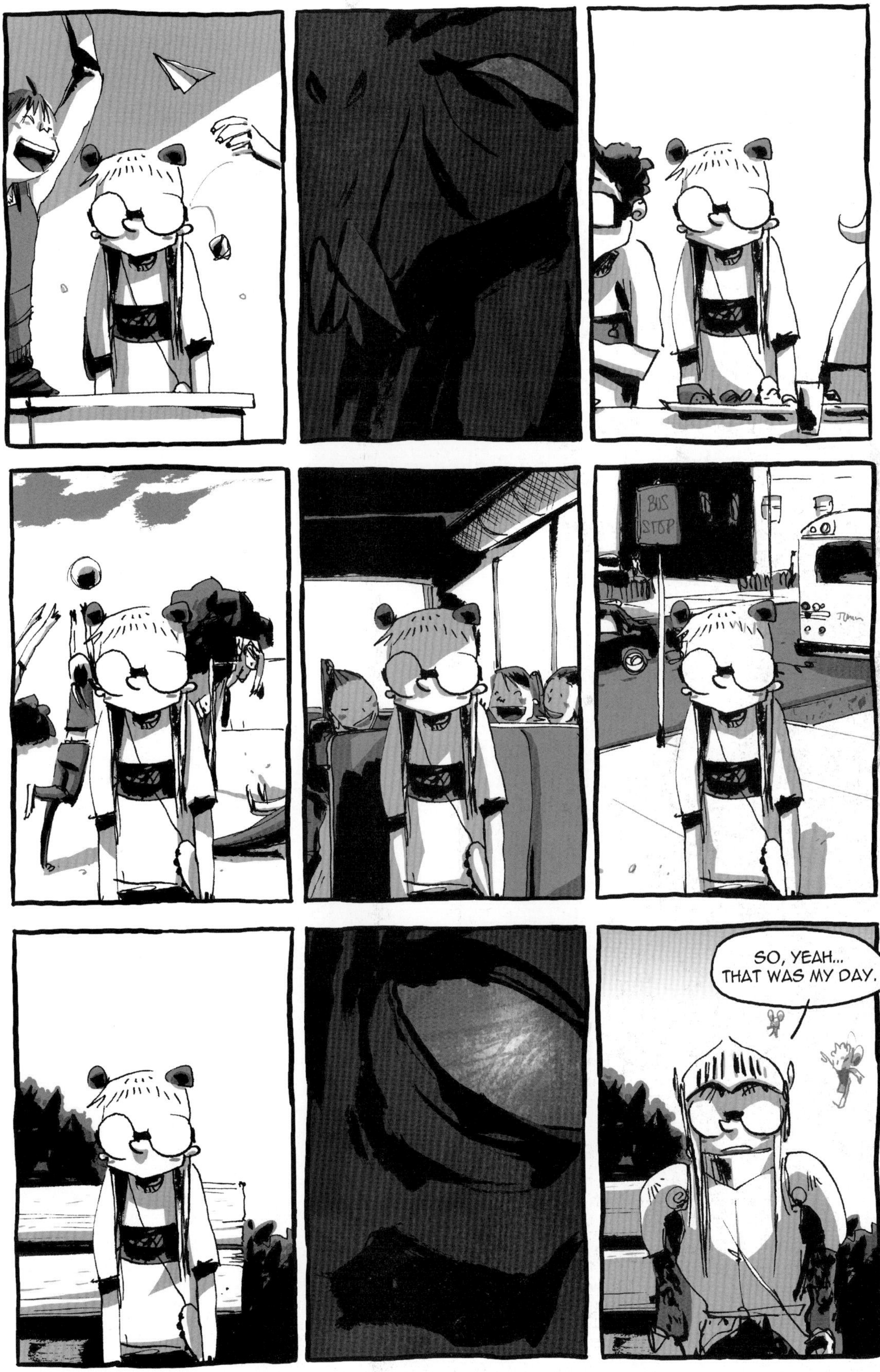
BUS STOP
SO, YEAH... THAT WAS MY DAY.

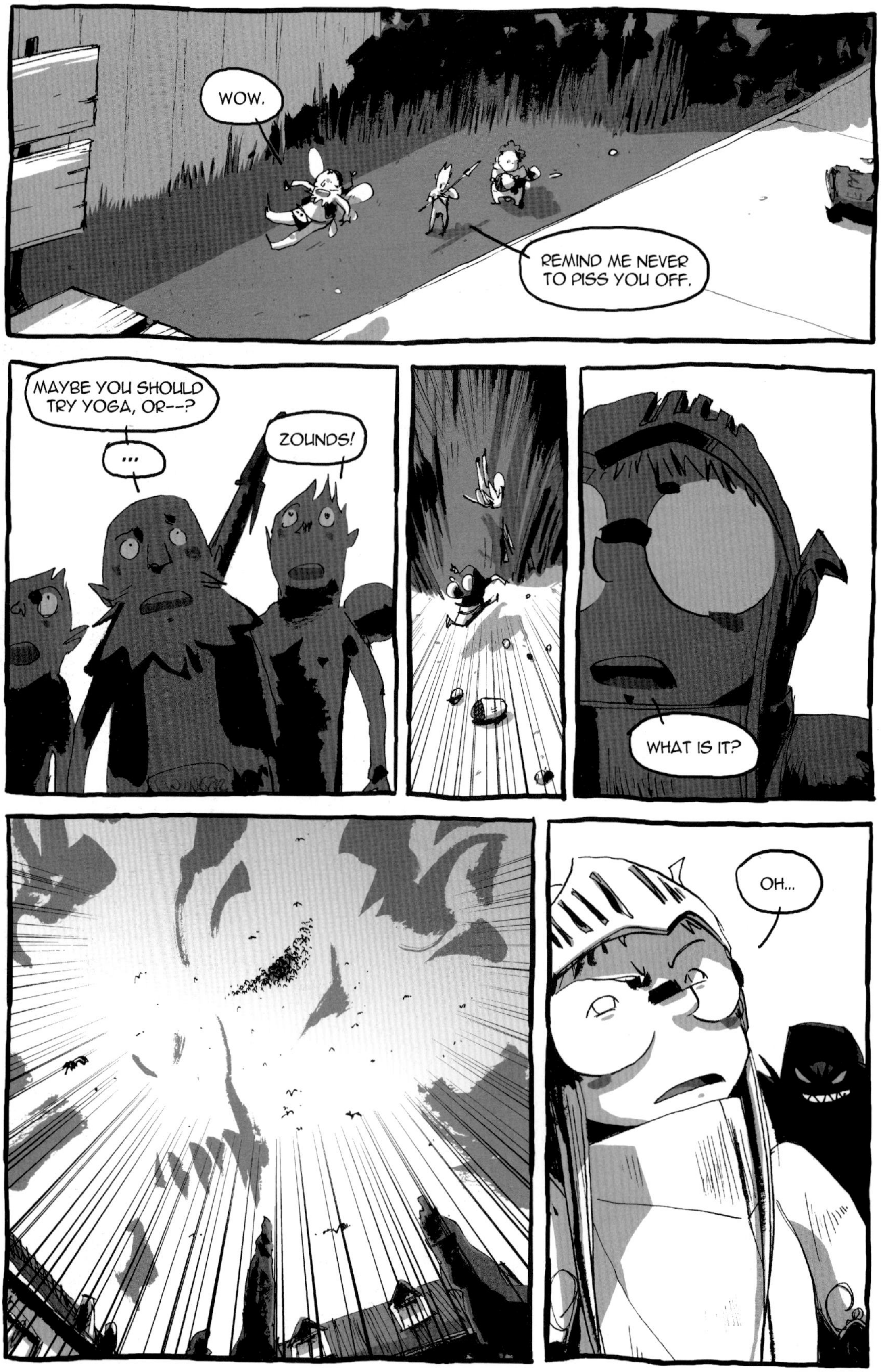
WOW.
REMIND ME NEVER TO PISS YOU OFF.
MAYBE YOU SHOULD TRY YOGA, OR--?
...
ZOUNDS!
WHAT IS IT?
OH...

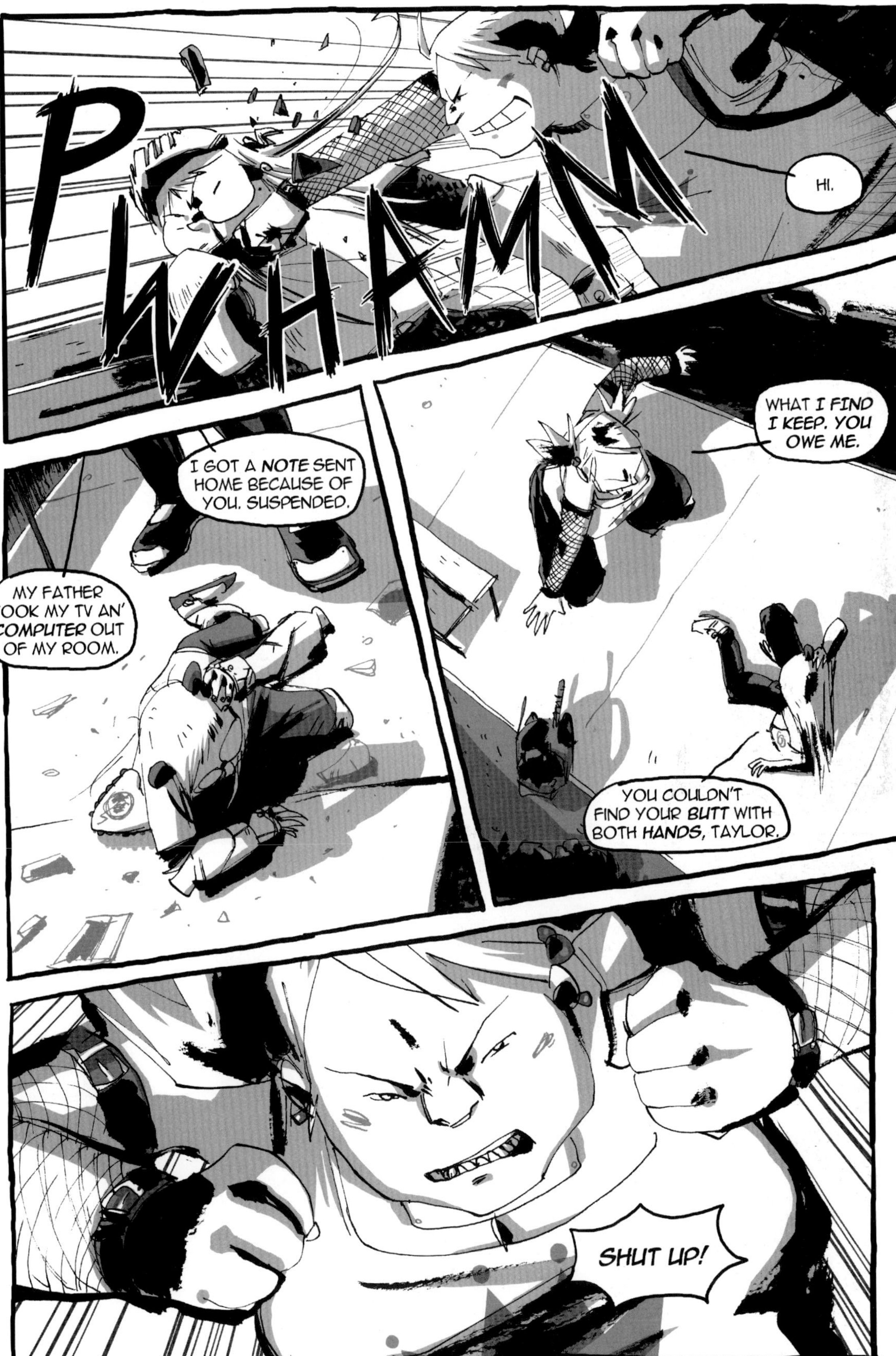
PWHAMM
HI.
I GOT A NOTE SENT HOME BECAUSE OF YOU. SUSPENDED.
MY FATHER TOOK MY TV AN' COMPUTER OUT OF MY ROOM.
WHAT I FIND I KEEP. YOU OWE ME.
YOU COULDN'T FIND YOUR BUTT WITH BOTH HANDS, TAYLOR.
SHUT UP!

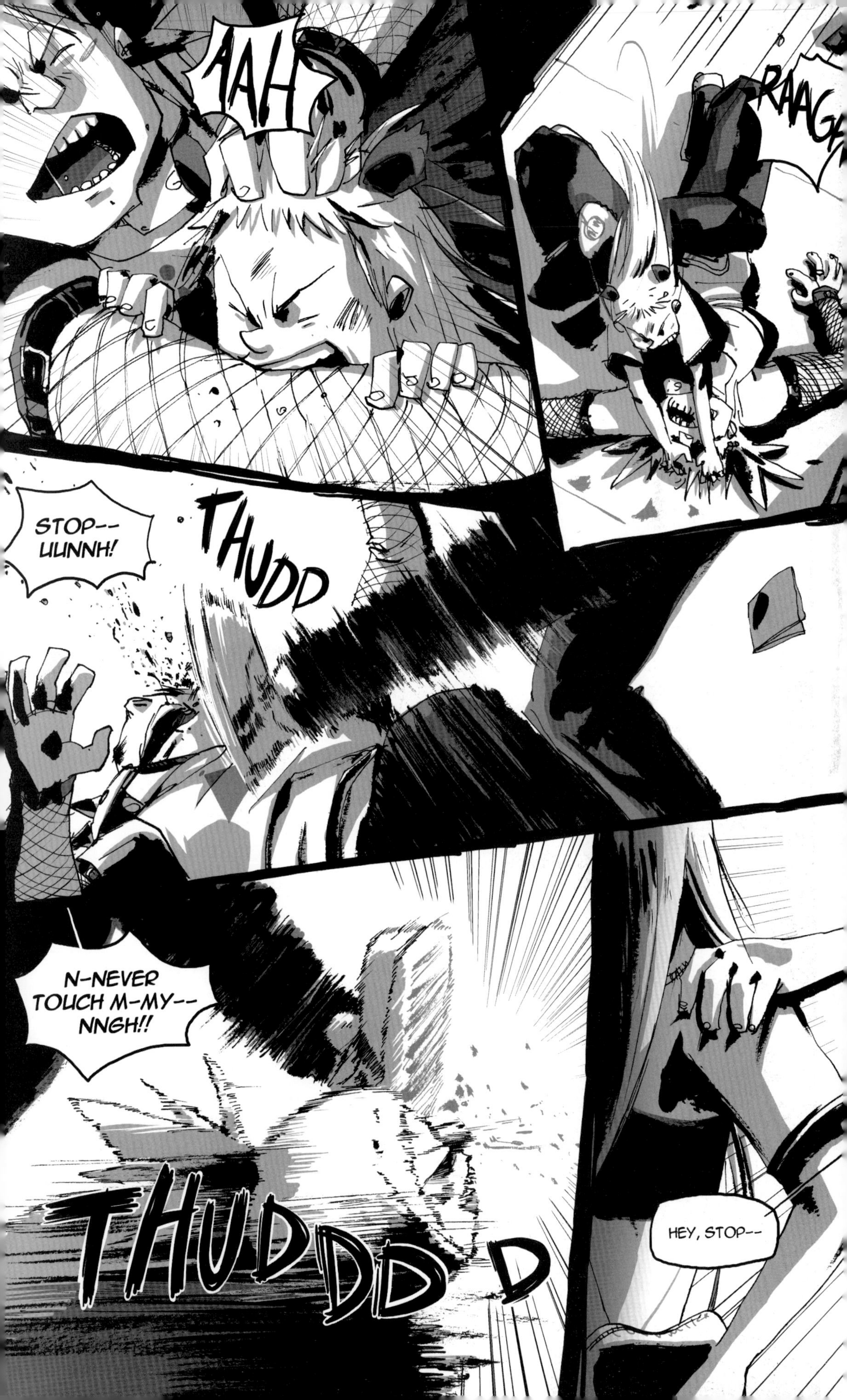
AAH
RAAGH
STOP--
UUNNH!
THUDD
N-NEVER
TOUCH M-MY--
NNGH!!
THUDDD D
HEY, STOP--

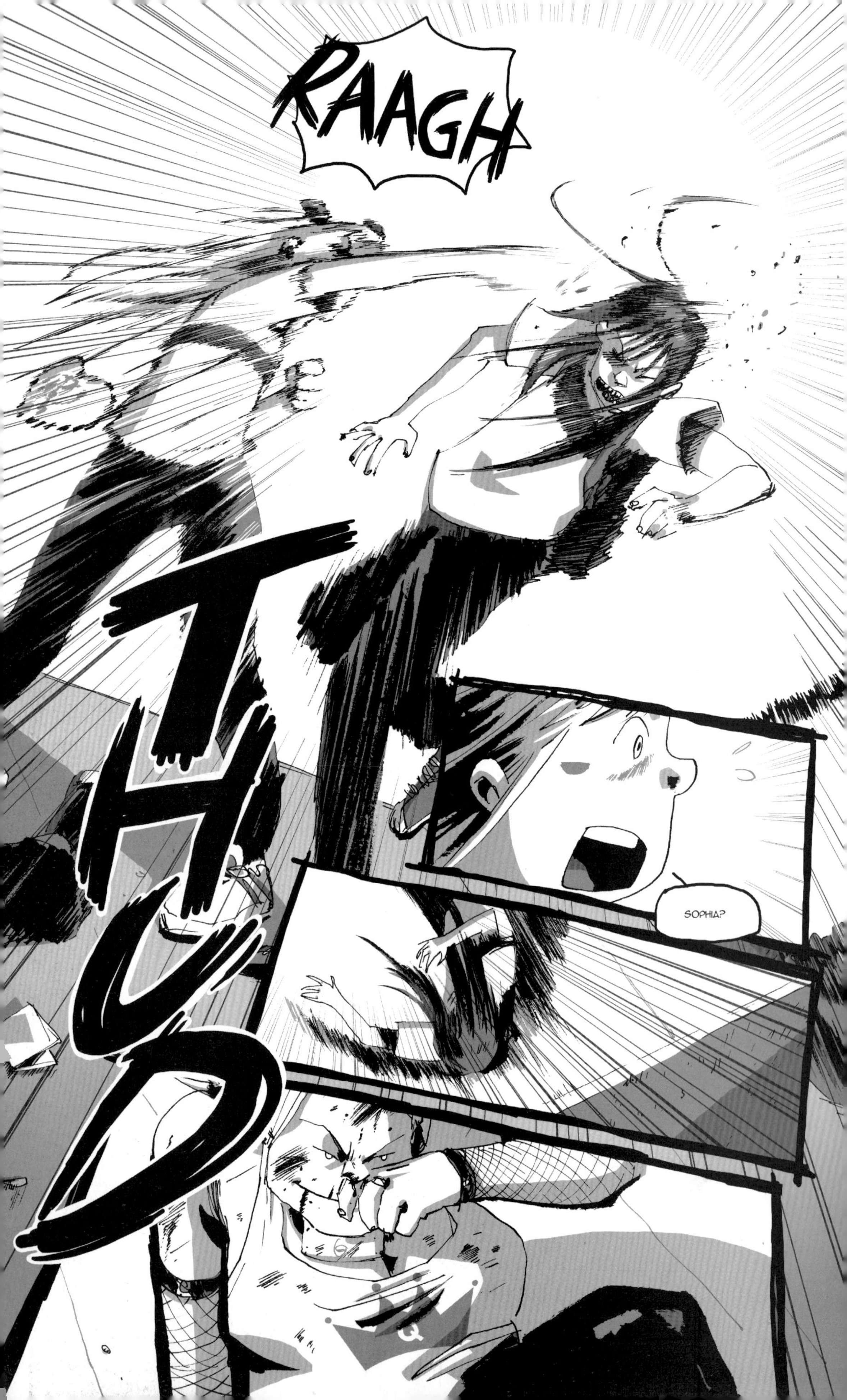
RAAGH
THUD
SOPHIA?

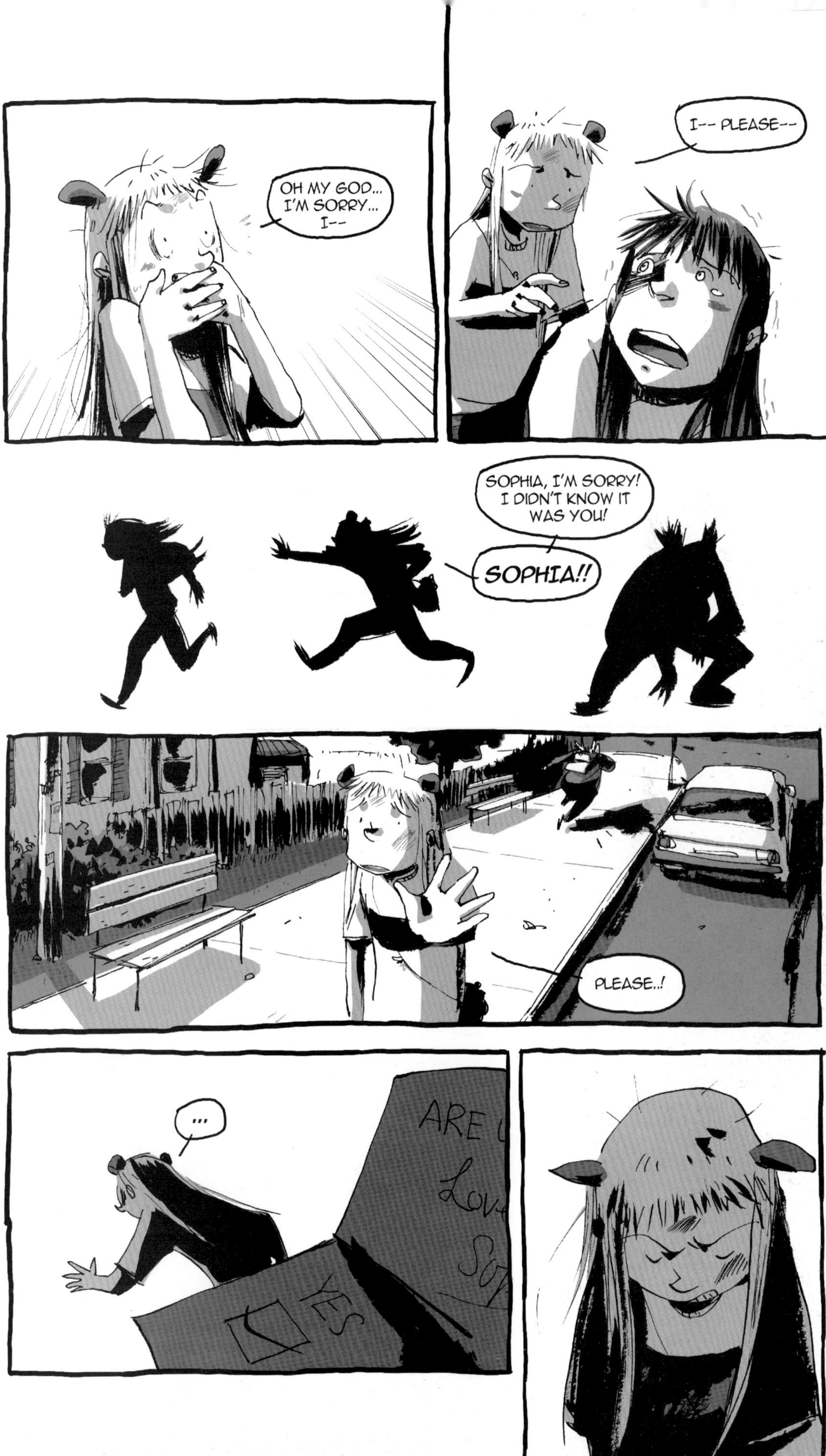
OH MY GOD... I'M SORRY... I--
I-- PLEASE--
SOPHIA, I'M SORRY! I DIDN'T KNOW IT WAS YOU!
SOPHIA!!
PLEASE..!
...

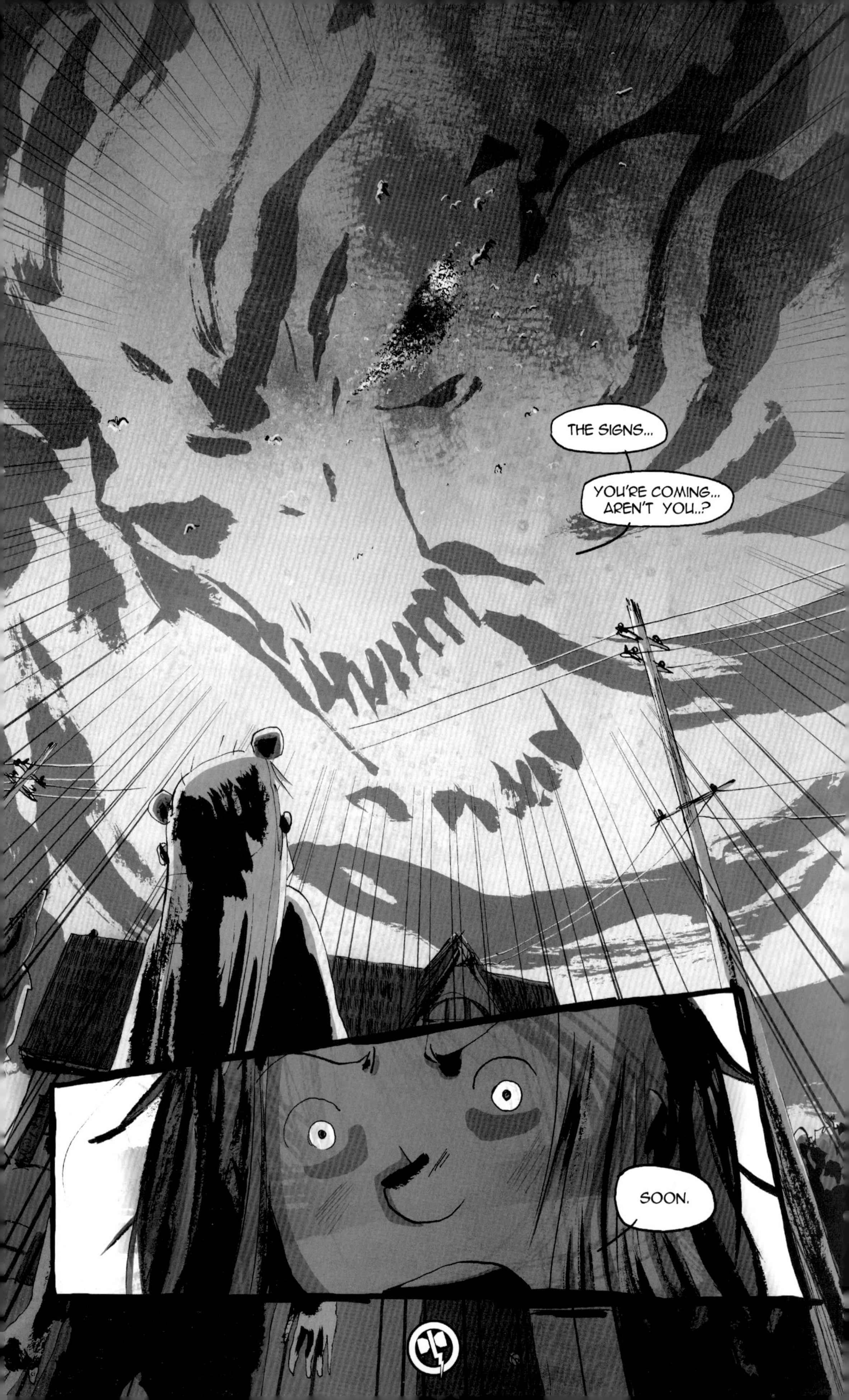
THE SIGNS...
YOU'RE COMING... AREN'T YOU..?
SOON.

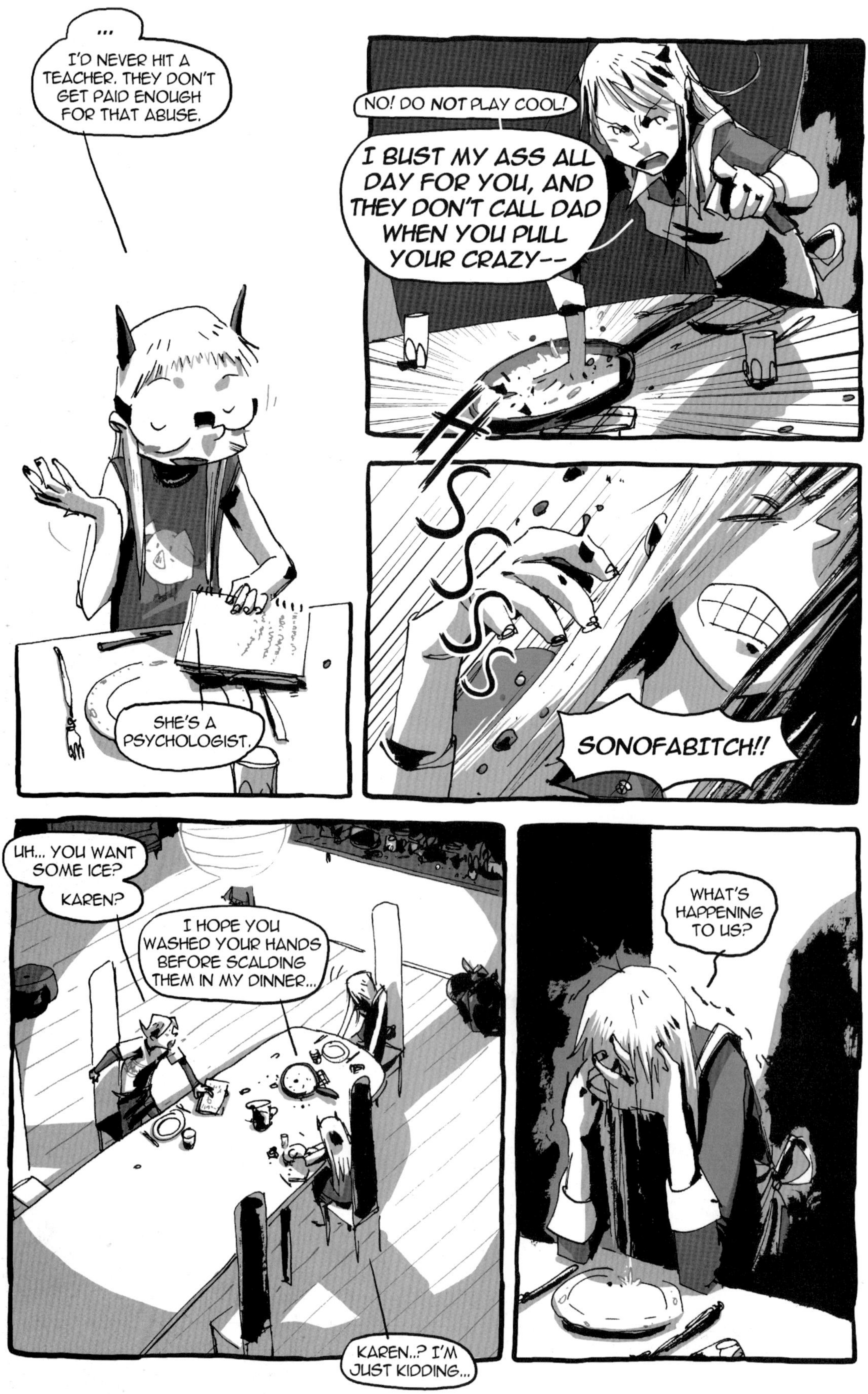
...
I'D NEVER HIT A TEACHER. THEY DON'T GET PAID ENOUGH FOR THAT ABUSE.
NO! DO NOT PLAY COOL!
I BUST MY ASS ALL DAY FOR YOU, AND THEY DON'T CALL DAD WHEN YOU PULL YOUR CRAZY--
SHE'S A PSYCHOLOGIST.
HISSSS
SONOFABITCH!!
UH... YOU WANT SOME ICE?
KAREN?
I HOPE YOU WASHED YOUR HANDS BEFORE SCALDING THEM IN MY DINNER...
KAREN..? I'M JUST KIDDING...
WHAT'S HAPPENING TO US?

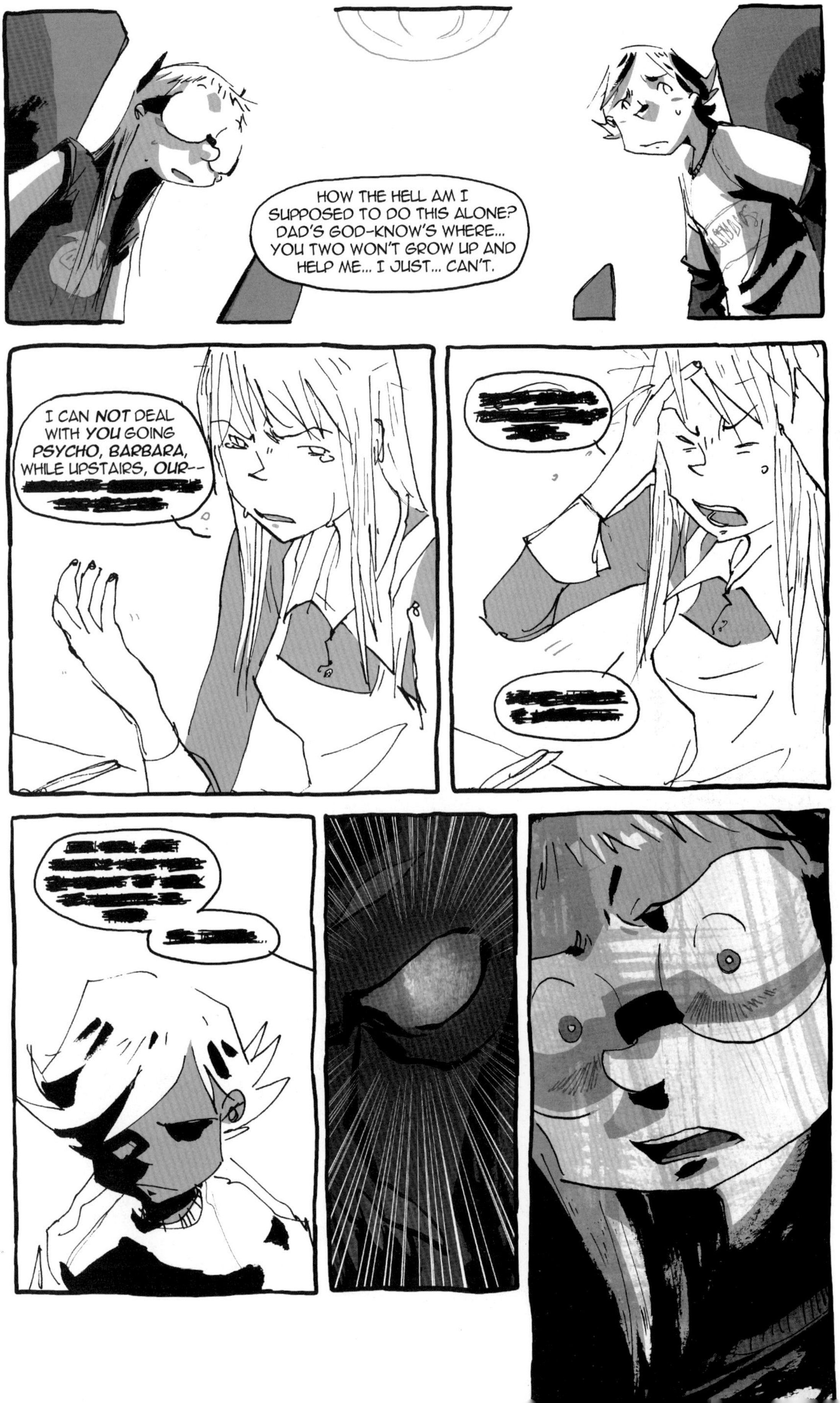
HOW THE HELL AM I SUPPOSED TO DO THIS ALONE? DAD'S GOD-KNOW'S WHERE... YOU TWO WON'T GROW UP AND HELP ME... I JUST... CAN'T.
I CAN **NOT** DEAL WITH ***YOU*** GOING ***PSYCHO***, BARBARA, WHILE UPSTAIRS, ***OUR***-- [redacted]
[redacted]
[redacted]
[redacted]
[redacted]...

IKG CHAPTER 4: THE GHOUL

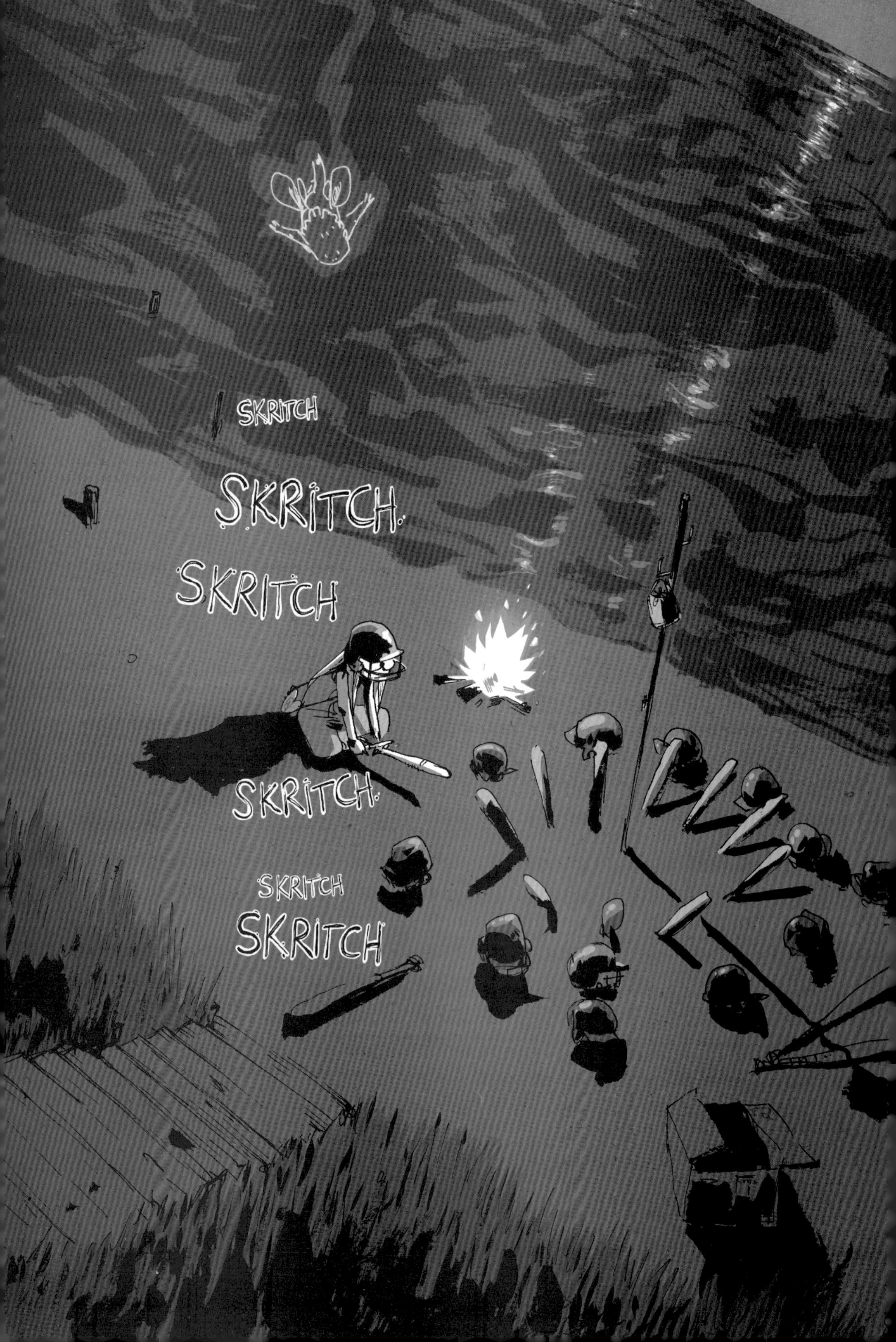
SKRITCH
SKRITCH
SKRITCH
SKRITCH
SKRITCH
SKRITCH

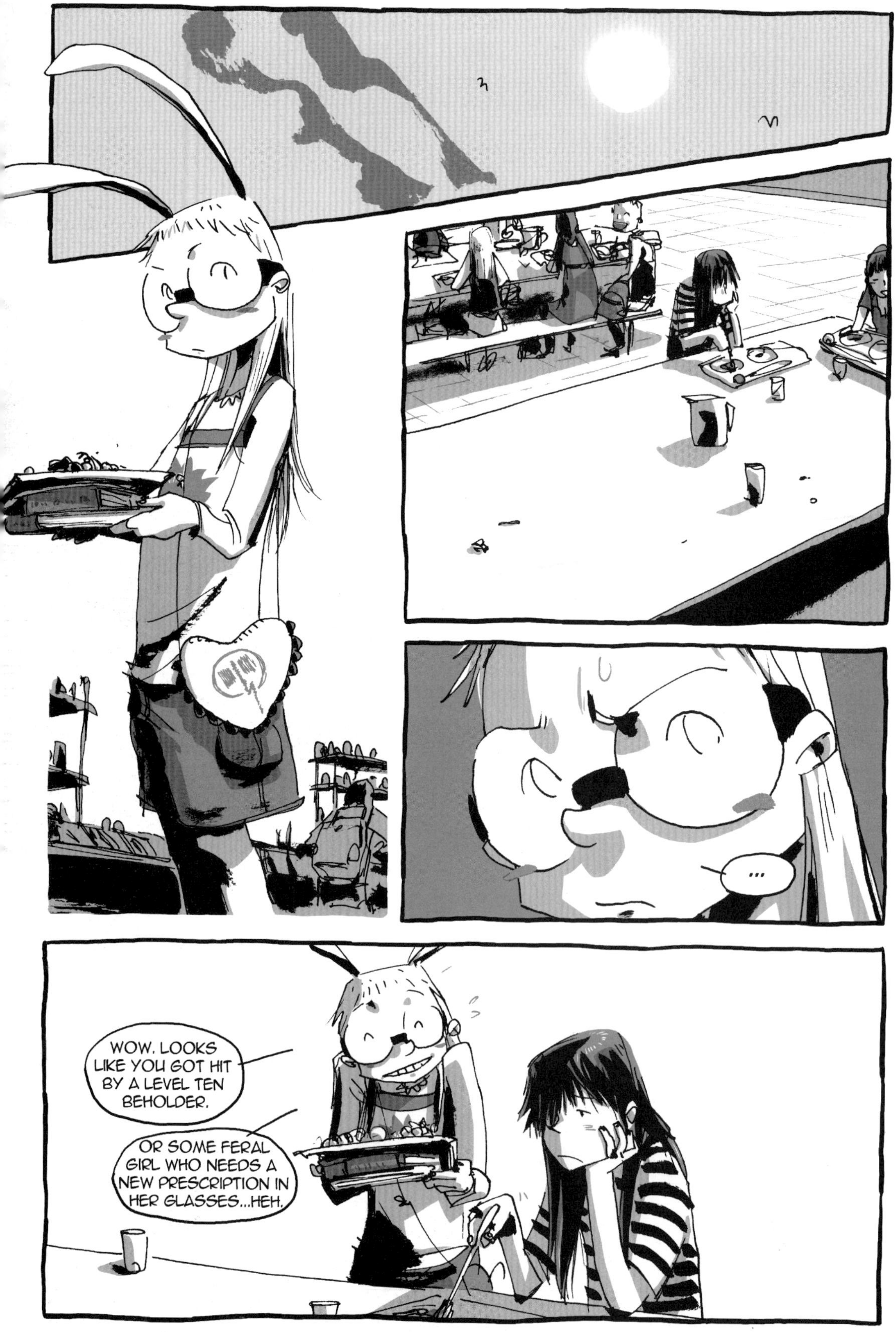
...
WOW. LOOKS LIKE YOU GOT HIT BY A LEVEL TEN BEHOLDER.
OR SOME FERAL GIRL WHO NEEDS A NEW PRESCRIPTION IN HER GLASSES...HEH.

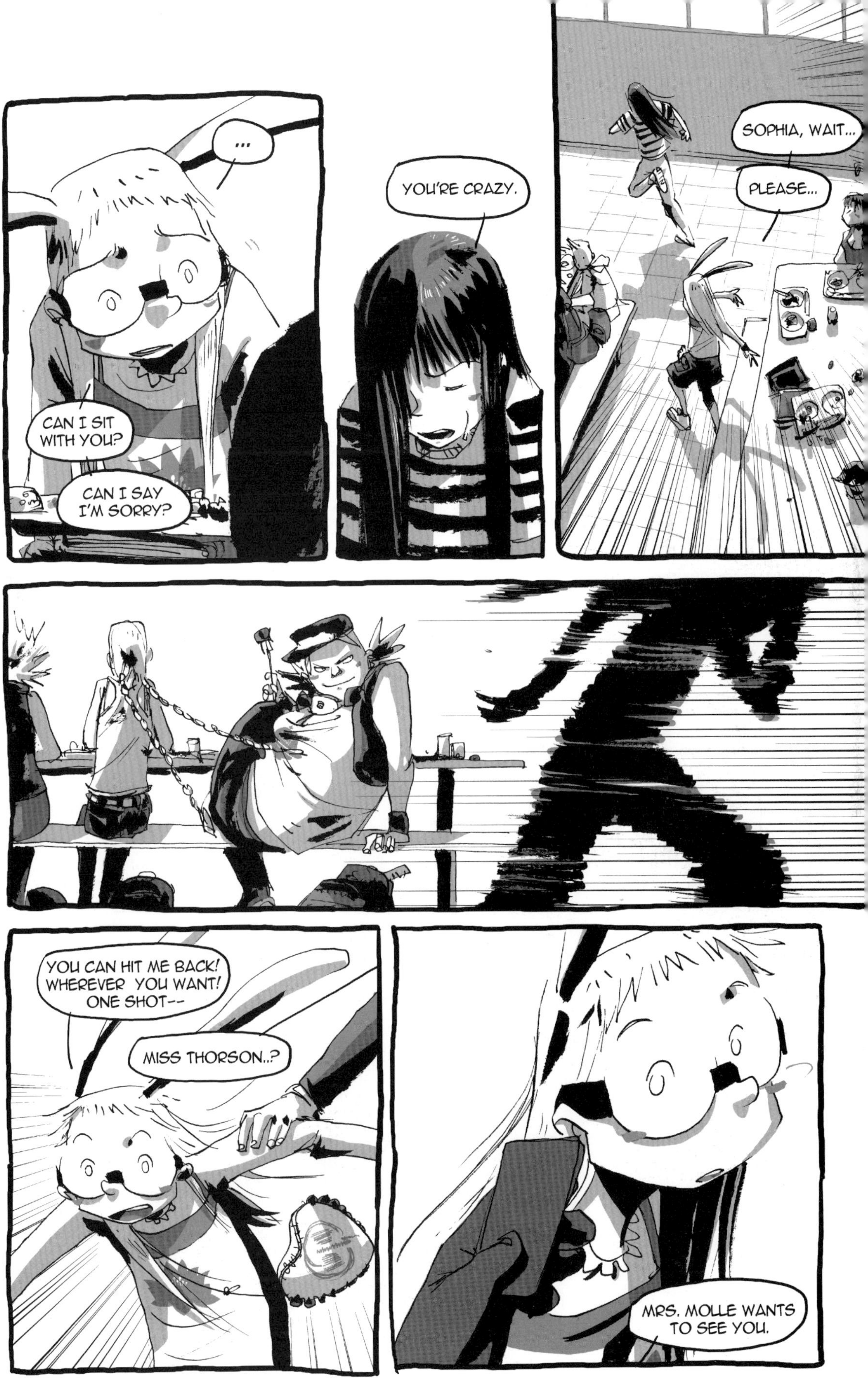
...
CAN I SIT WITH YOU?
CAN I SAY I'M SORRY?
YOU'RE CRAZY.
SOPHIA, WAIT...
PLEASE...
YOU CAN HIT ME BACK! WHEREVER YOU WANT! ONE SHOT--
MISS THORSON..?
MRS. MOLLE WANTS TO SEE YOU.

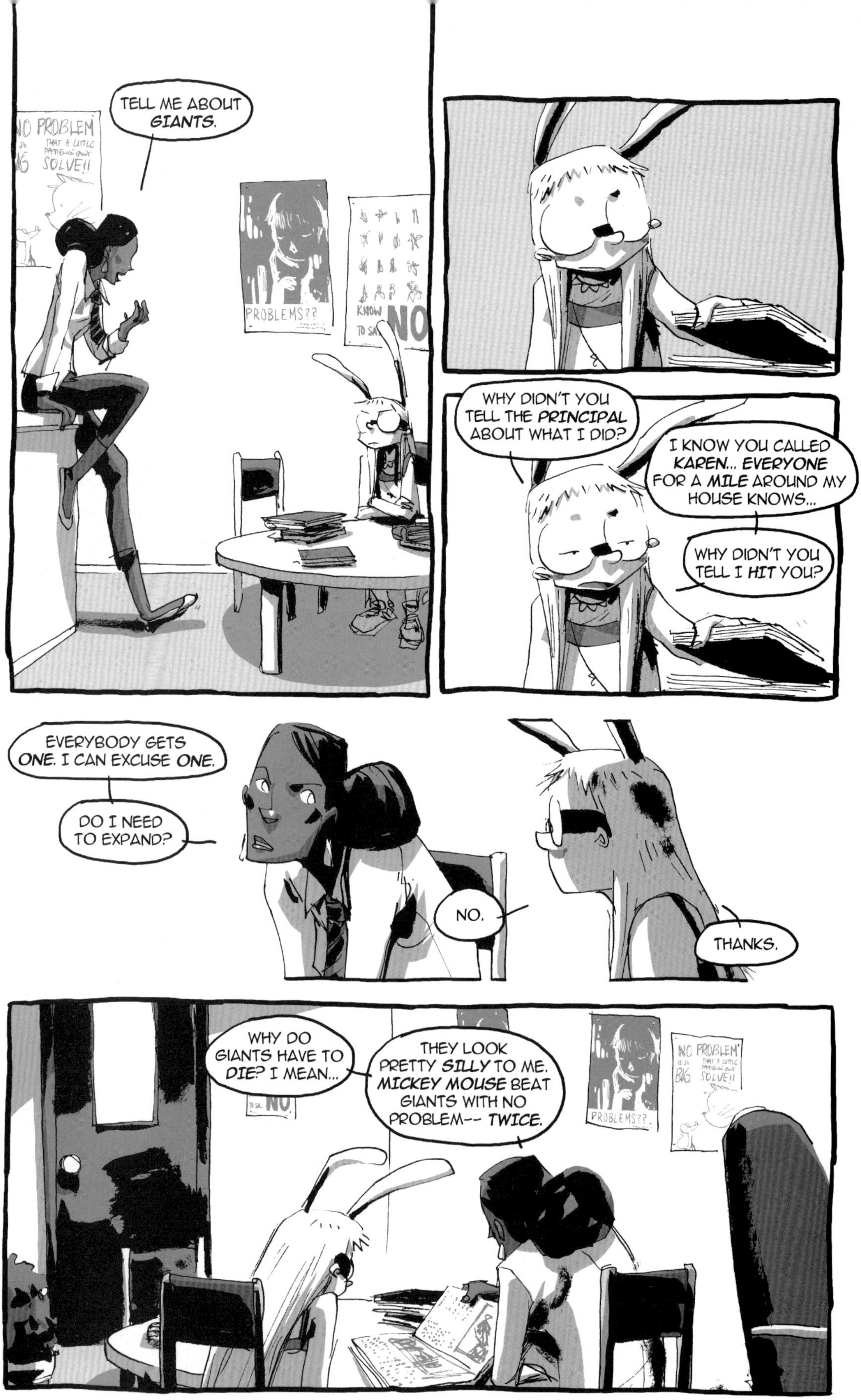
TELL ME ABOUT GIANTS.
WHY DIDN'T YOU TELL THE PRINCIPAL ABOUT WHAT I DID?
I KNOW YOU CALLED KAREN... EVERYONE FOR A MILE AROUND MY HOUSE KNOWS...
WHY DIDN'T YOU TELL I HIT YOU?
EVERYBODY GETS ONE. I CAN EXCUSE ONE.
DO I NEED TO EXPAND?
NO.
THANKS.
WHY DO GIANTS HAVE TO DIE? I MEAN...
THEY LOOK PRETTY SILLY TO ME. MICKEY MOUSE BEAT GIANTS WITH NO PROBLEM-- TWICE.

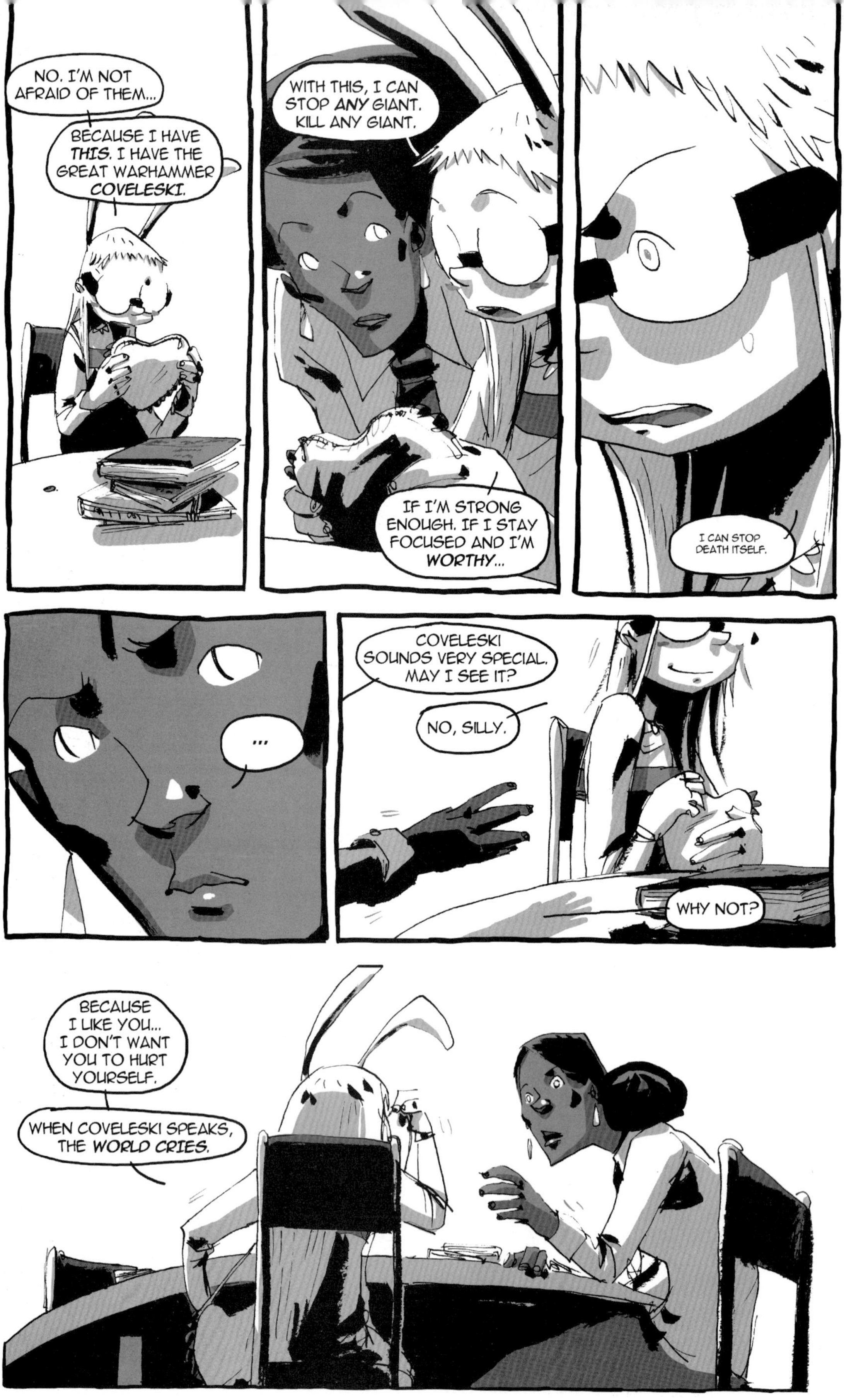
NO. I'M NOT AFRAID OF THEM...
BECAUSE I HAVE THIS. I HAVE THE GREAT WARHAMMER COVELESKI.
WITH THIS, I CAN STOP ANY GIANT. KILL ANY GIANT.
IF I'M STRONG ENOUGH. IF I STAY FOCUSED AND I'M WORTHY...
I CAN STOP DEATH ITSELF.
...
COVELESKI SOUNDS VERY SPECIAL. MAY I SEE IT?
NO, SILLY.
WHY NOT?
BECAUSE I LIKE YOU... I DON'T WANT YOU TO HURT YOURSELF.
WHEN COVELESKI SPEAKS, THE WORLD CRIES.

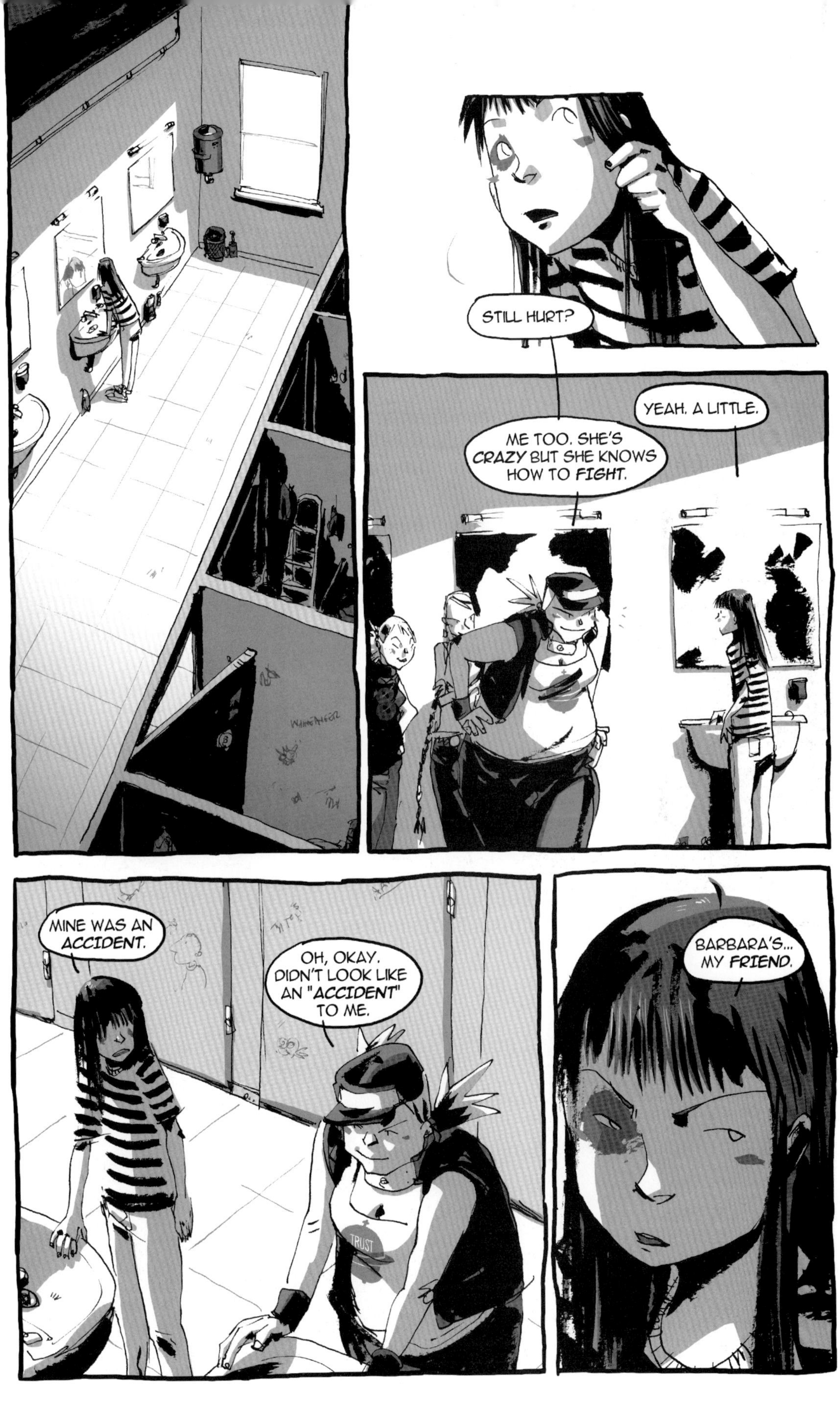
STILL HURT?
YEAH. A LITTLE.
ME TOO. SHE'S CRAZY BUT SHE KNOWS HOW TO FIGHT.
MINE WAS AN ACCIDENT.
OH, OKAY. DIDN'T LOOK LIKE AN "ACCIDENT" TO ME.
BARBARA'S... MY FRIEND.

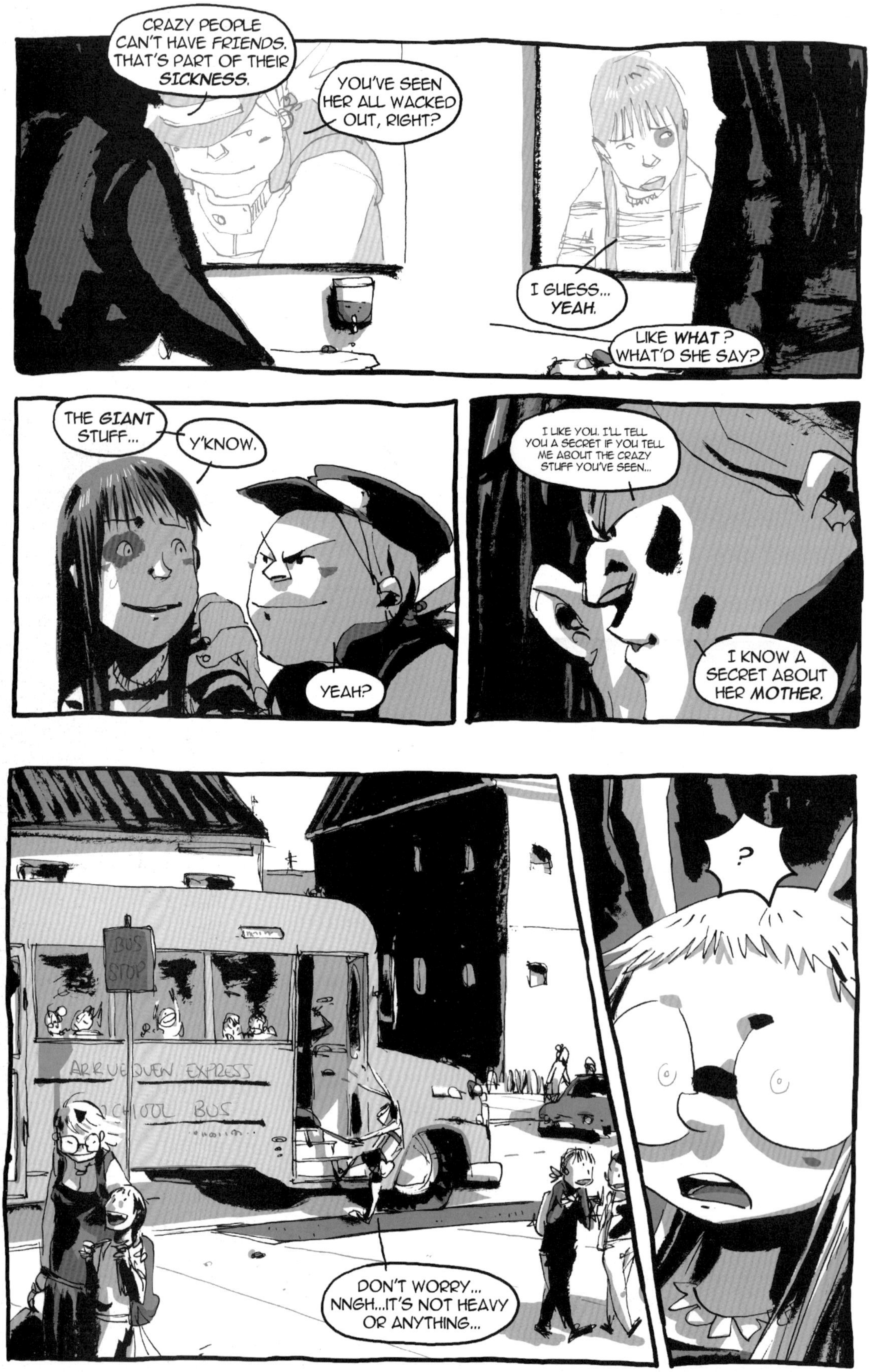
CRAZY PEOPLE CAN'T HAVE FRIENDS. THAT'S PART OF THEIR SICKNESS.
YOU'VE SEEN HER ALL WACKED OUT, RIGHT?
I GUESS... YEAH.
LIKE WHAT? WHAT'D SHE SAY?
THE GIANT STUFF...
Y'KNOW.
YEAH?
I LIKE YOU. I'LL TELL YOU A SECRET IF YOU TELL ME ABOUT THE CRAZY STUFF YOU'VE SEEN...
I KNOW A SECRET ABOUT HER MOTHER.
BUS STOP
ARRUEQUEN EXPRESS
SCHOOL BUS
DON'T WORRY... NNGH...IT'S NOT HEAVY OR ANYTHING...
?

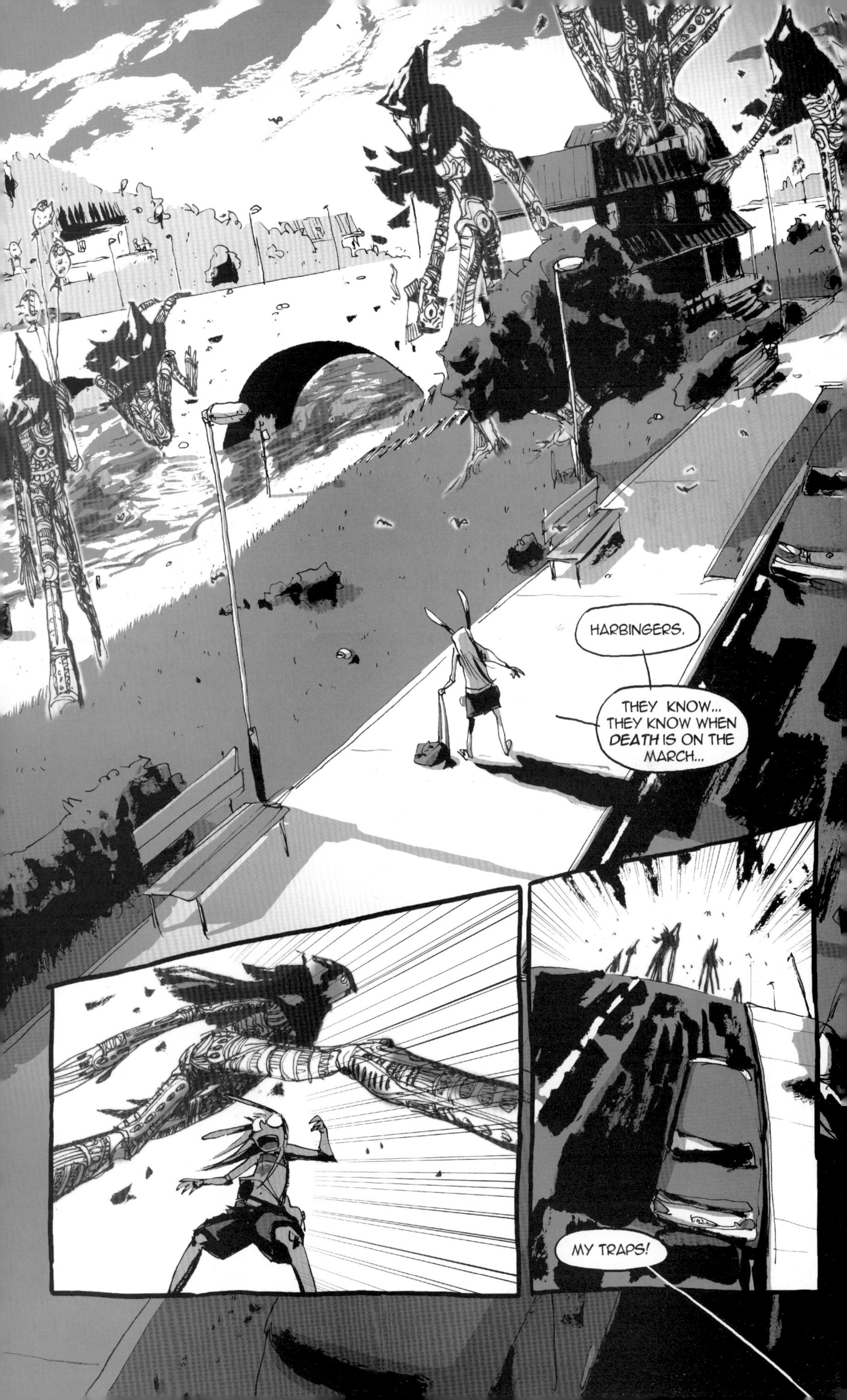
HARBINGERS.
THEY KNOW... THEY KNOW WHEN DEATH IS ON THE MARCH...
MY TRAPS!

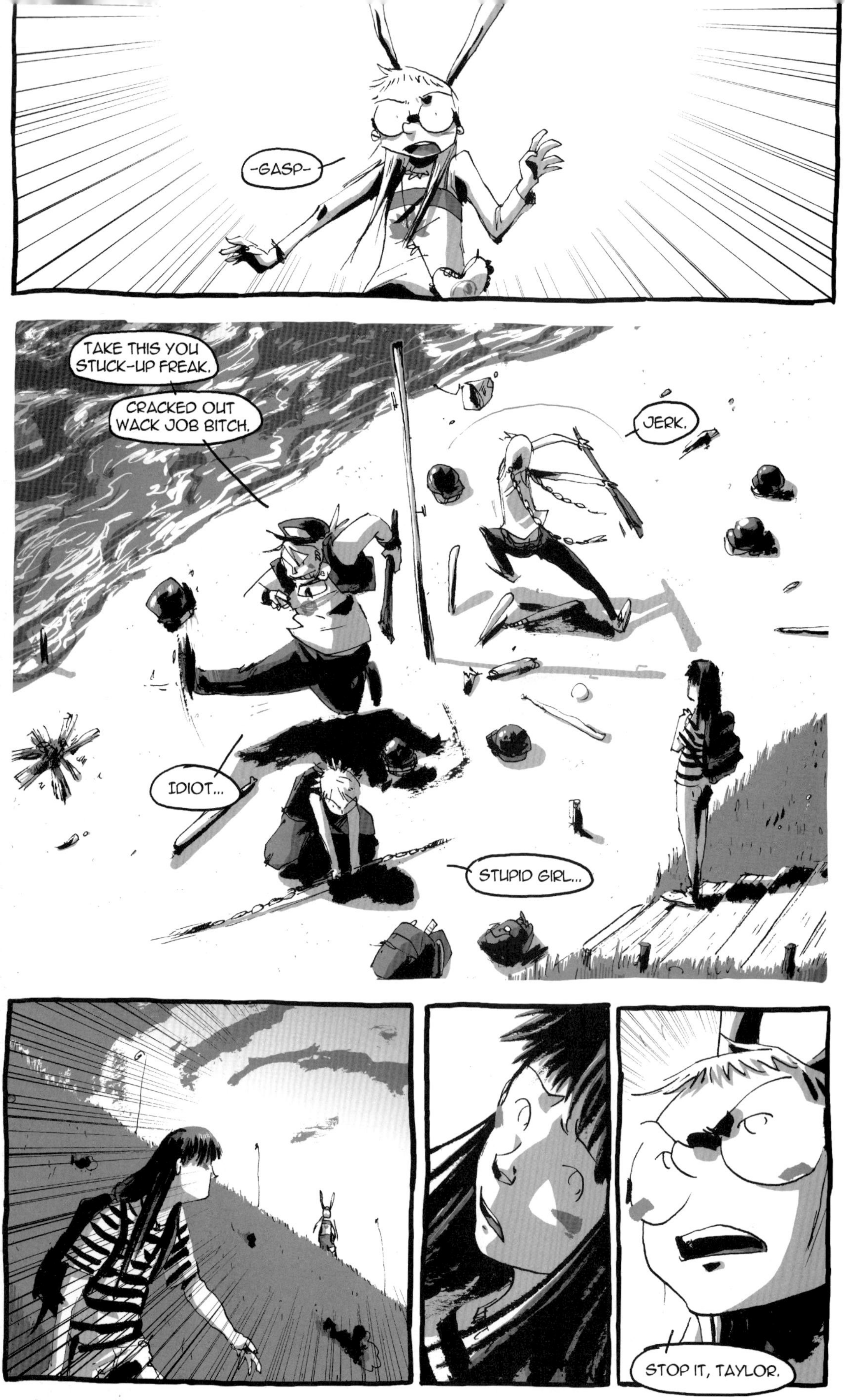
-GASP-
TAKE THIS YOU STUCK-UP FREAK.
CRACKED OUT WACK JOB BITCH.
JERK.
IDIOT...
STUPID GIRL...
STOP IT, TAYLOR.

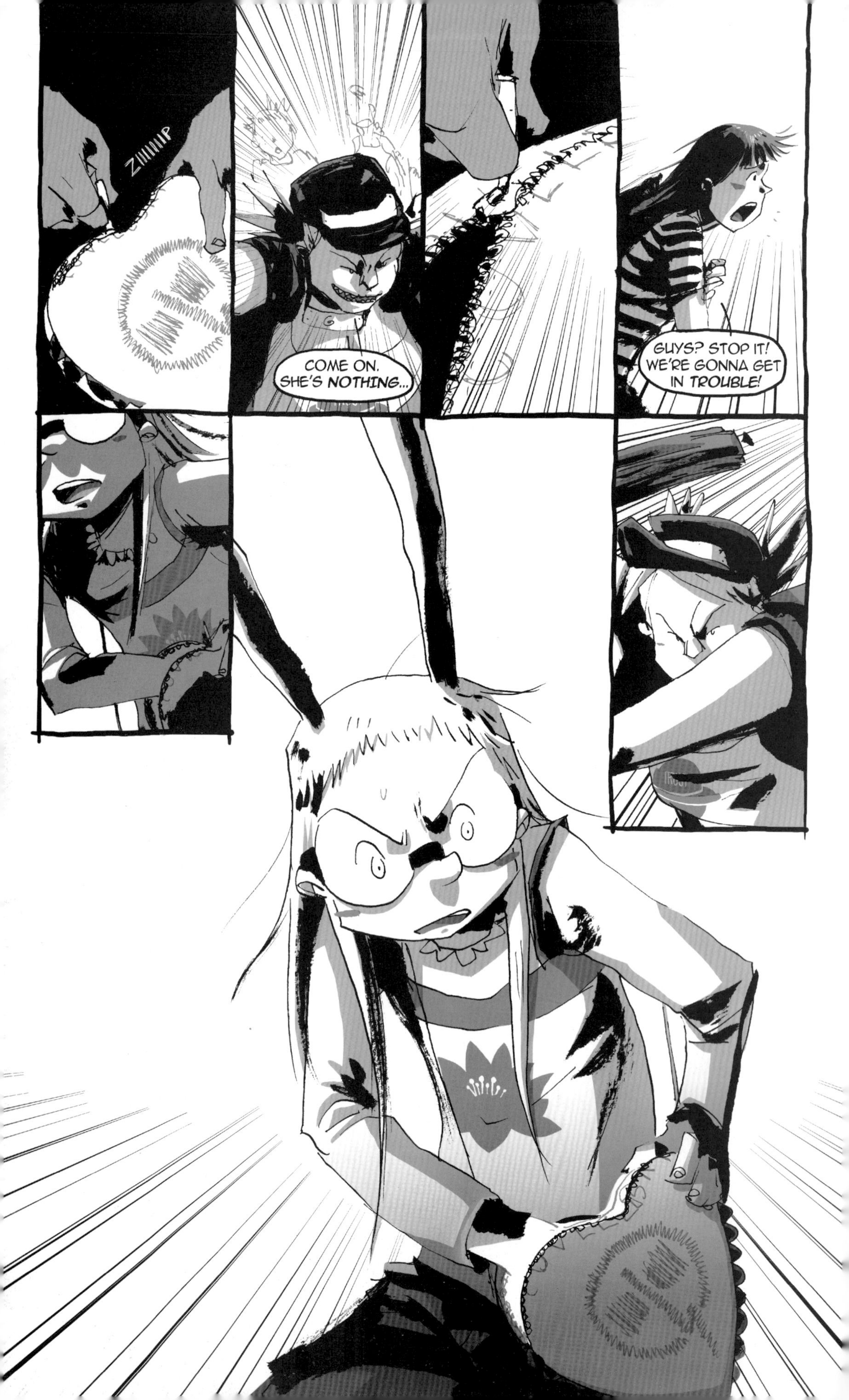
ZIIIIIIP
COME ON. SHE'S NOTHING...
GUYS? STOP IT! WE'RE GONNA GET IN TROUBLE!

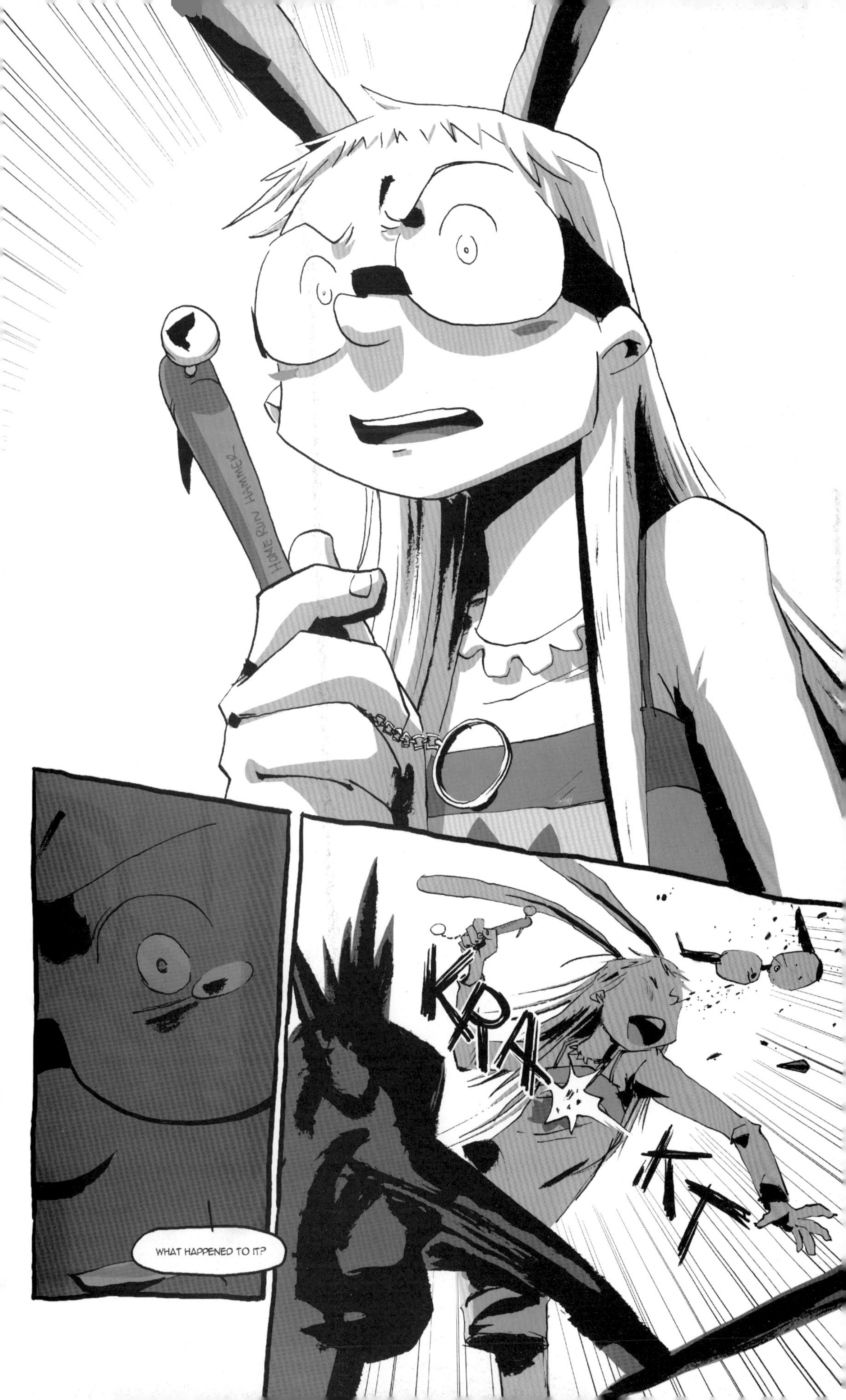
HOME RUN HAMMER
WHAT HAPPENED TO IT?
KRAKT

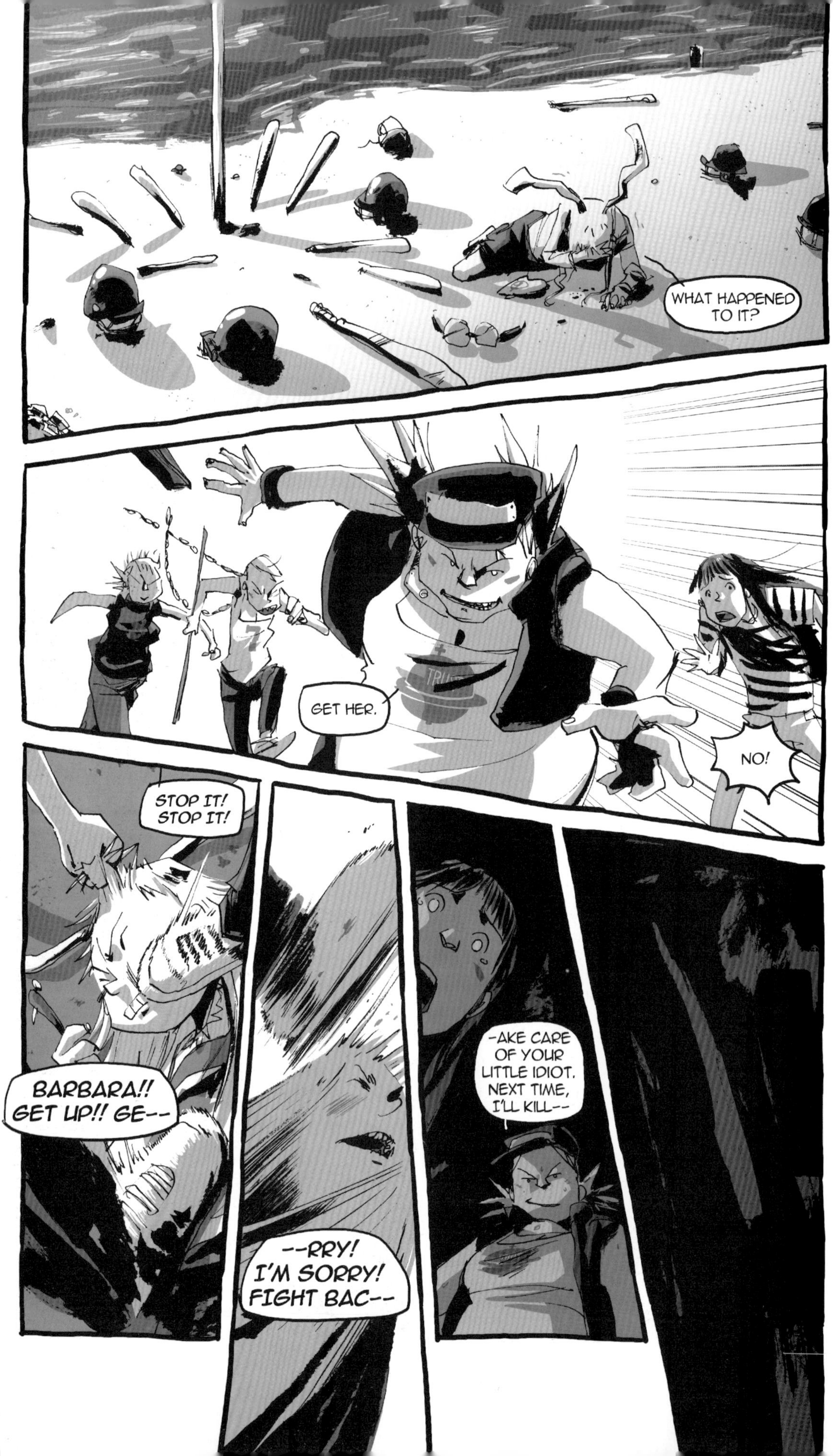
WHAT HAPPENED TO IT?
GET HER.
NO!
STOP IT! STOP IT!
BARBARA!! GET UP!! GE--
--RRY! I'M SORRY! FIGHT BAC--
-AKE CARE OF YOUR LITTLE IDIOT. NEXT TIME, I'LL KILL--

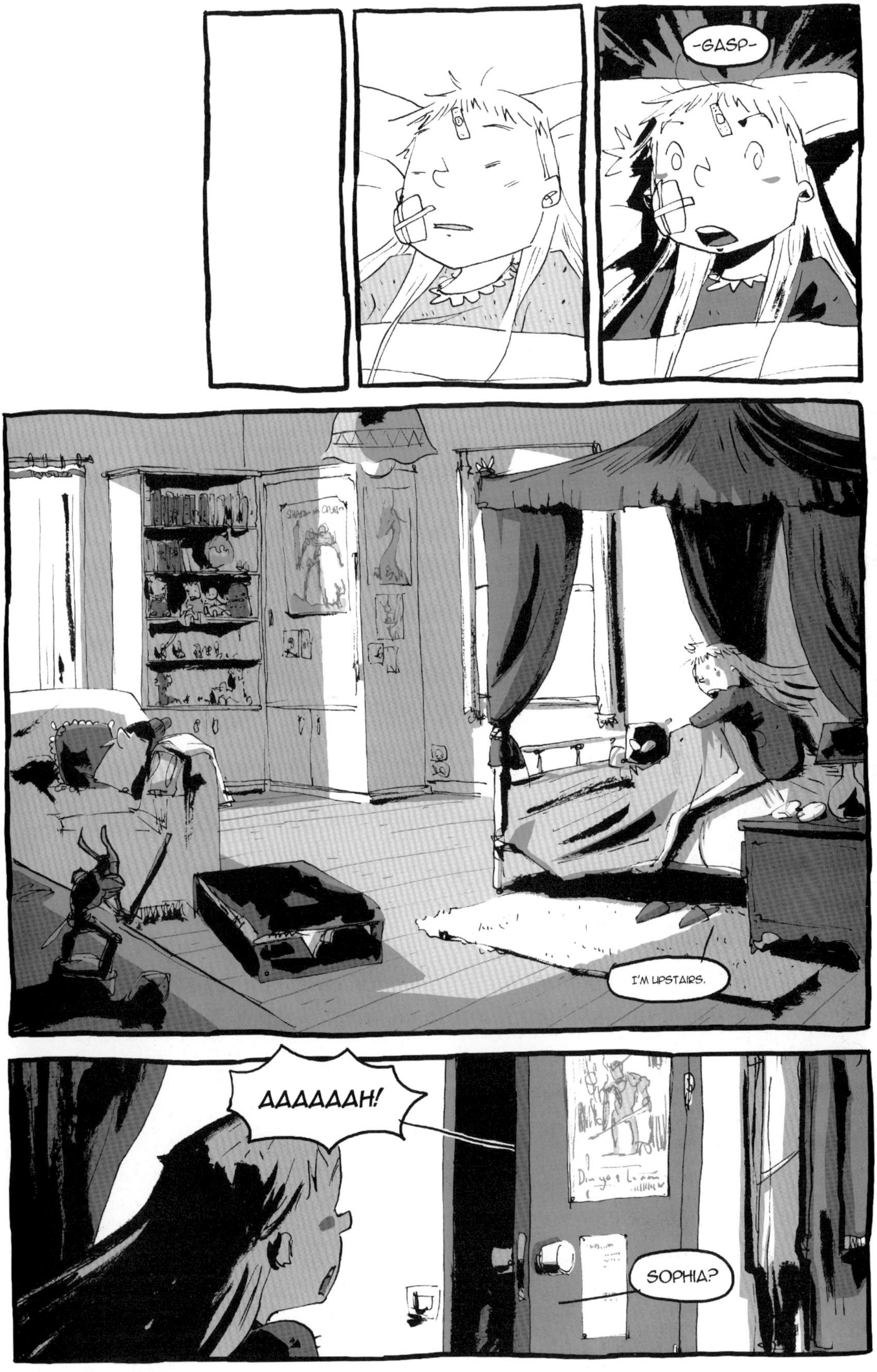
-GASP-
I'M UPSTAIRS.
AAAAAAH!
SOPHIA?

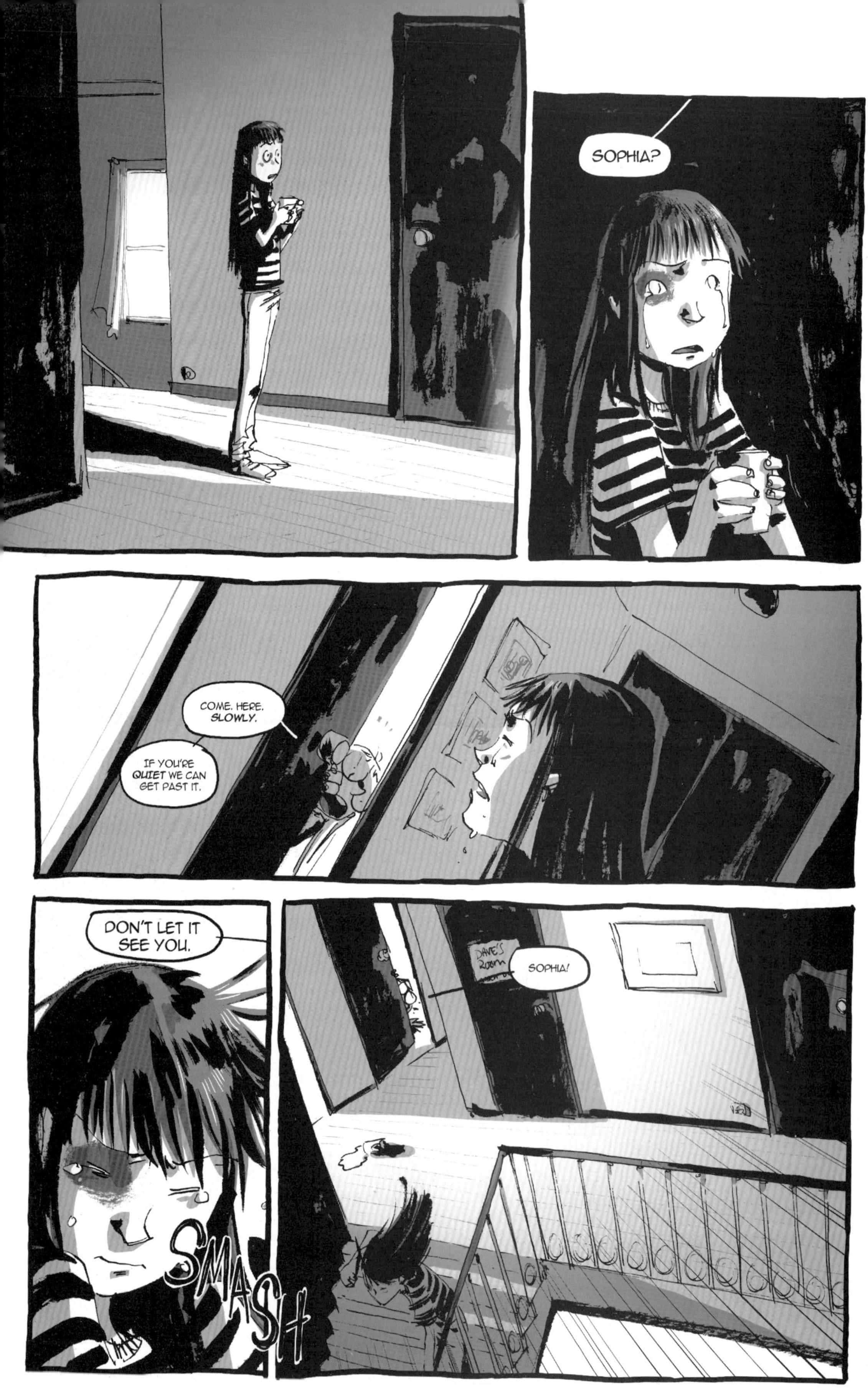
SOPHIA?
COME. HERE. SLOWLY.
IF YOU'RE QUIET WE CAN GET PAST IT.
DON'T LET IT SEE YOU.
SMASH
DAVE'S Room
SOPHIA!

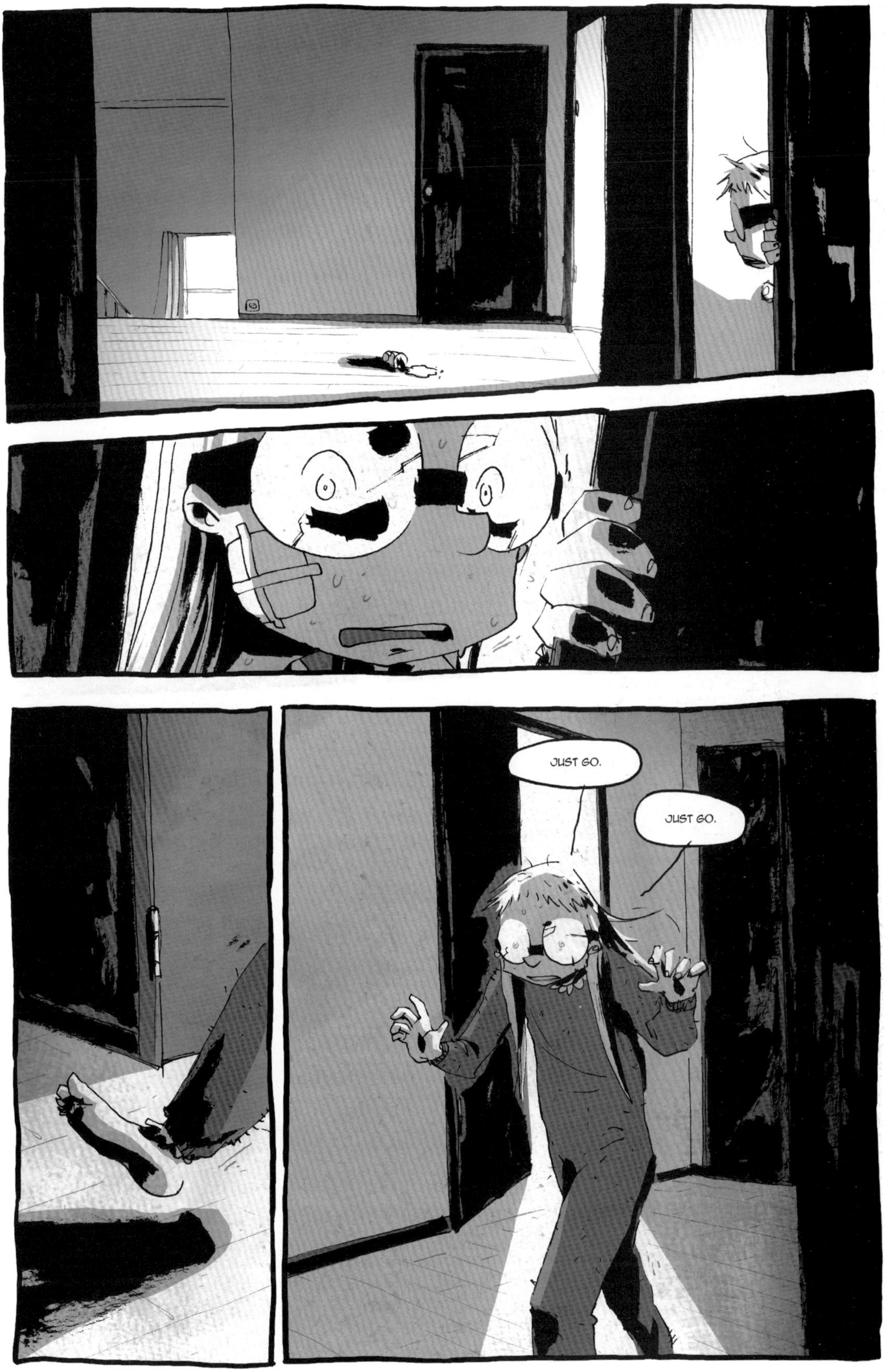
JUST GO.
JUST GO.

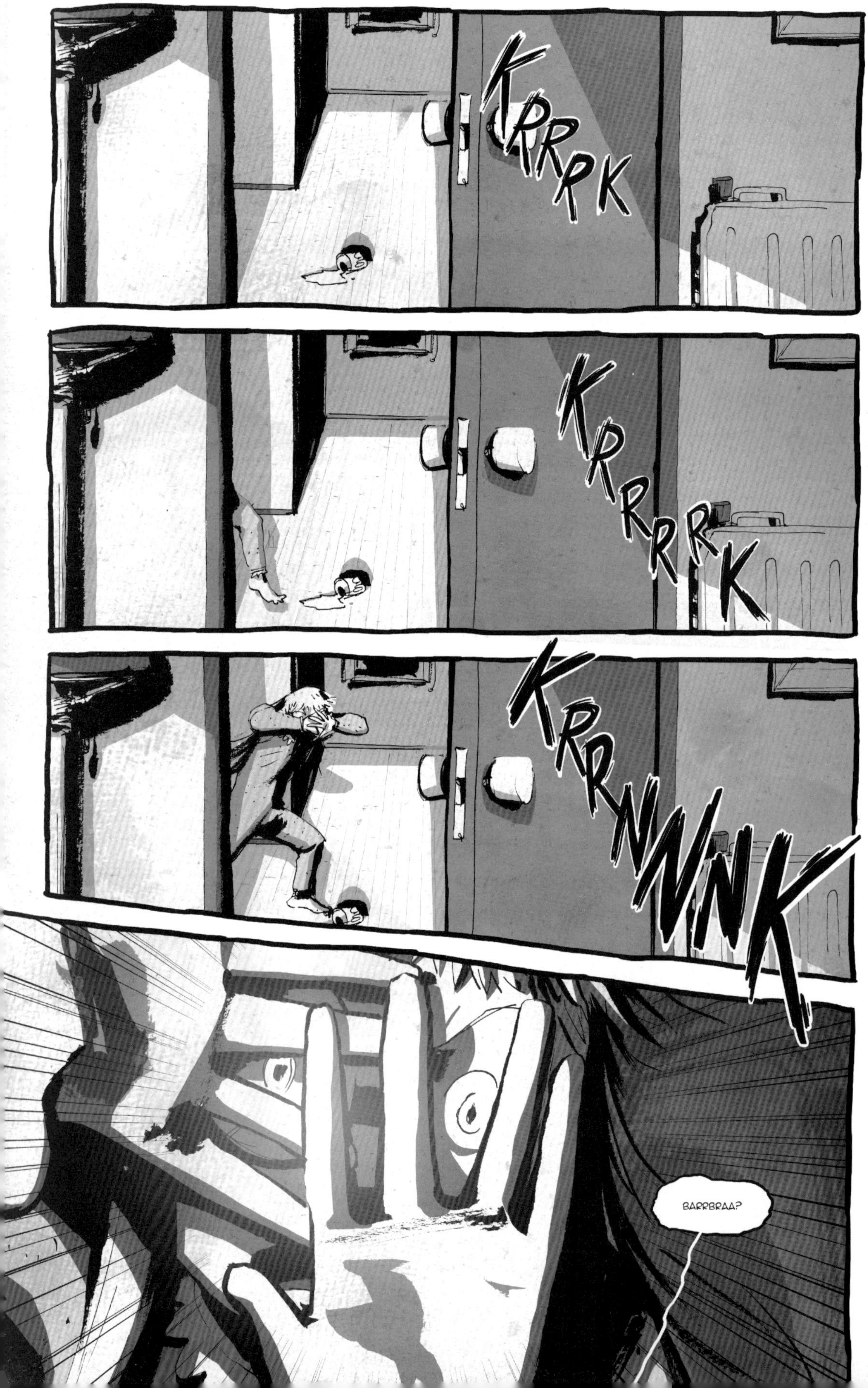
KRRRRK
KRRRRRRK
KRRNNNK
BARRBRAA?

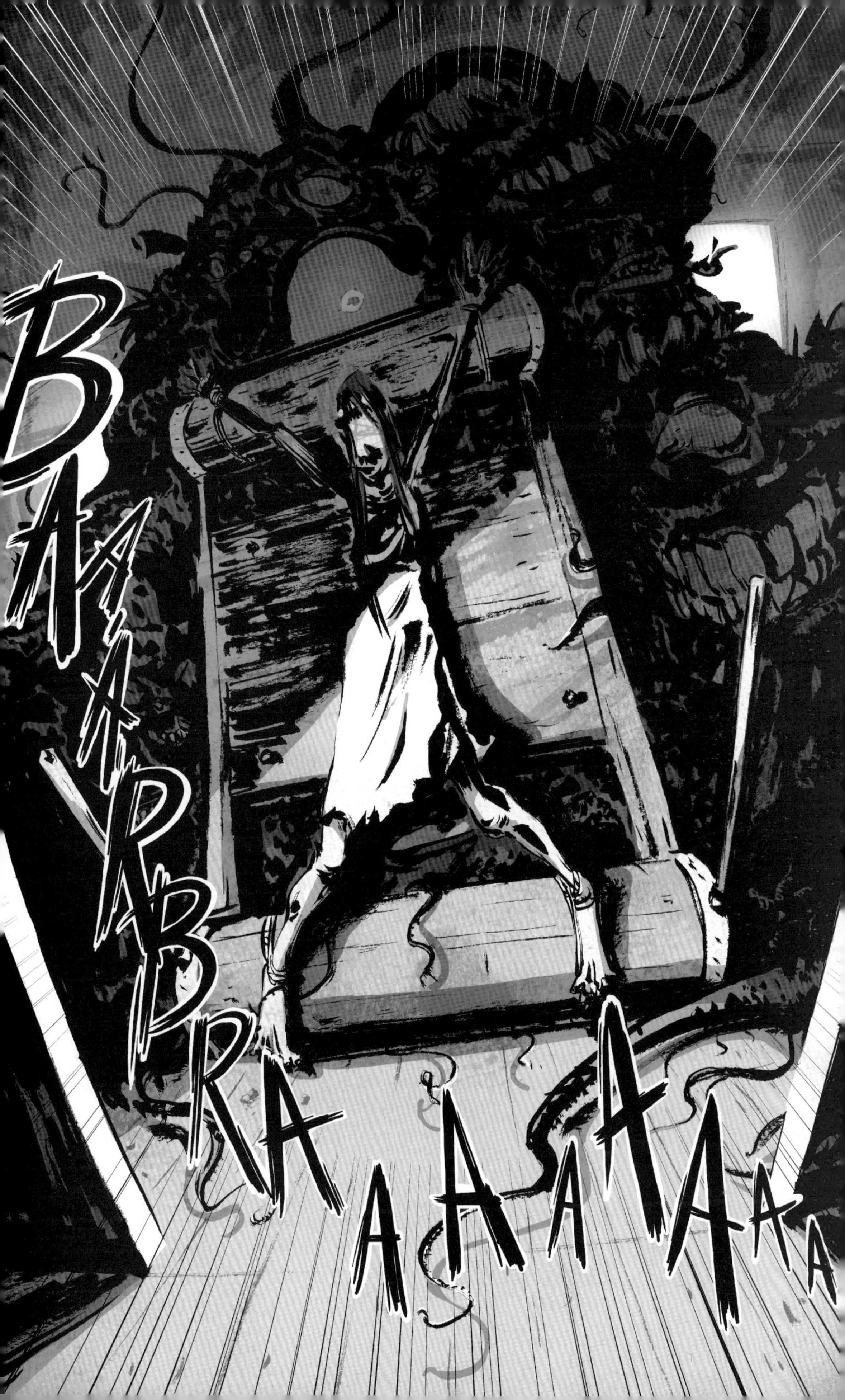
BAAAARABRA AAAAAAAA

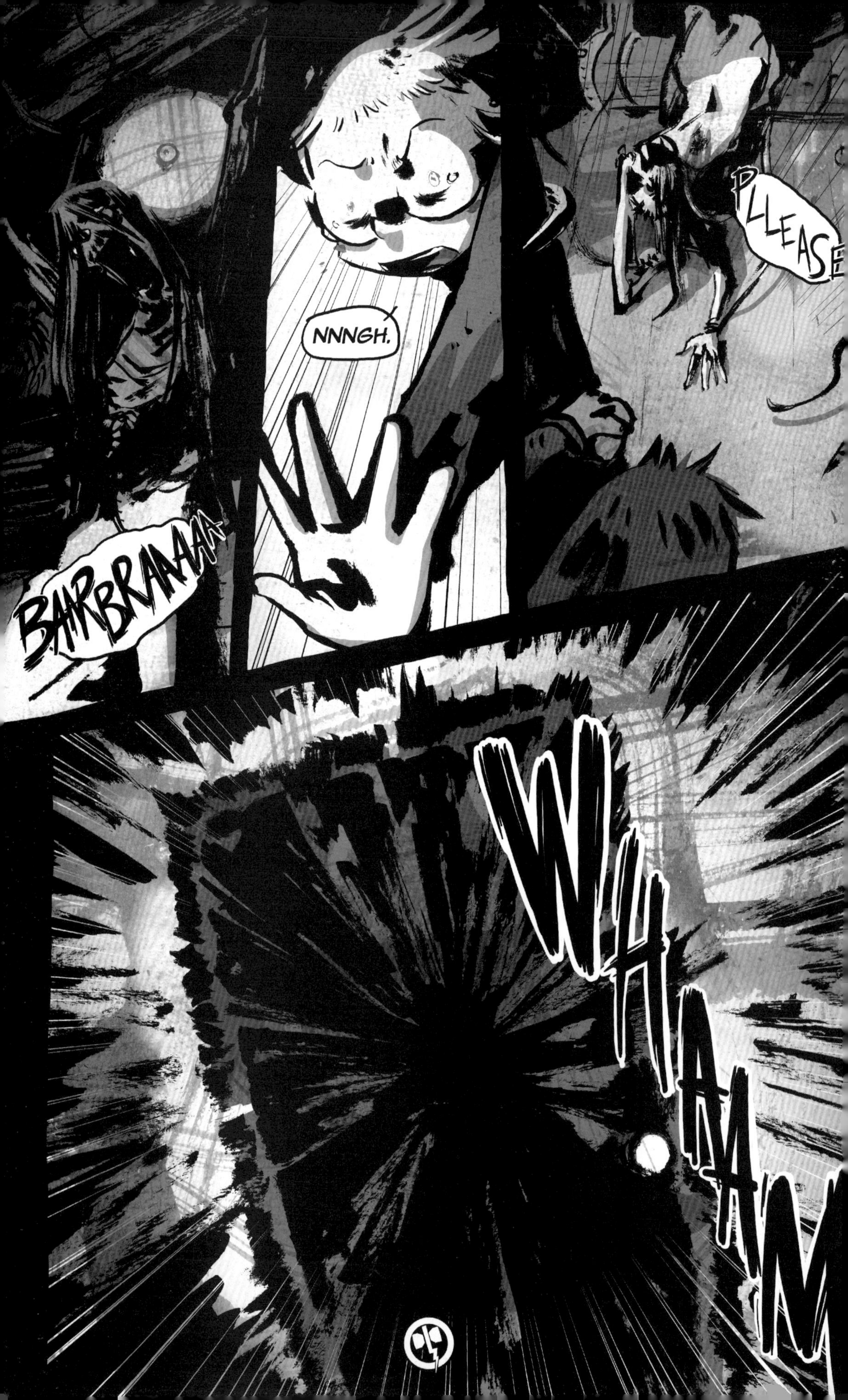
PLLEASE
NNNGH.
BAARBRAAAAA
WHAAM

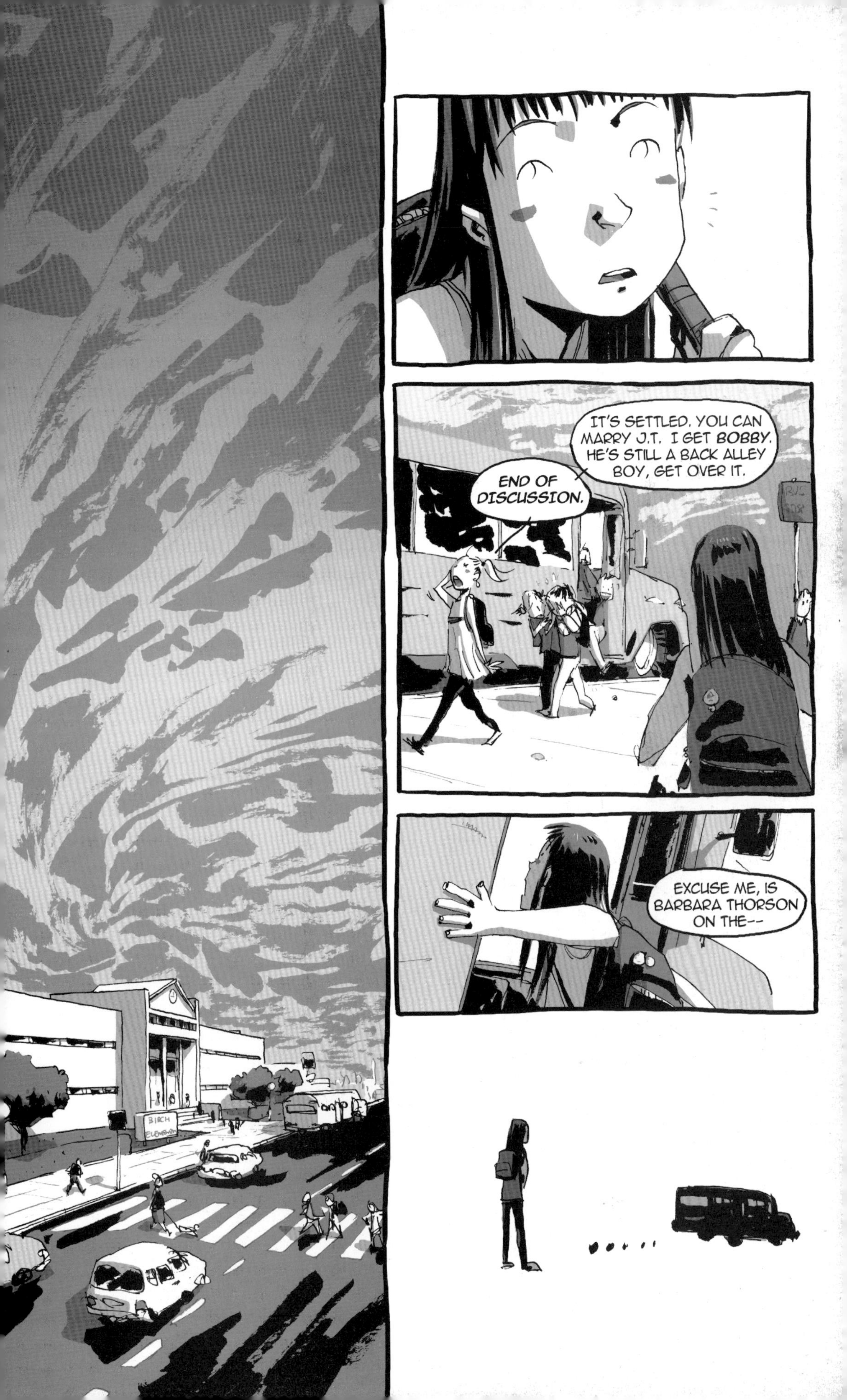
IT'S SETTLED. YOU CAN MARRY J.T. I GET BOBBY. HE'S STILL A BACK ALLEY BOY, GET OVER IT.
END OF DISCUSSION.
EXCUSE ME, IS BARBARA THORSON ON THE--
....

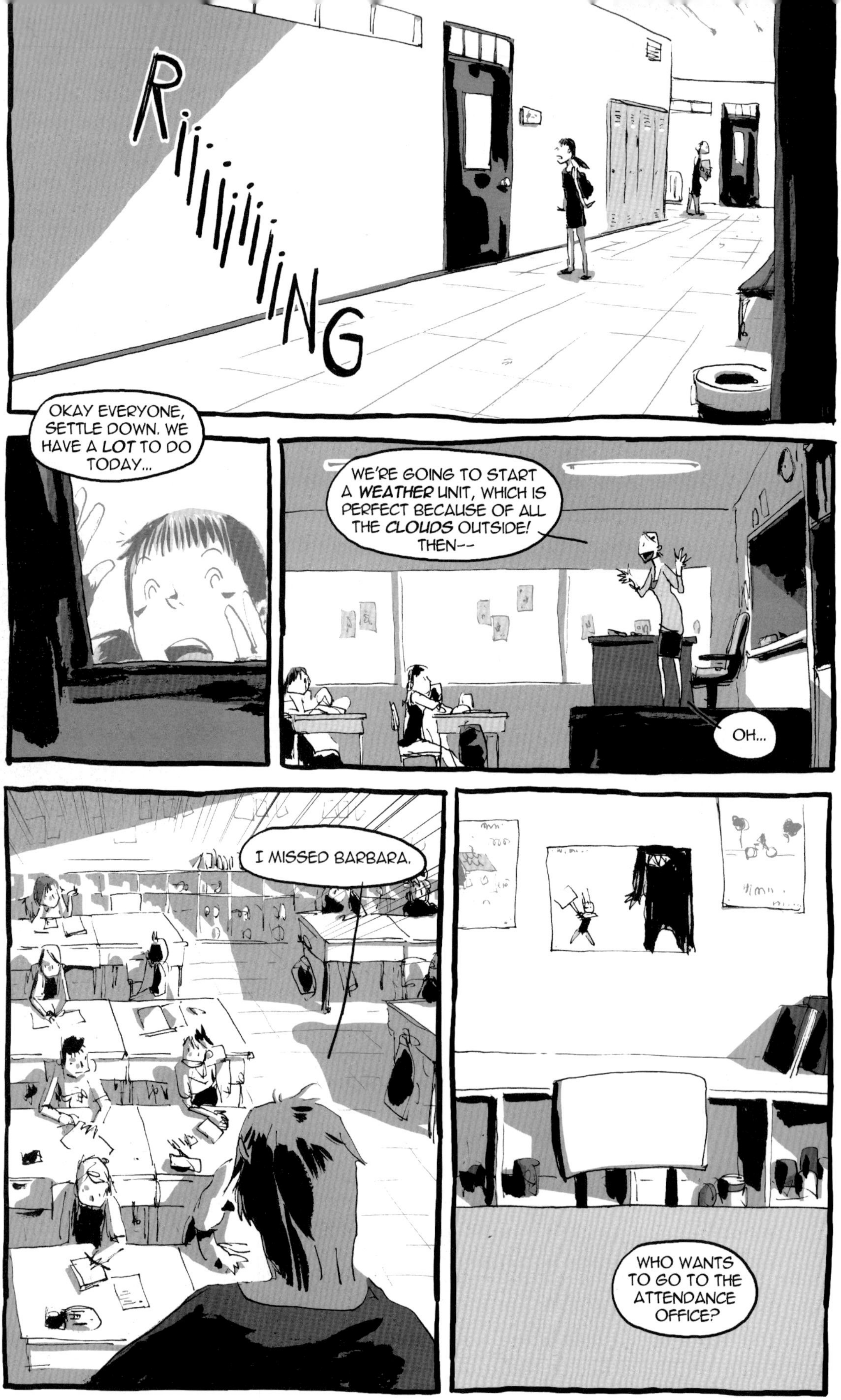
RIIIIIIIIIING
OKAY EVERYONE, SETTLE DOWN. WE HAVE A LOT TO DO TODAY...
WE'RE GOING TO START A WEATHER UNIT, WHICH IS PERFECT BECAUSE OF ALL THE CLOUDS OUTSIDE! THEN--
OH...
I MISSED BARBARA.
WHO WANTS TO GO TO THE ATTENDANCE OFFICE?

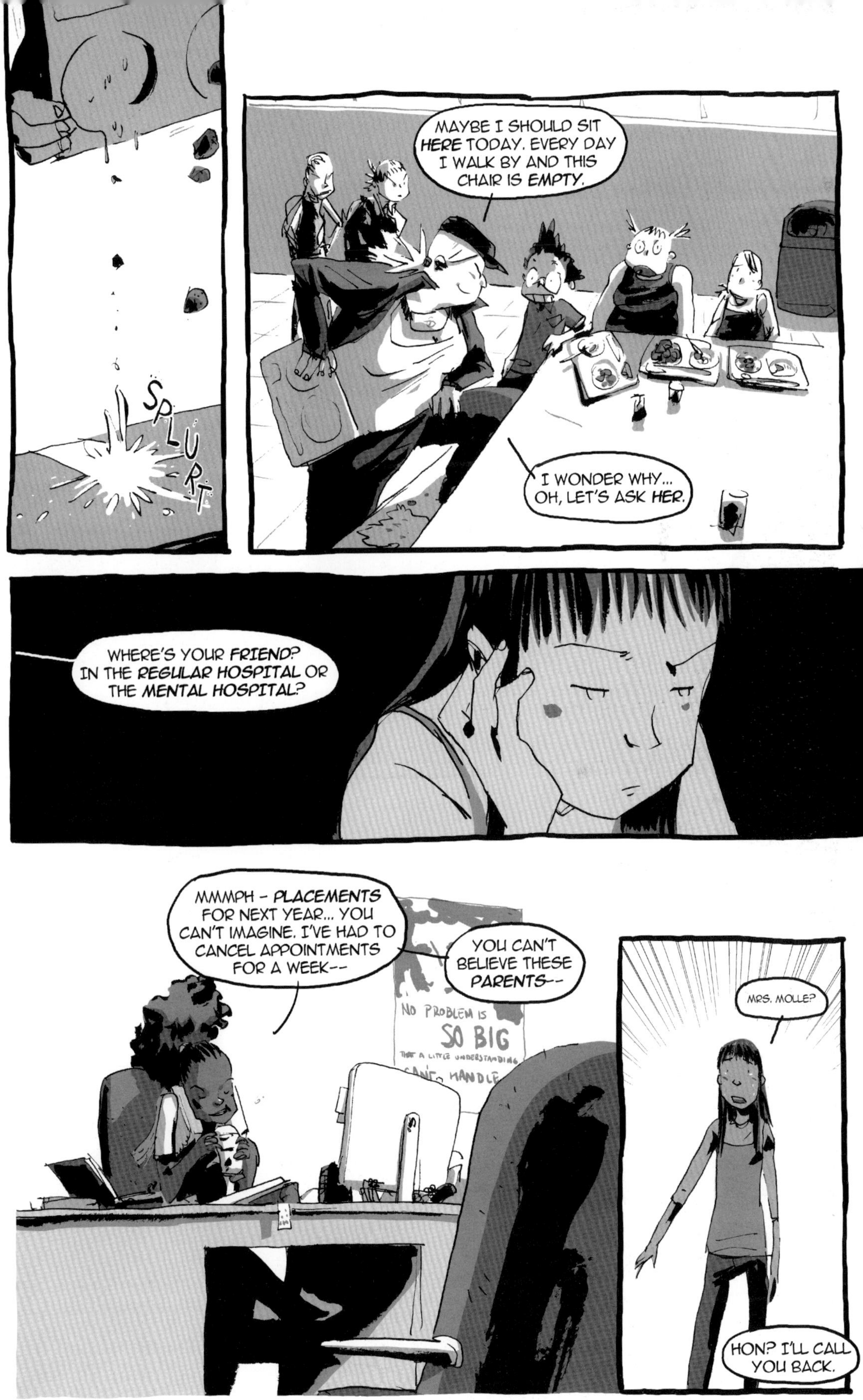
SPLURT
MAYBE I SHOULD SIT HERE TODAY. EVERY DAY I WALK BY AND THIS CHAIR IS EMPTY.
I WONDER WHY... OH, LET'S ASK HER.
WHERE'S YOUR FRIEND? IN THE REGULAR HOSPITAL OR THE MENTAL HOSPITAL?
MMMPH - PLACEMENTS FOR NEXT YEAR... YOU CAN'T IMAGINE. I'VE HAD TO CANCEL APPOINTMENTS FOR A WEEK--
YOU CAN'T BELIEVE THESE PARENTS--
NO PROBLEM IS
SO BIG
MRS. MOLLE?
HON? I'LL CALL YOU BACK.

IKG CHAPTER 5: THE SACRIFICE

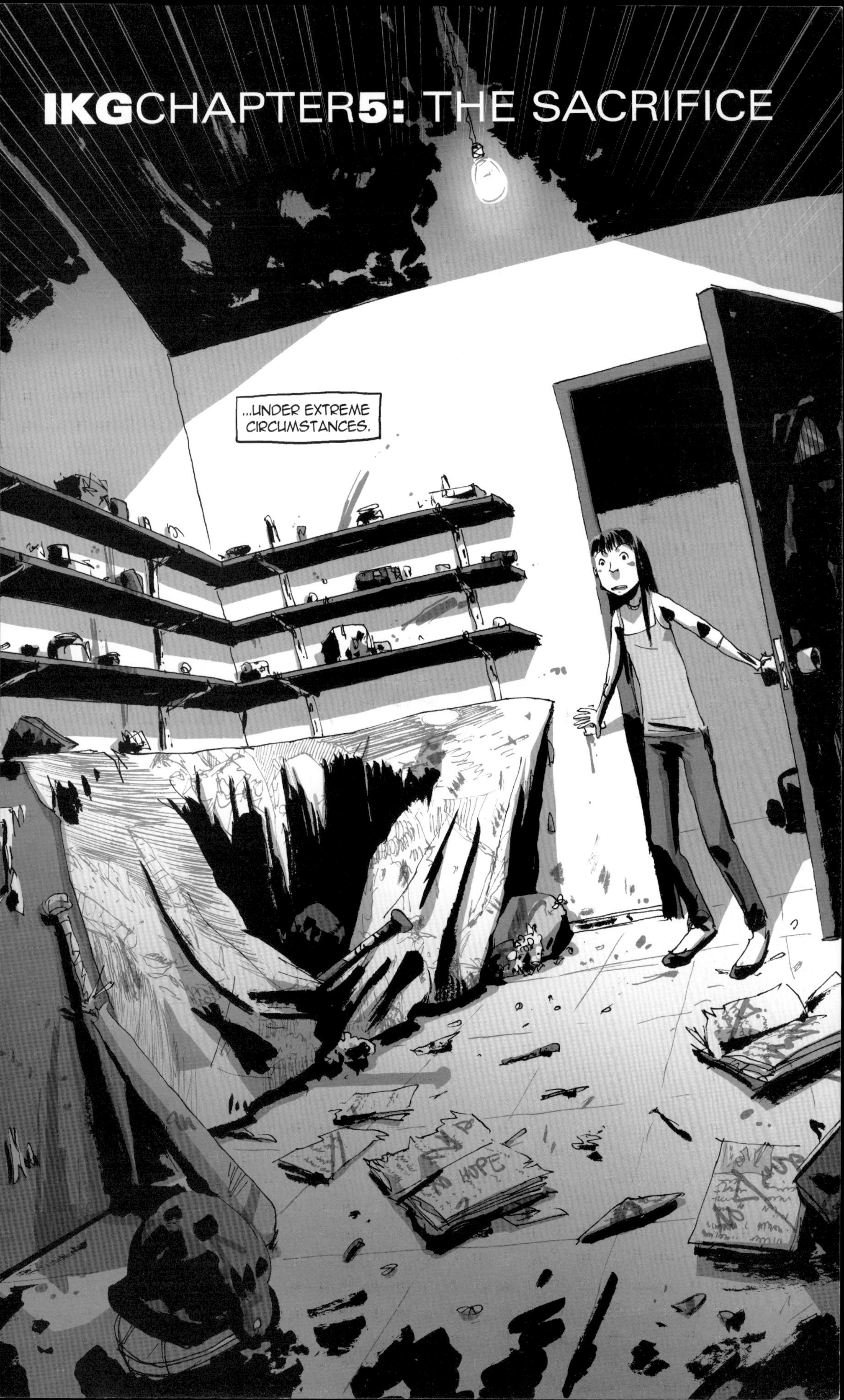
...UNDER EXTREME CIRCUMSTANCES.
NO HOPE

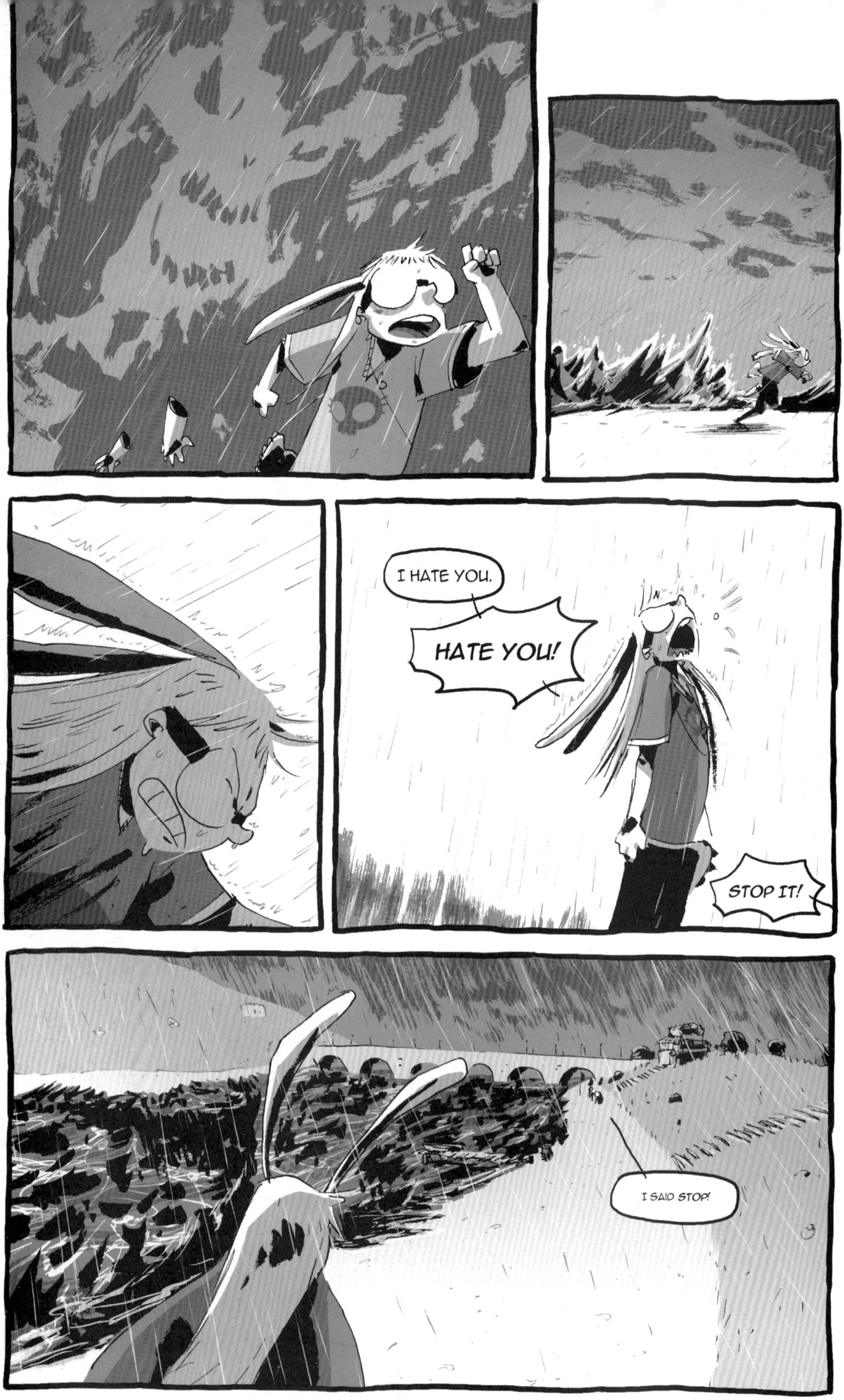
I HATE YOU.
HATE YOU!
STOP IT!
I SAID STOP!

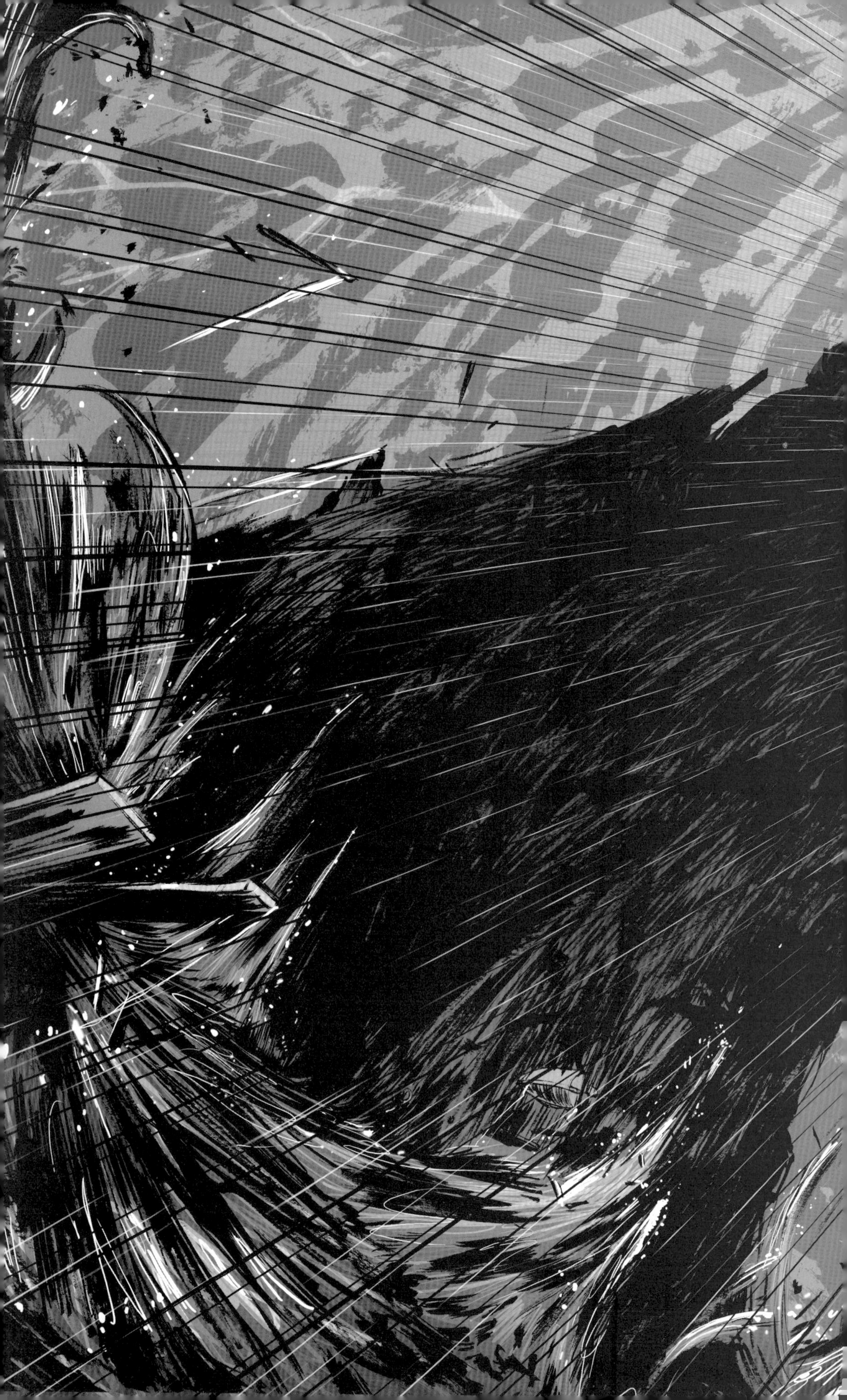

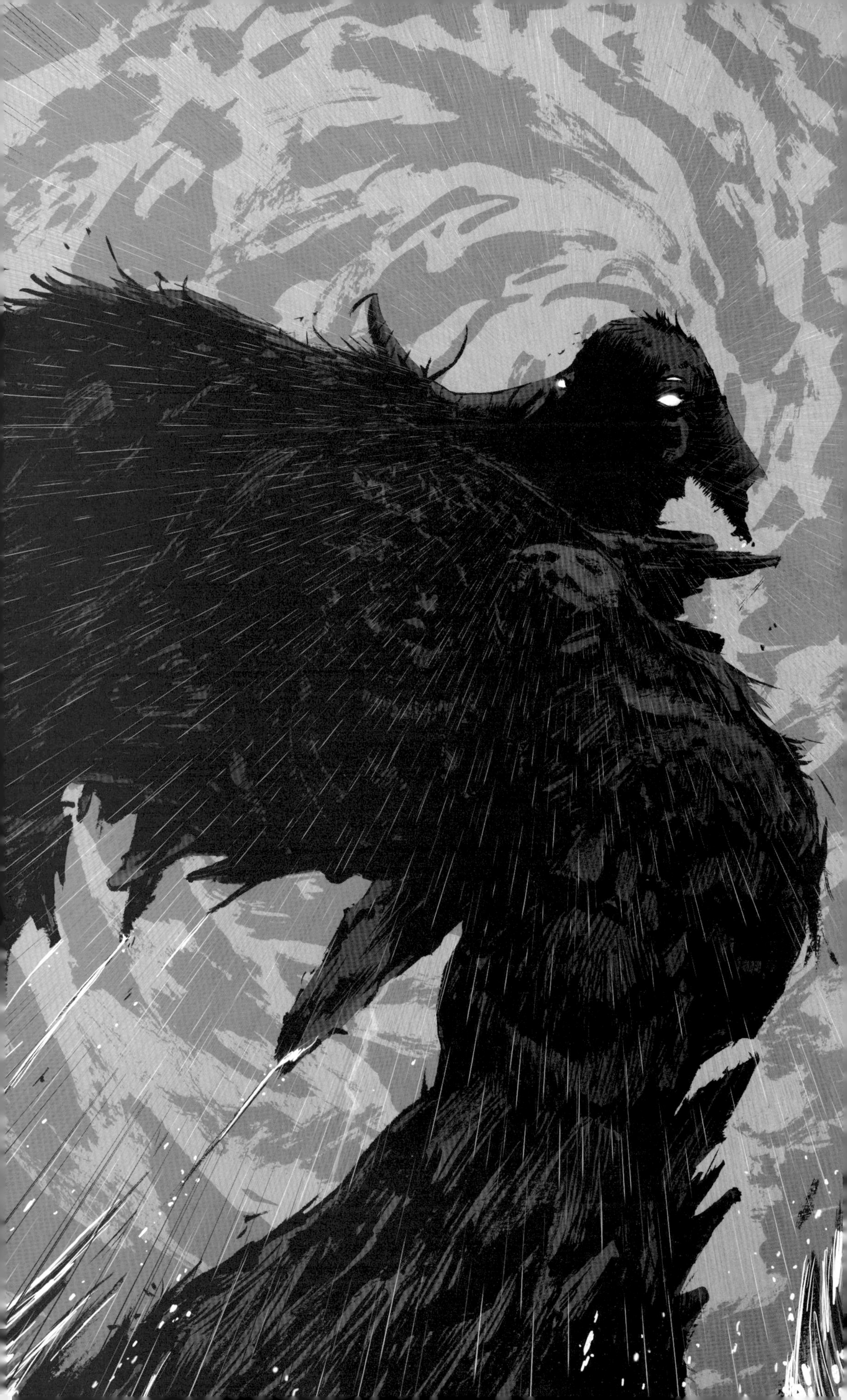

IKG CHAPTER 6: THE TITAN

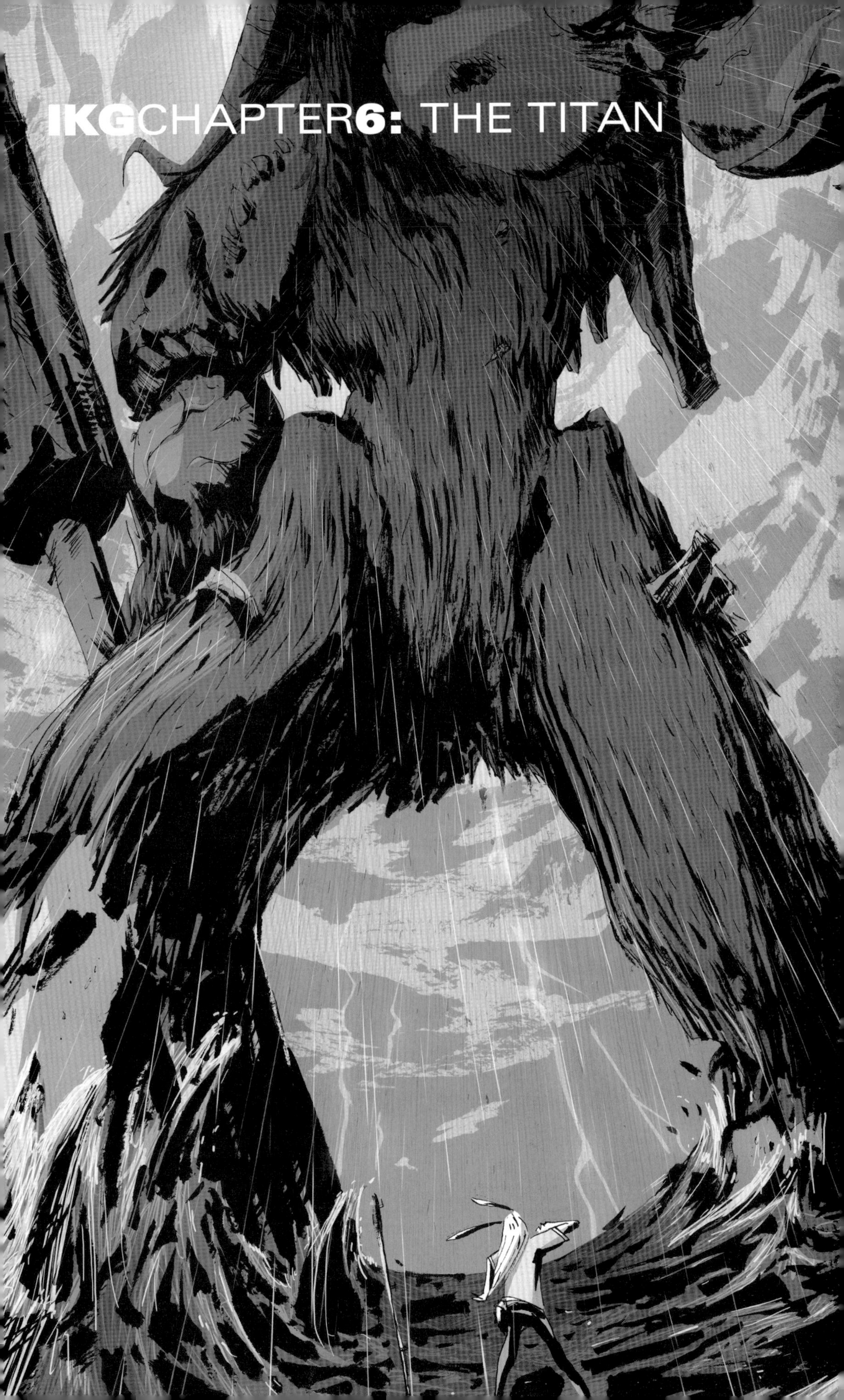

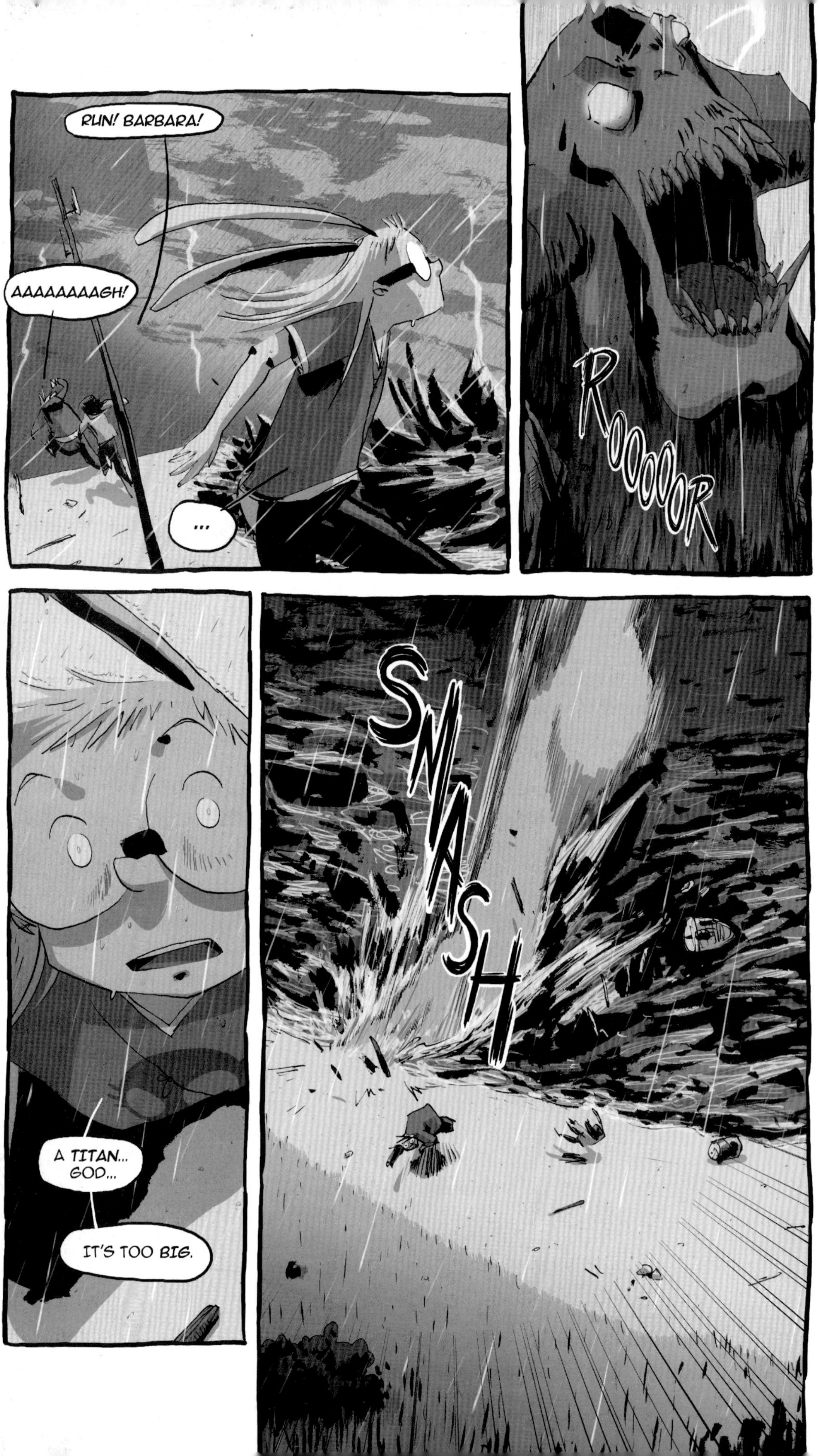
RUN! BARBARA!
AAAAAAAAGH!
...
ROOOOOR
A TITAN... GOD...
IT'S TOO BIG.
SMASH

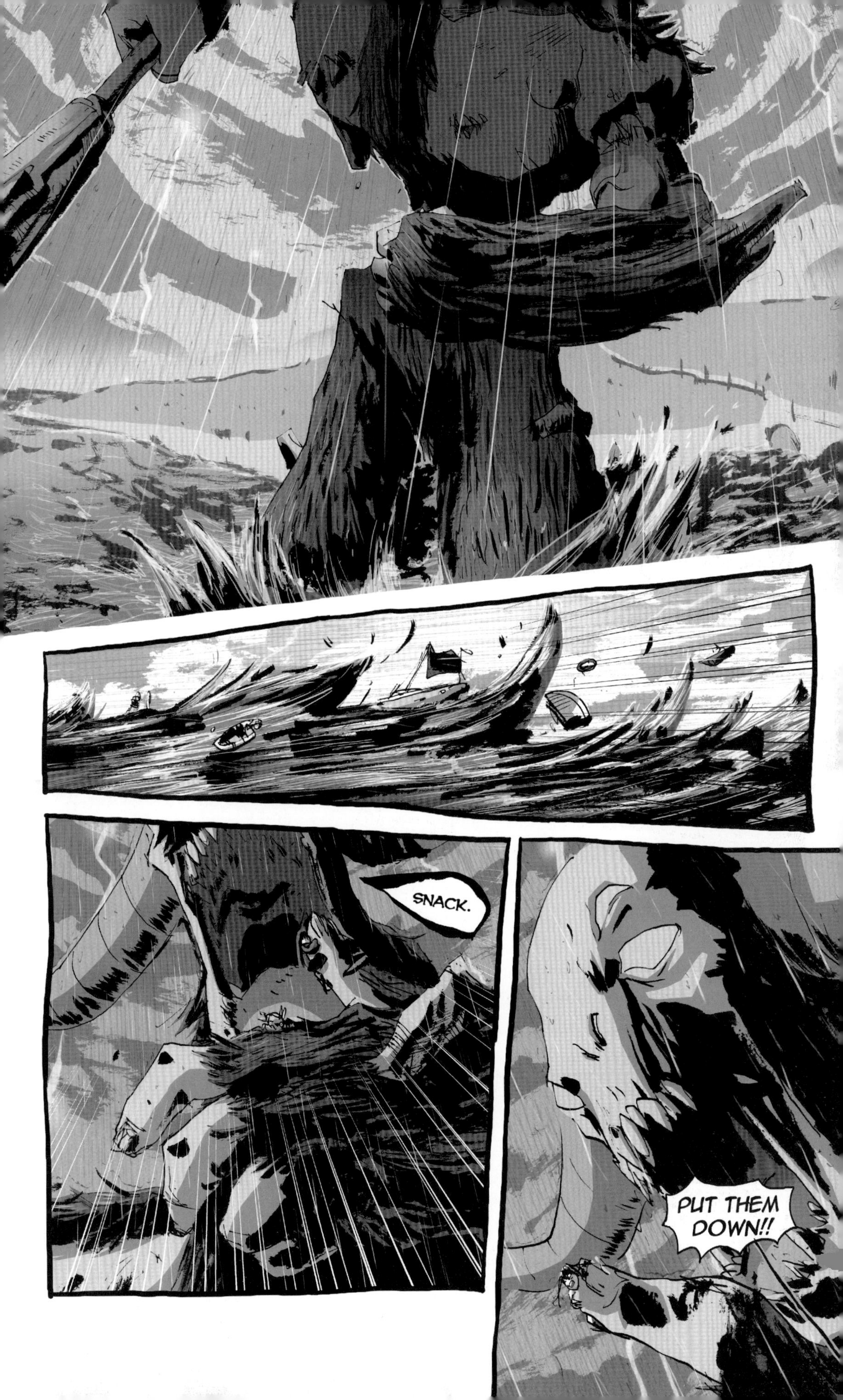
SNACK.
PUT THEM DOWN!!

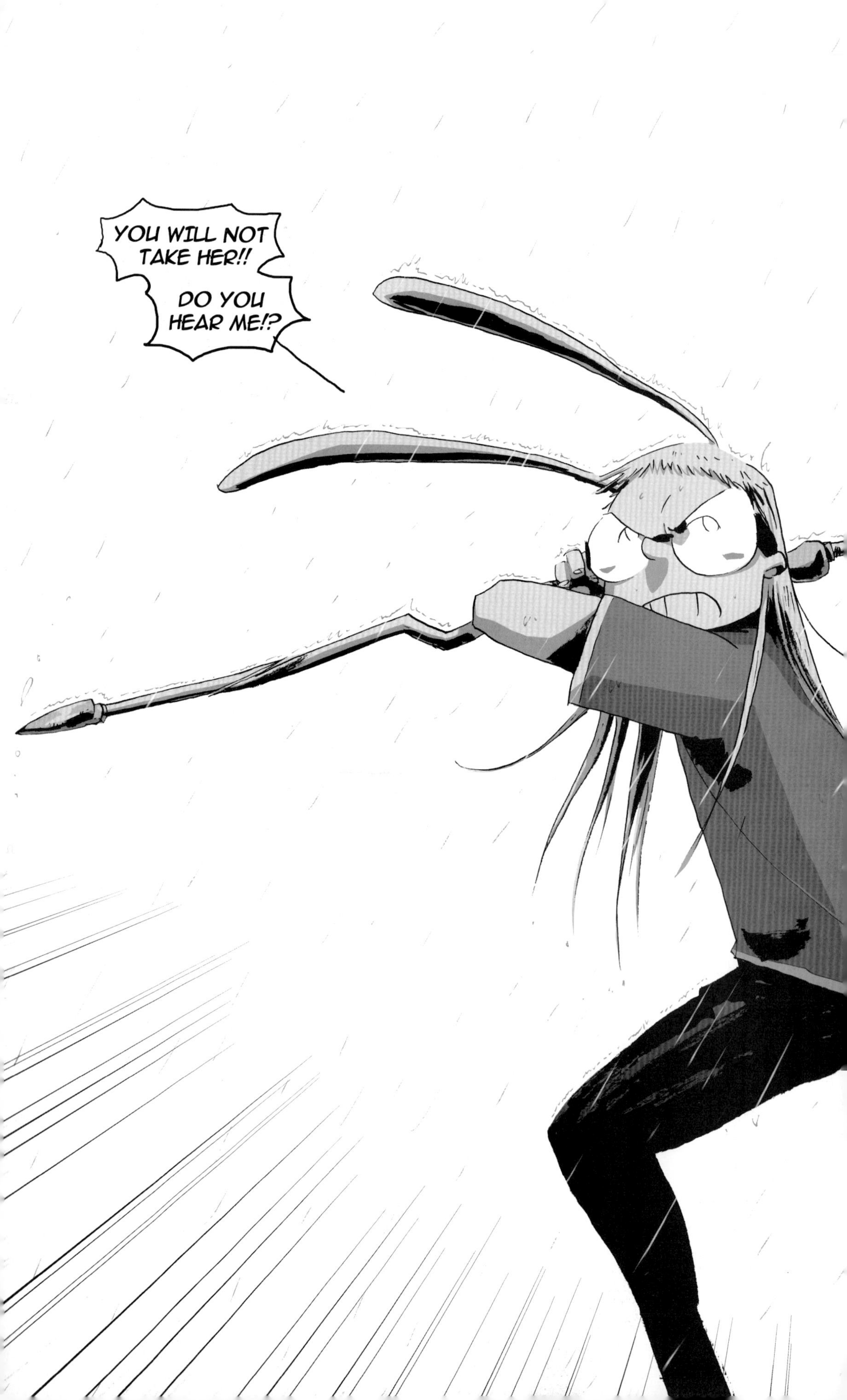
YOU WILL NOT TAKE HER!!
DO YOU HEAR ME!?

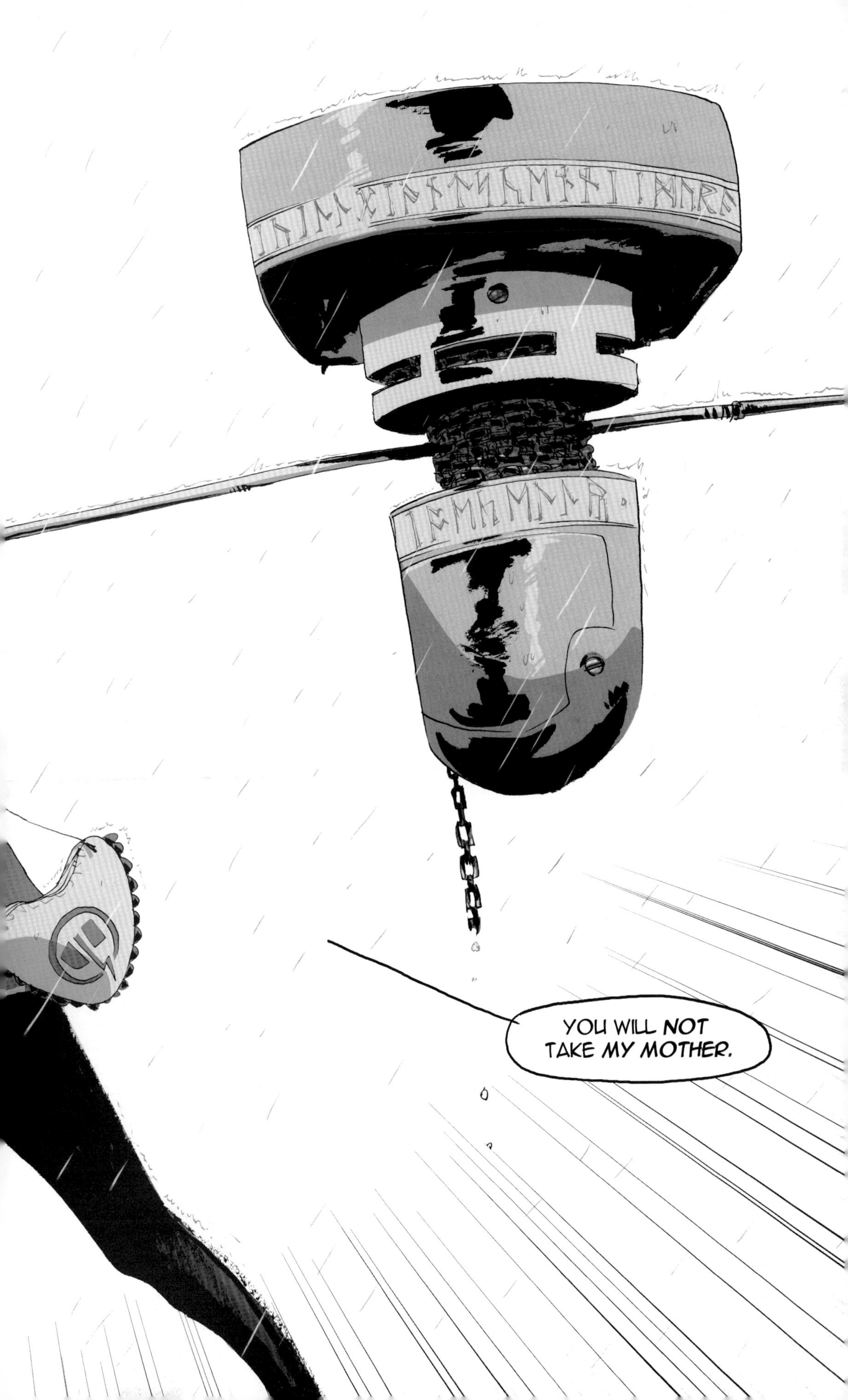
YOU WILL NOT TAKE MY MOTHER.

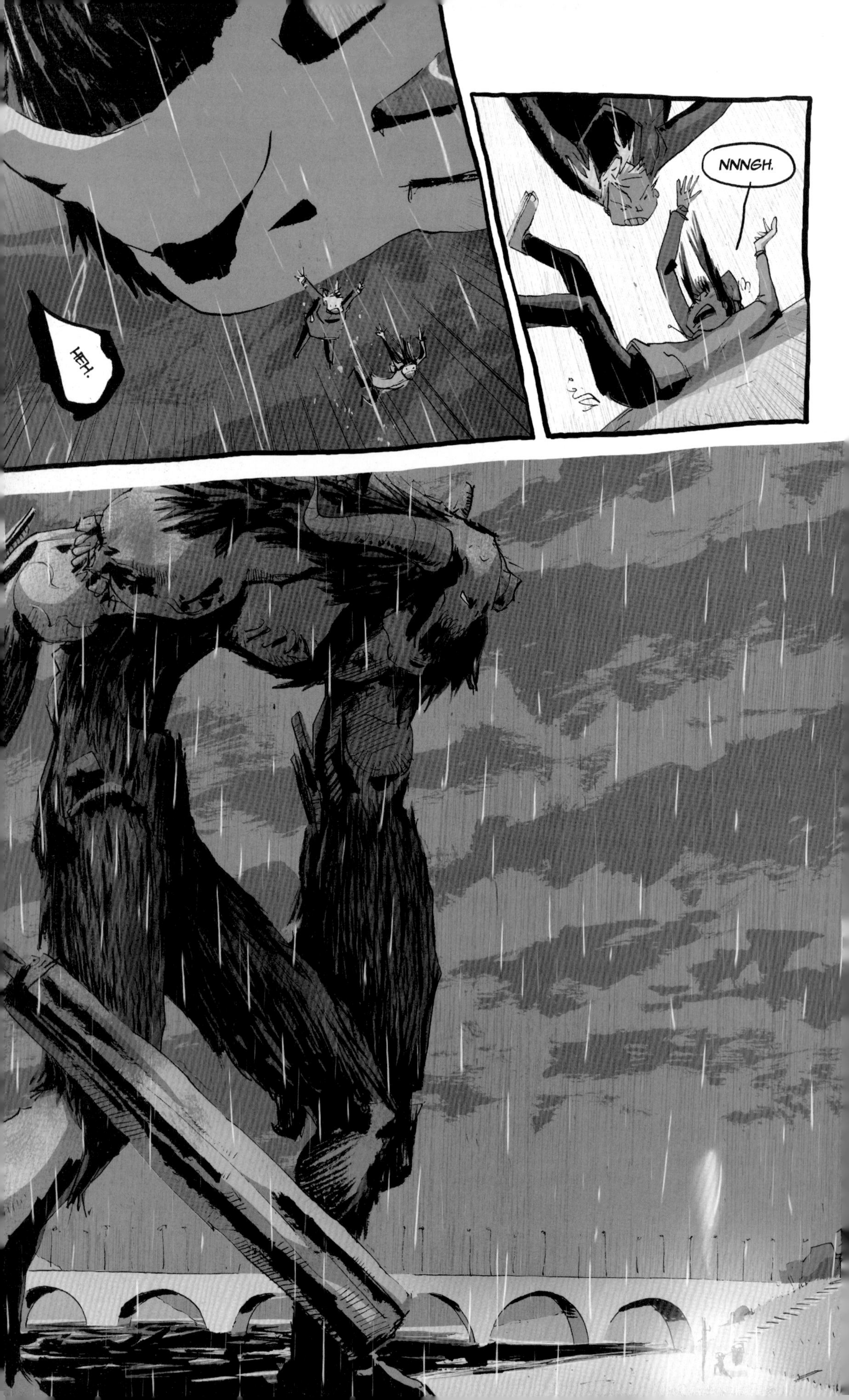
HEH.
NNNGH.

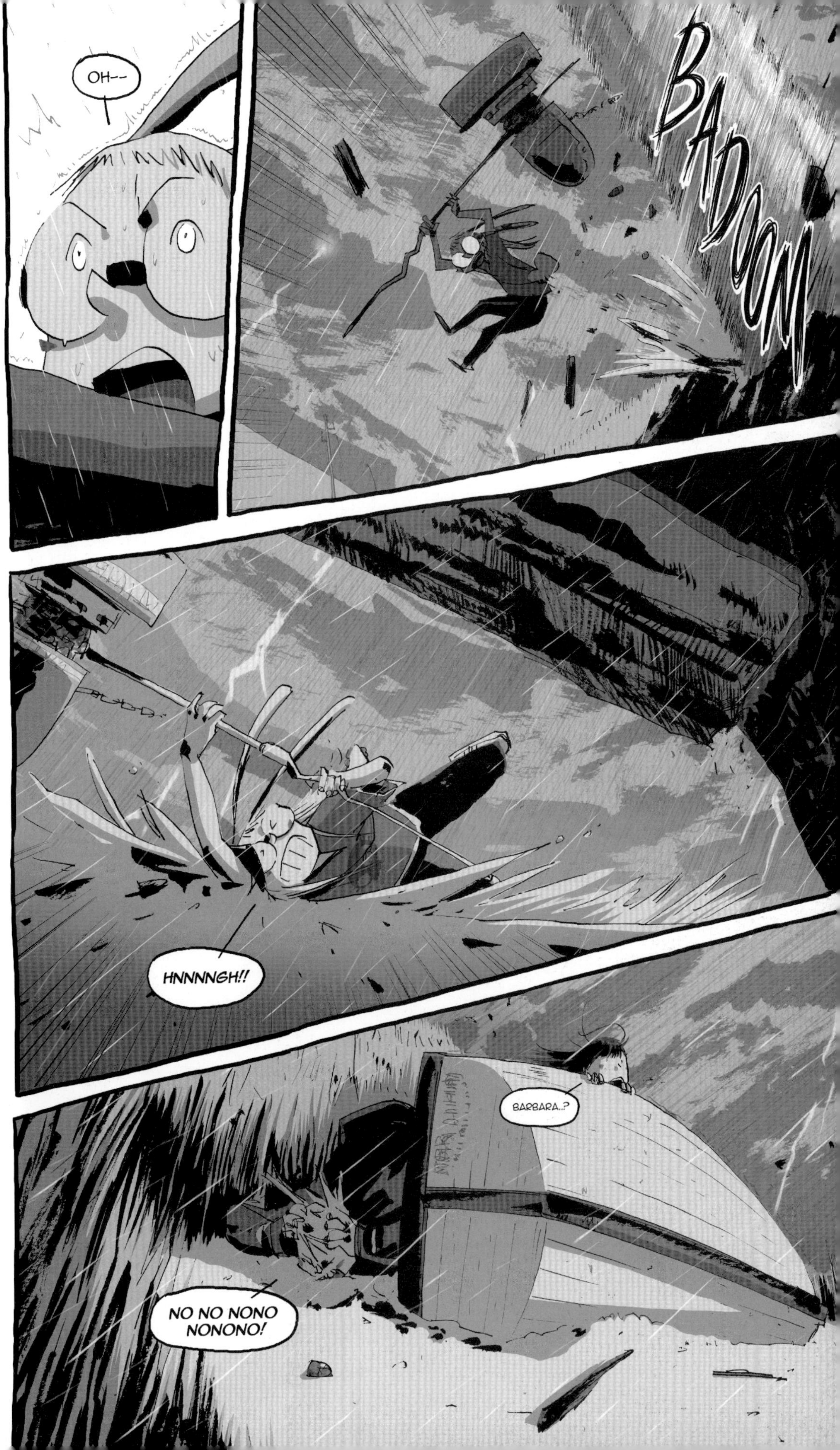
OH--
BADOOM
HNNNNGH!!
BARBARA..?
NO NO NONO
NONONO!

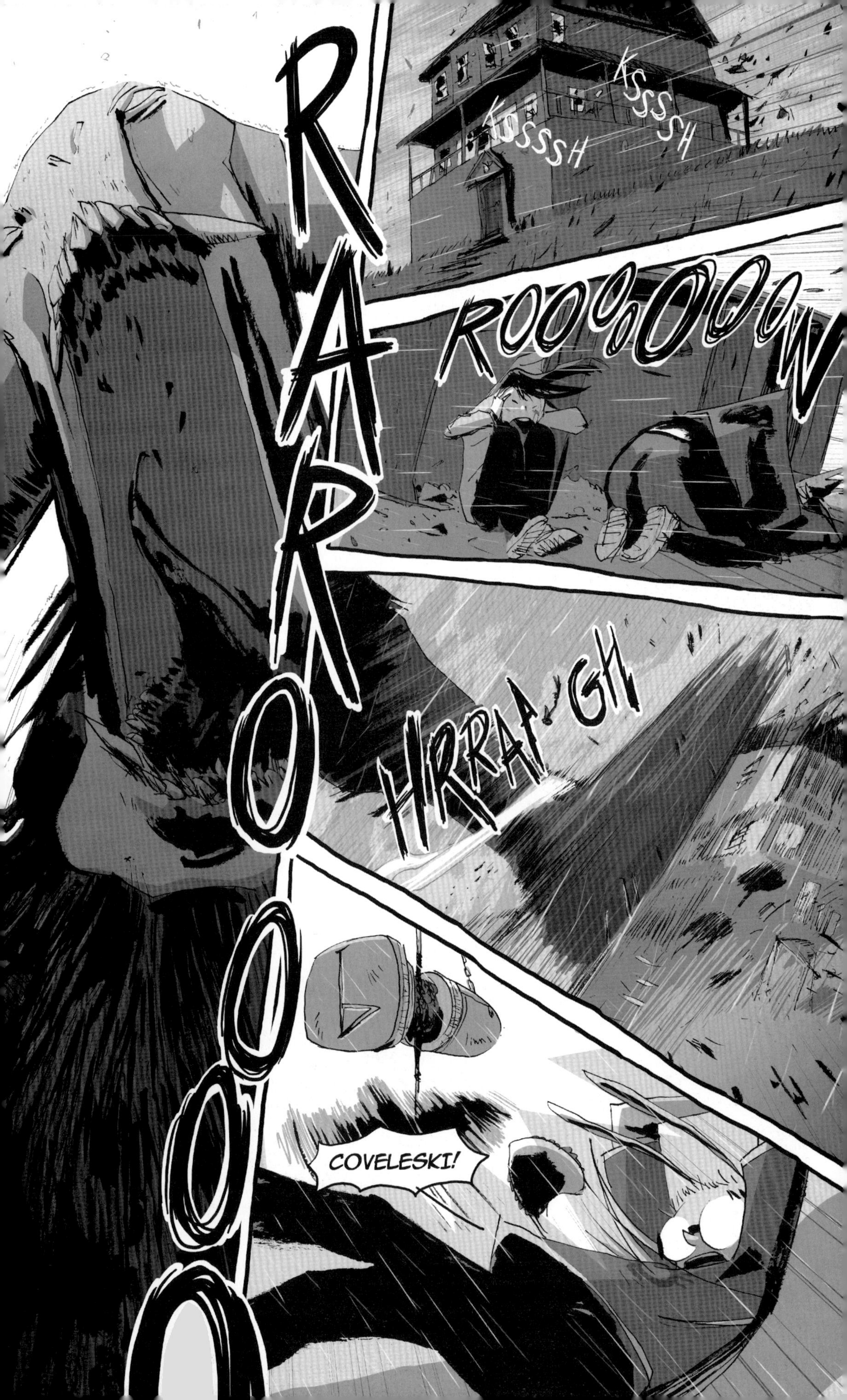
KSSSSH
KSSSSH
ROOOOOOOW
HRRAAGH
RAAROOOOOO
COVELESKI!

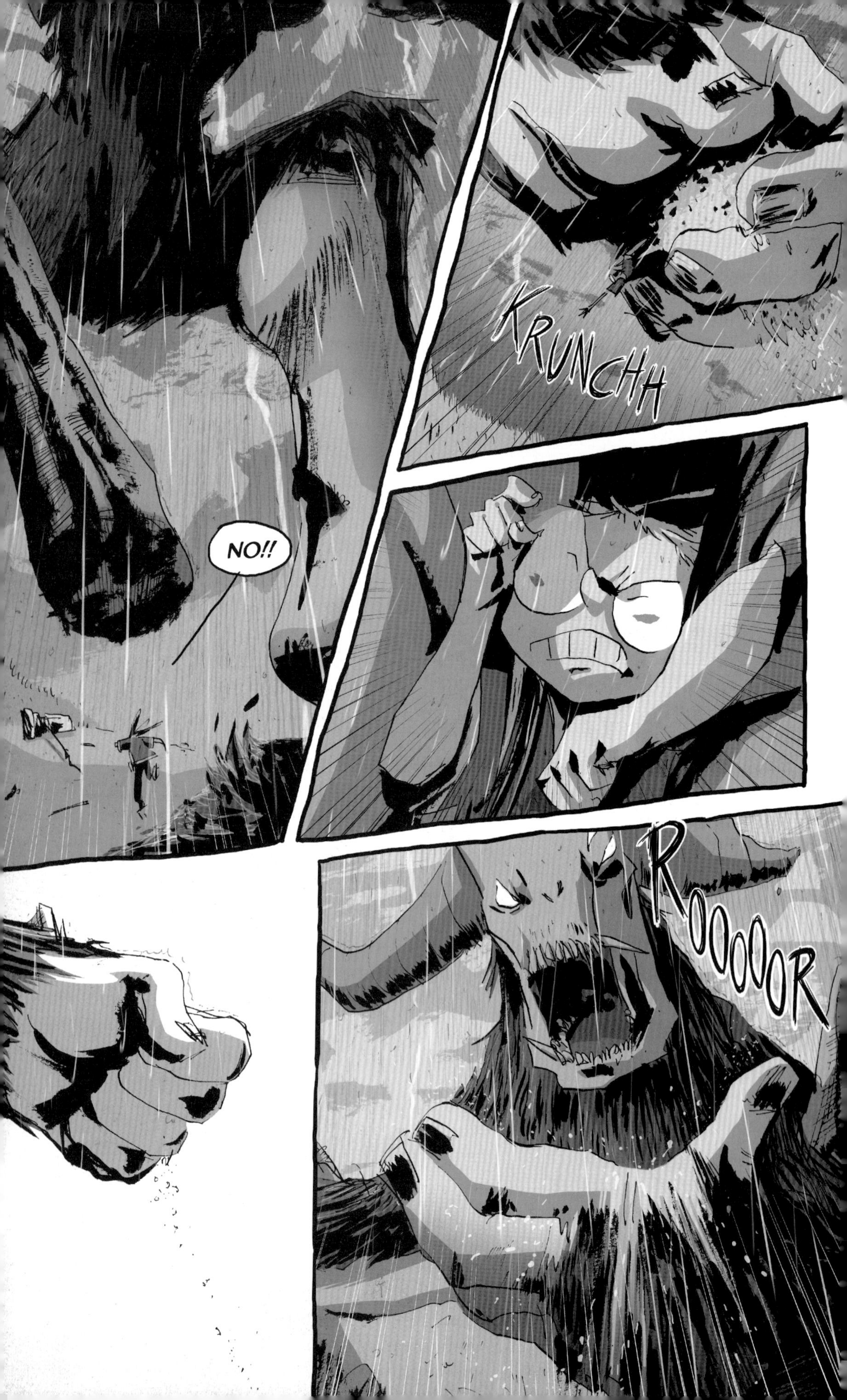
NO!!
KRUNCHH
ROOOOOR

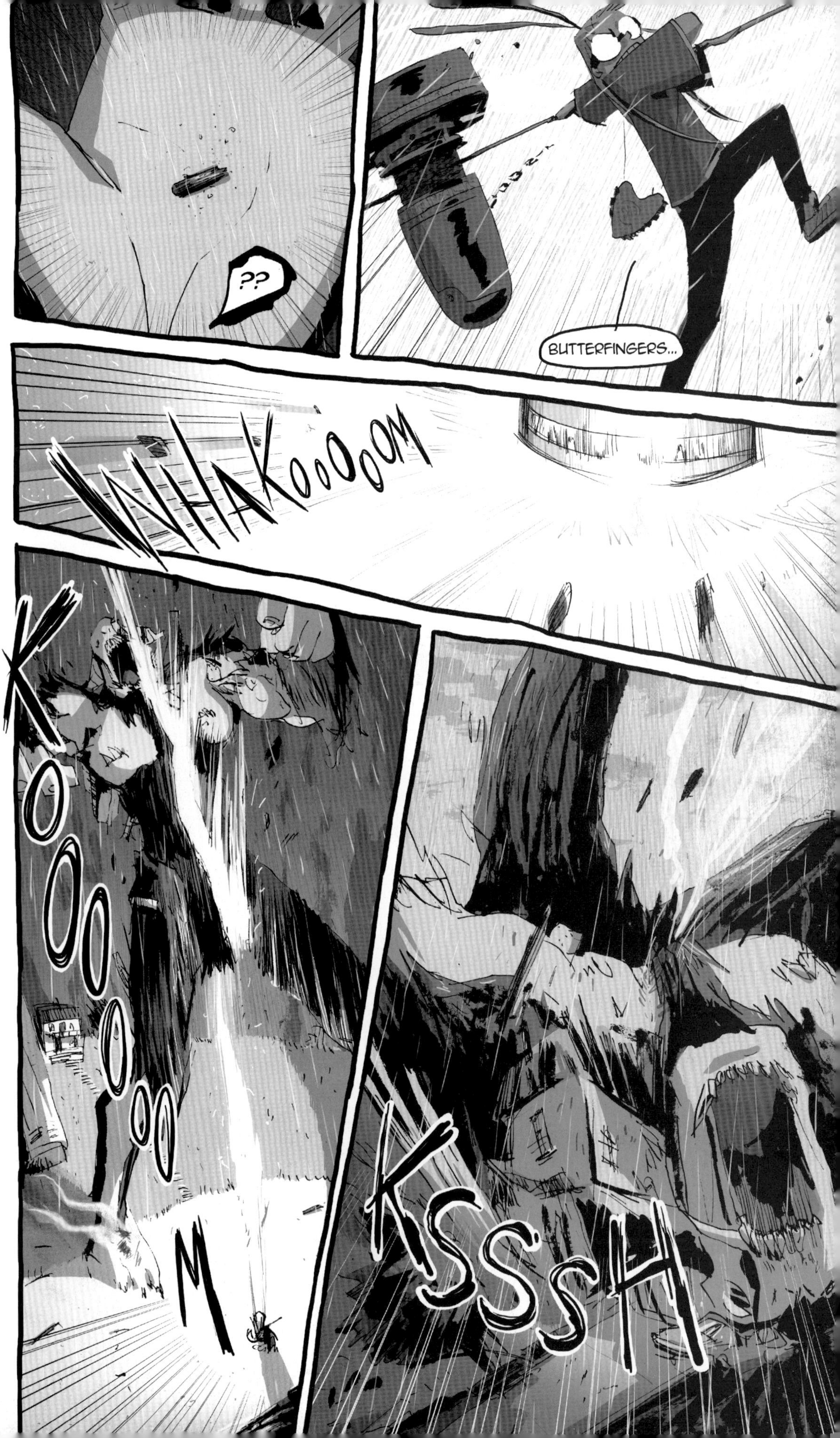
??
BUTTERFINGERS...
WHAKOOOOOM
KOOOOOOOM
KSSSH

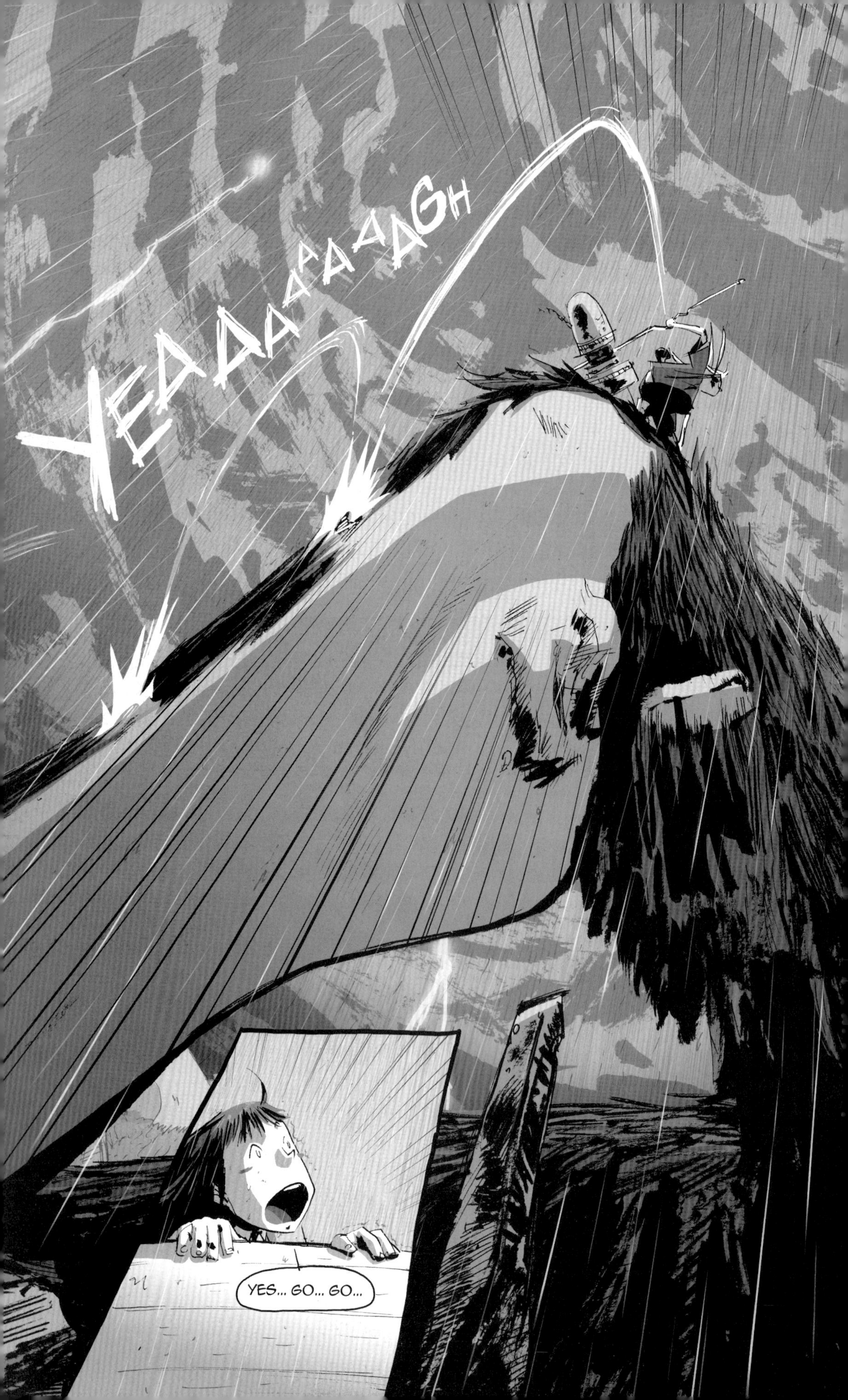
YEAAAAAAAAGH
YES... GO... GO...

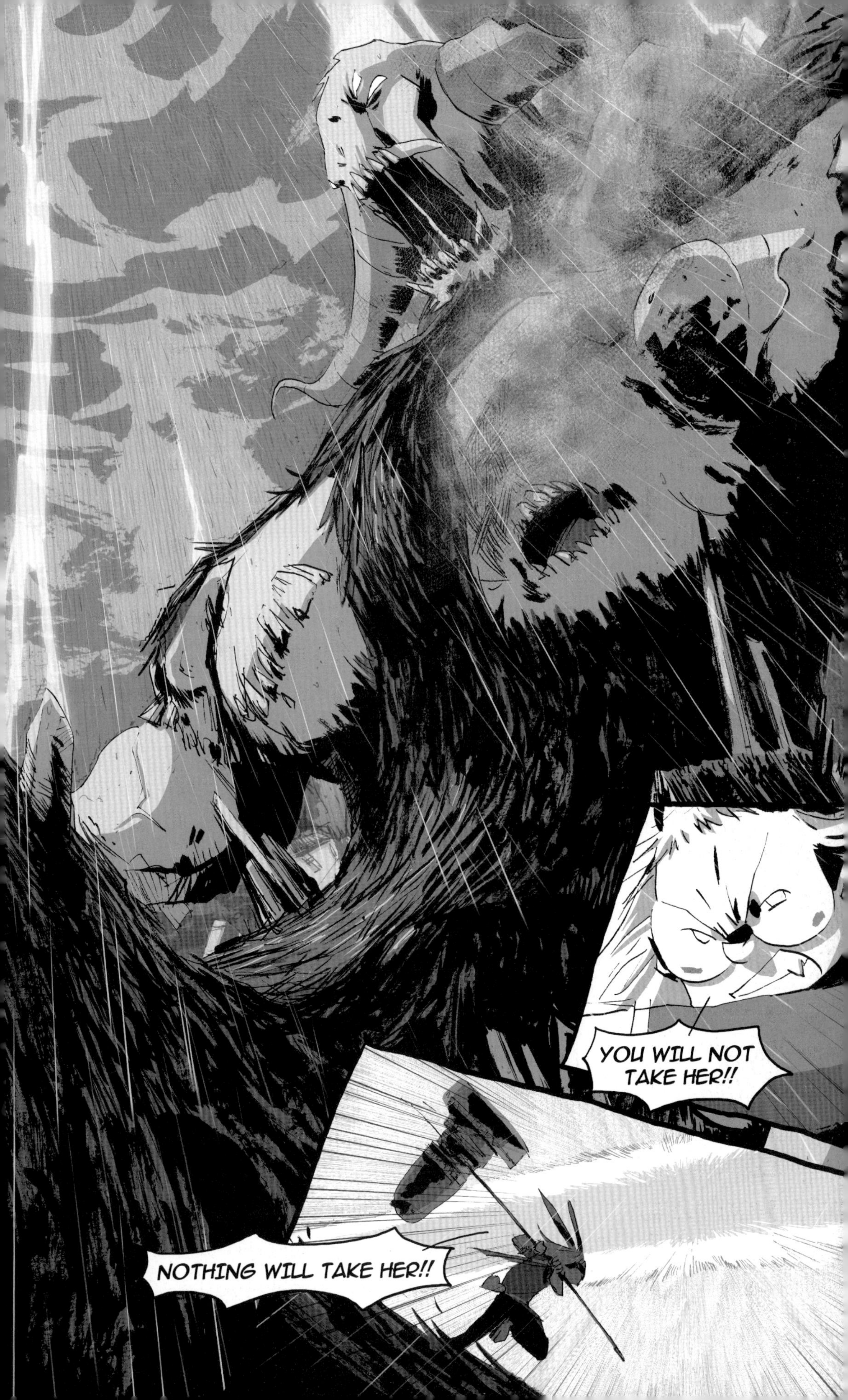
YOU WILL NOT TAKE HER!!
NOTHING WILL TAKE HER!!

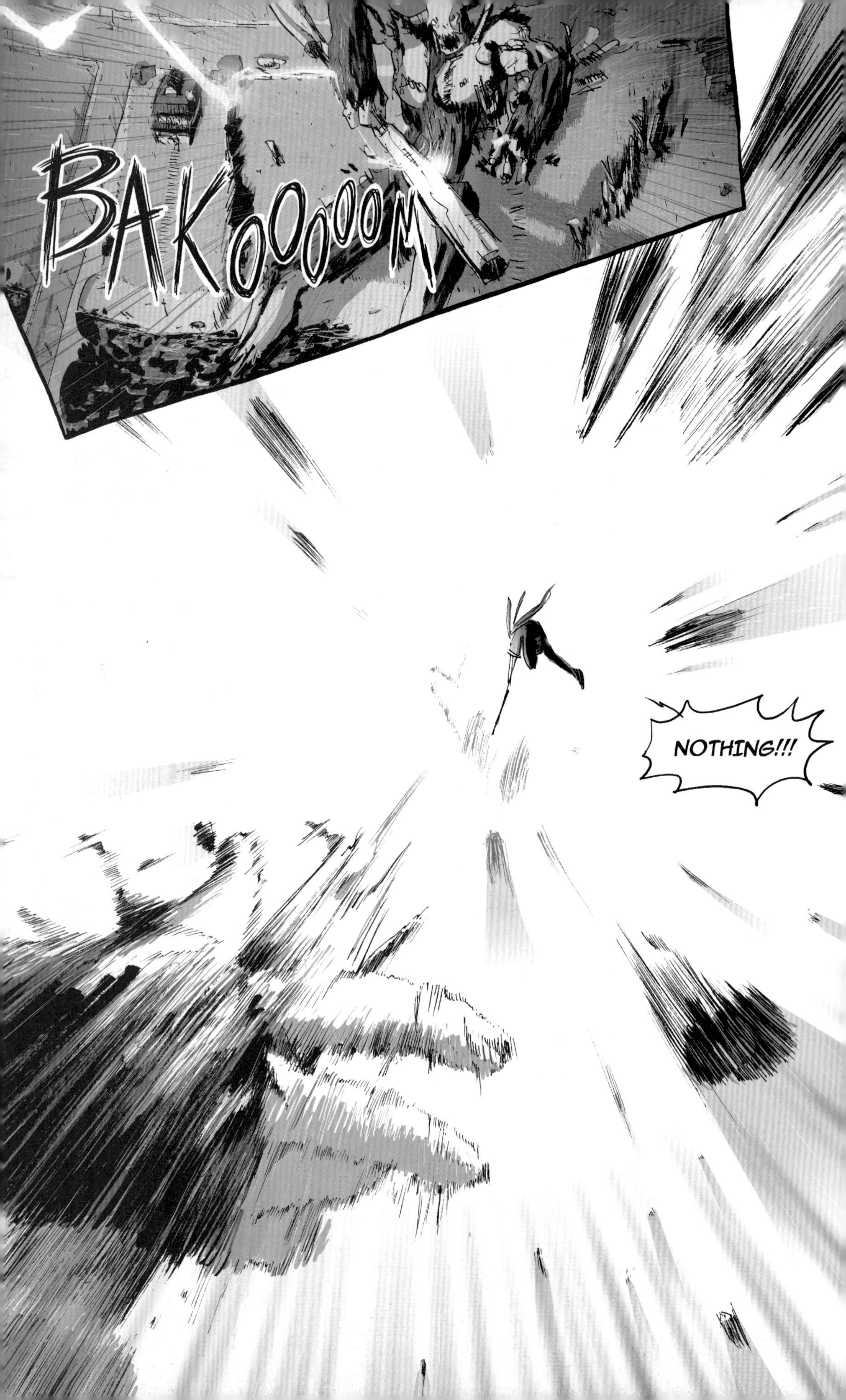
BAKOOOOOM
NOTHING!!!

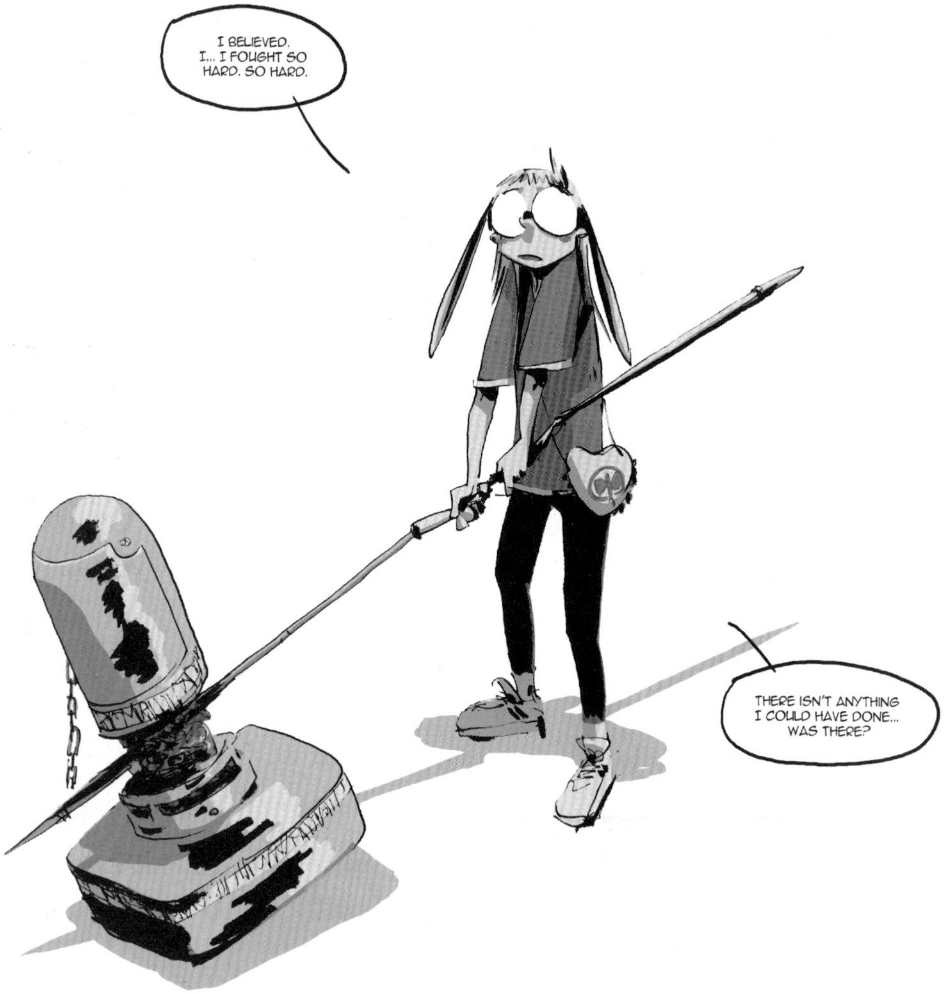
I BELIEVED.
I... I FOUGHT SO HARD. SO HARD.
THERE ISN'T ANYTHING I COULD HAVE DONE... WAS THERE?

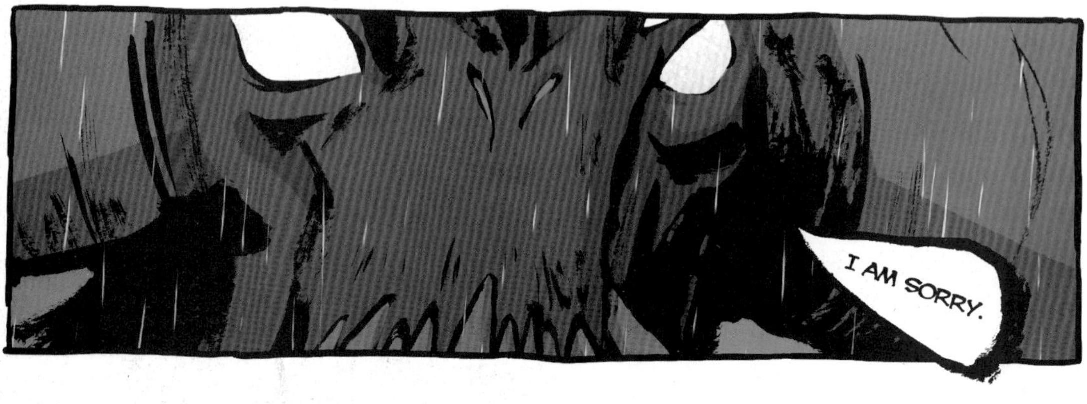
I AM SORRY.

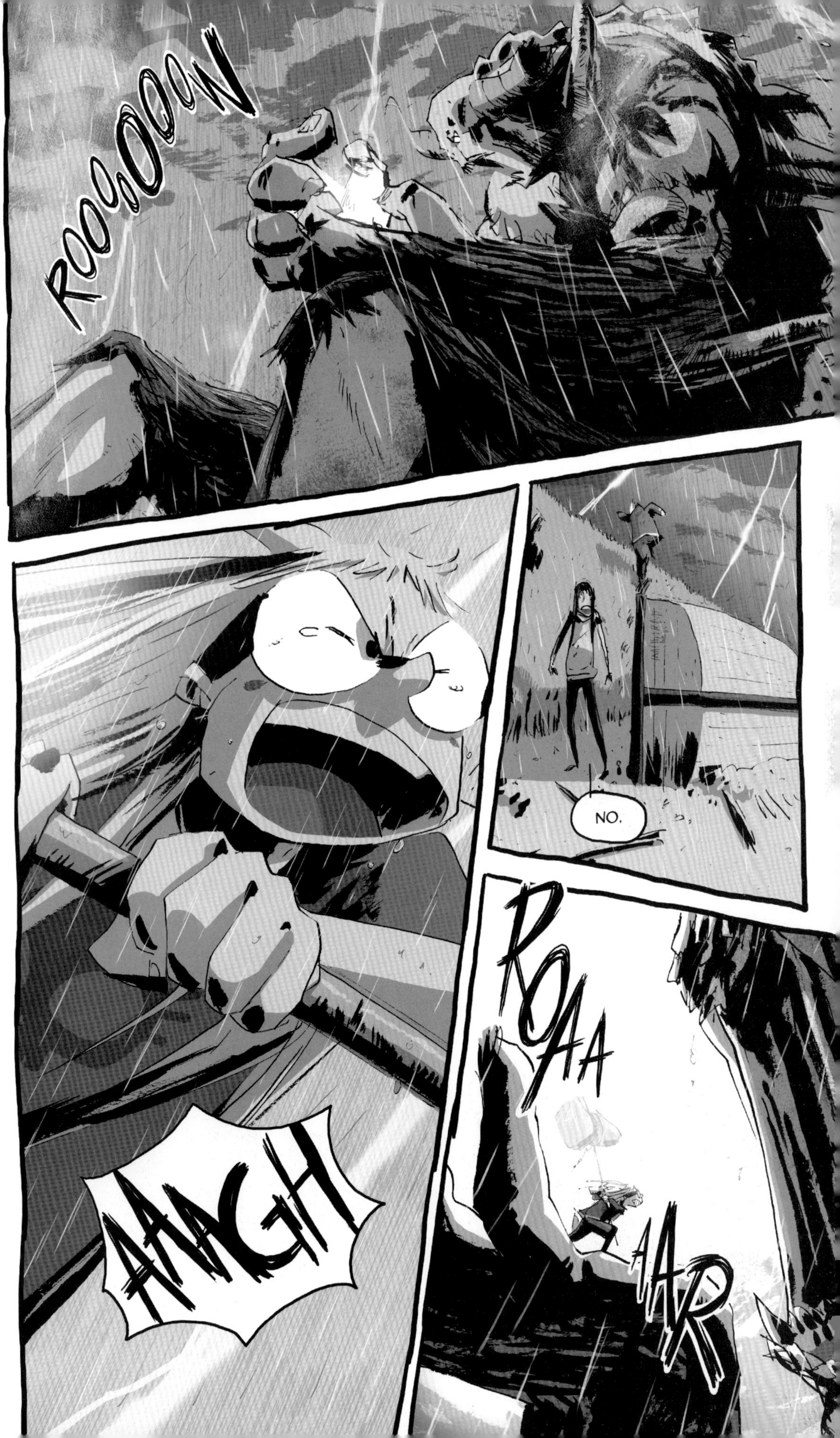
ROOOOOOOW
AAAGH
NO.
ROAAAAR

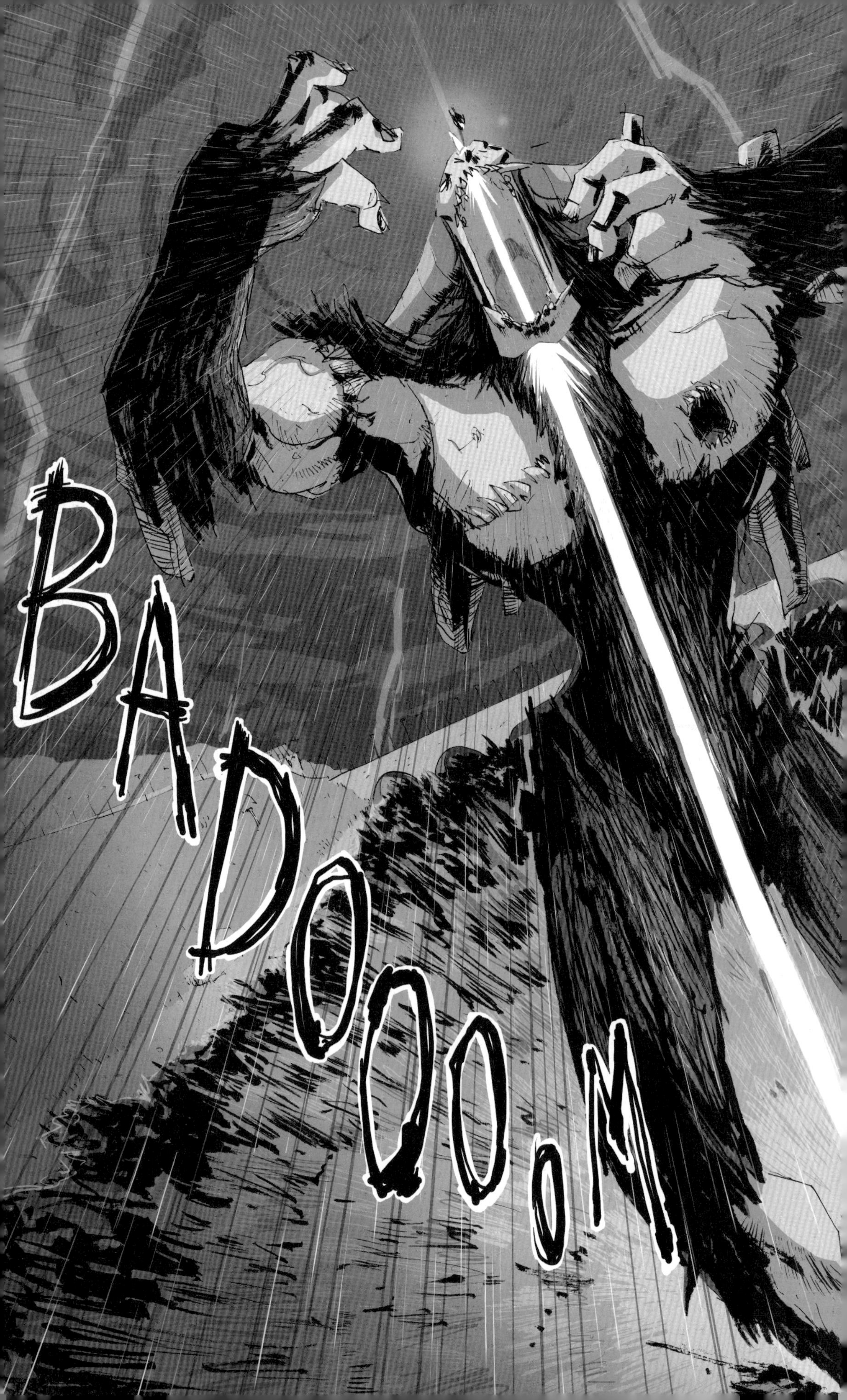
BADOOOoM

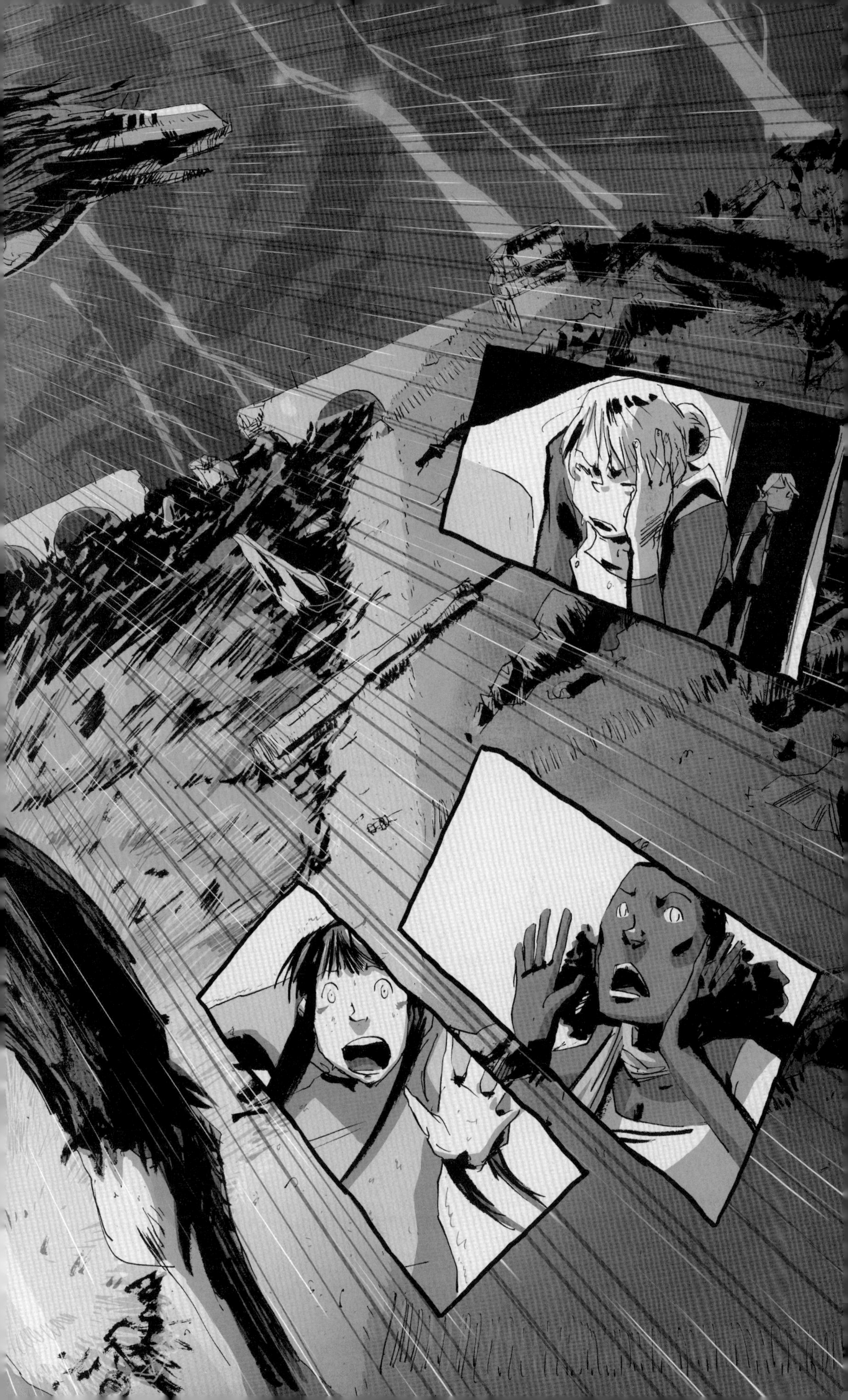

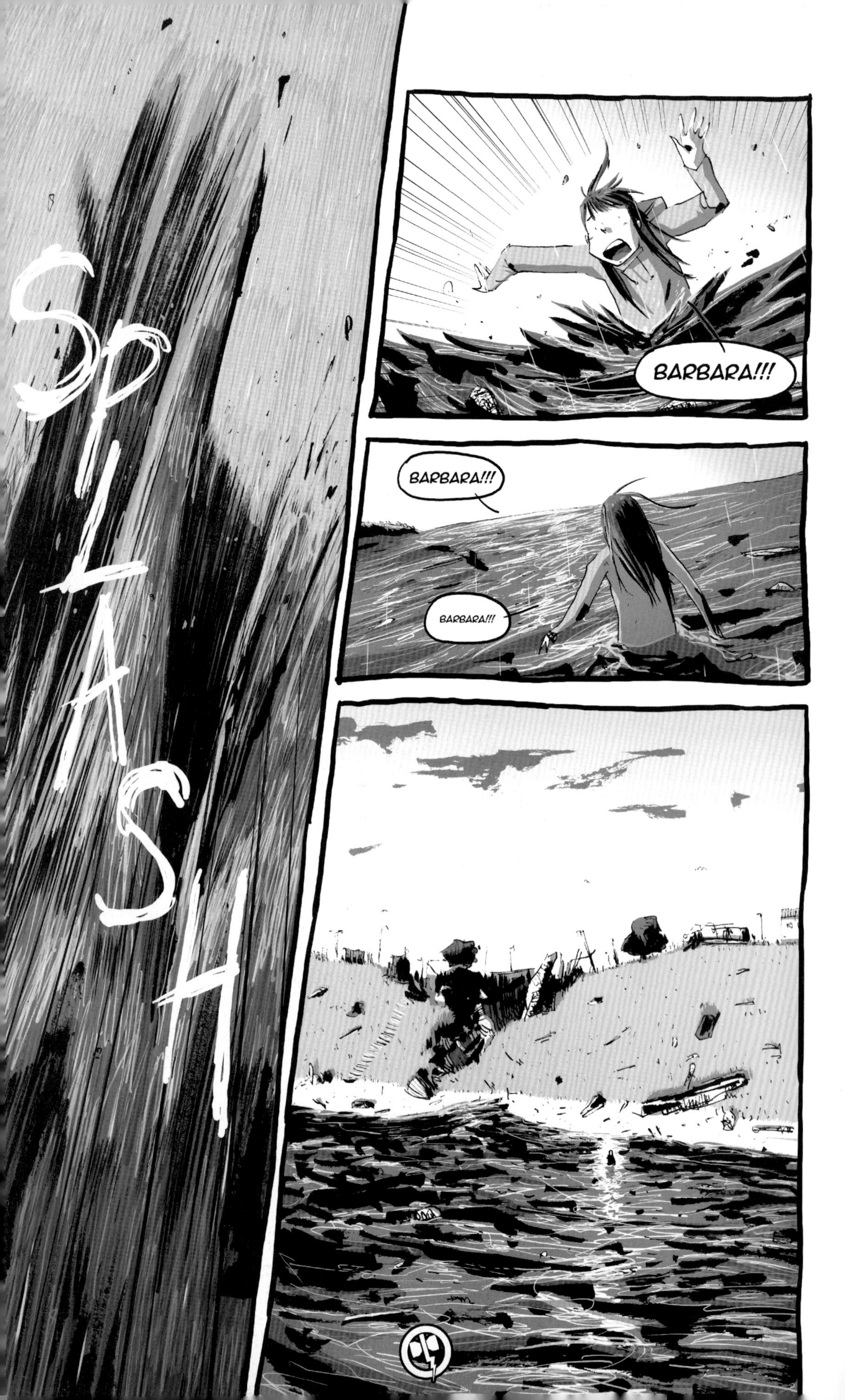
SPLASH
BARBARA!!!
BARBARA!!!
BARBARA!!!

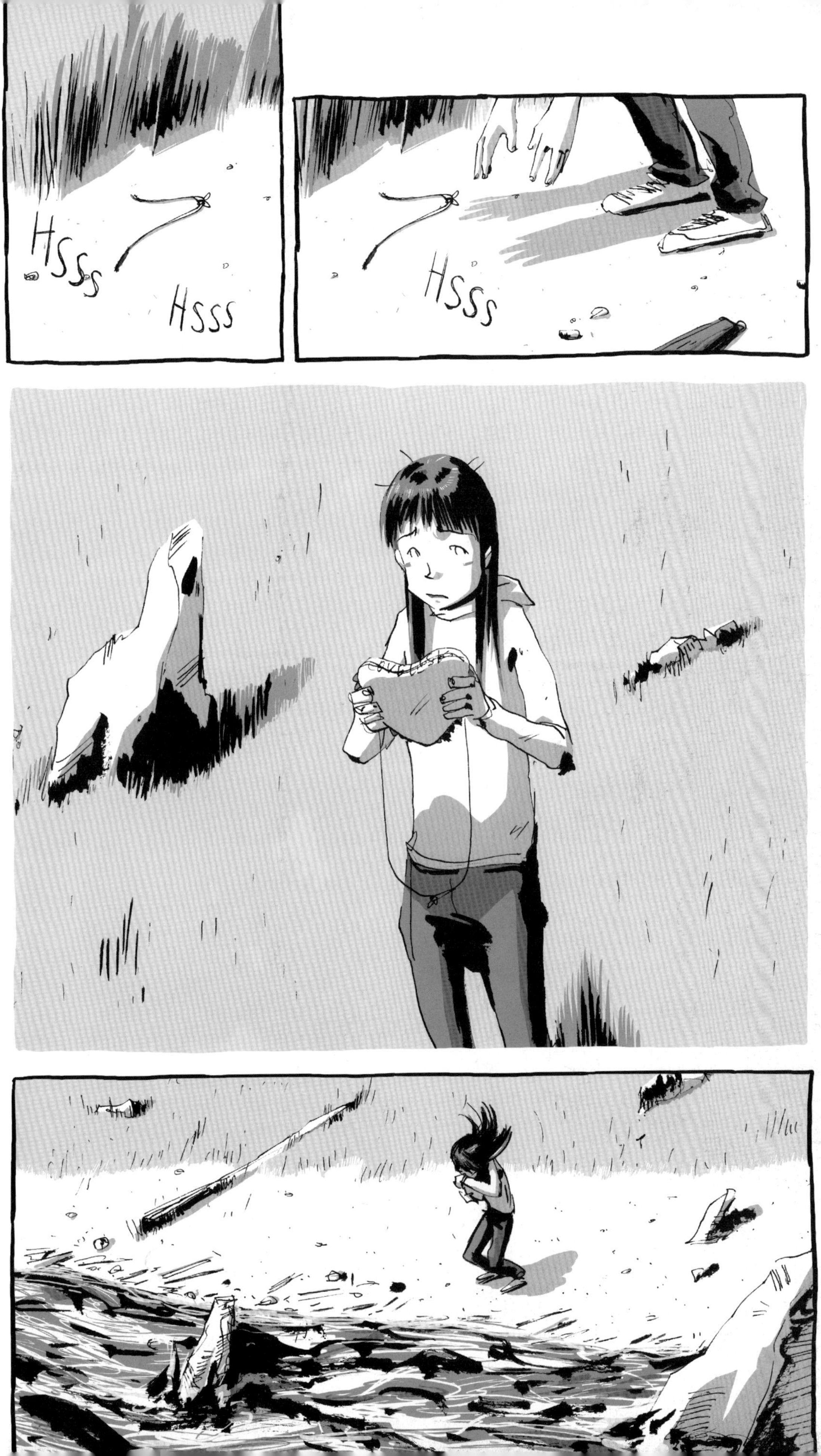
Hssss
Hsss
Hssss

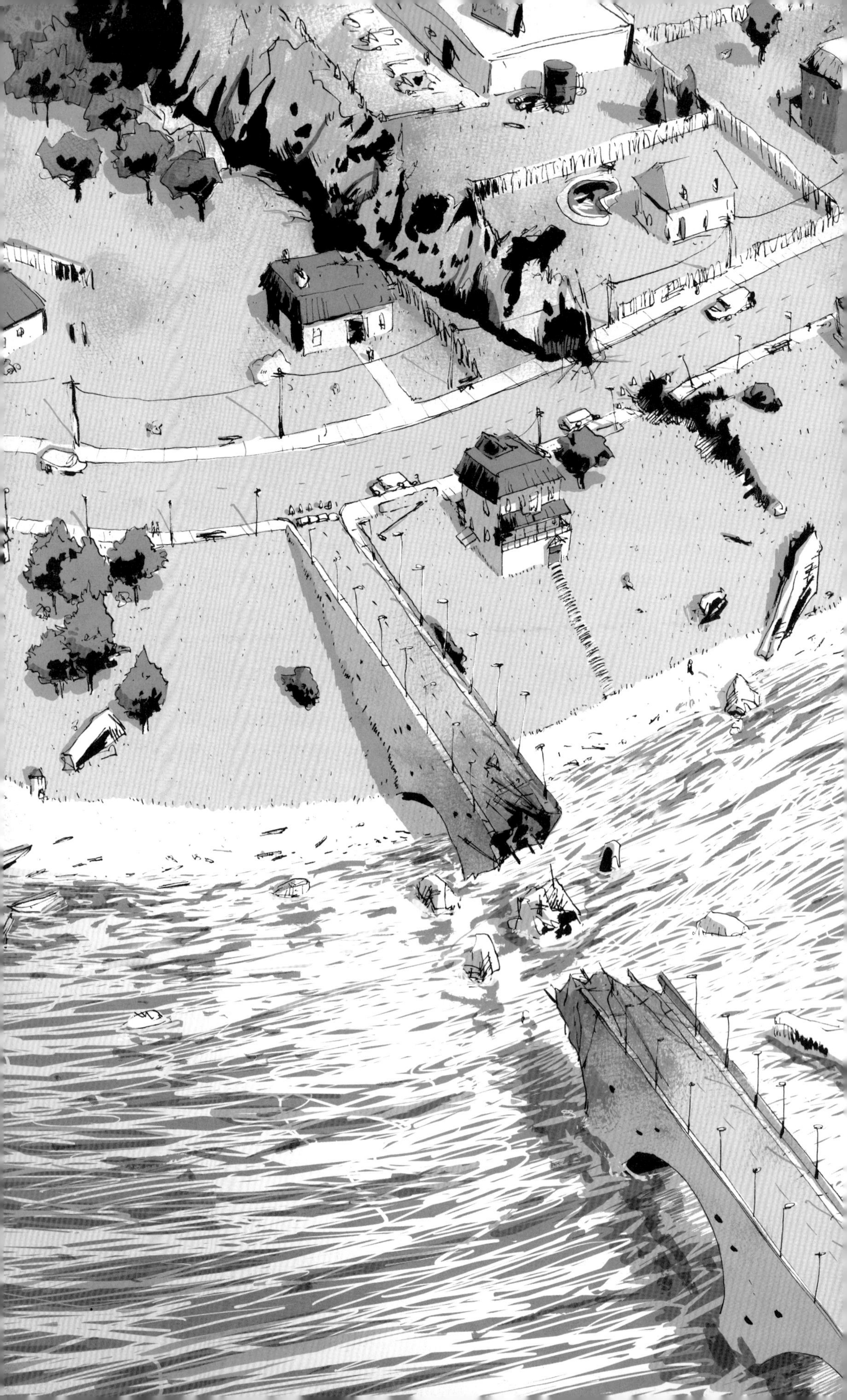

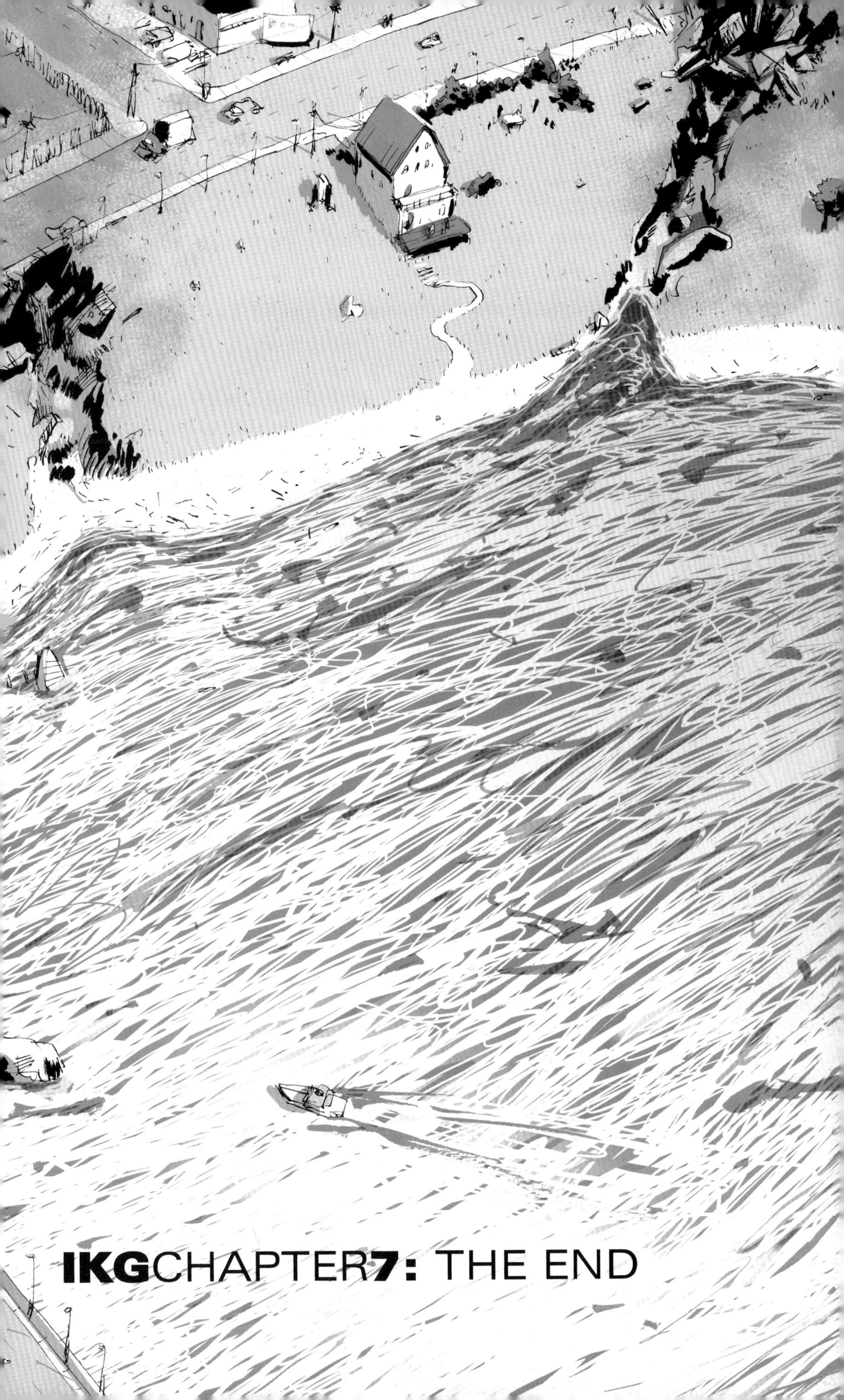

IKGCHAPTER7: THE END

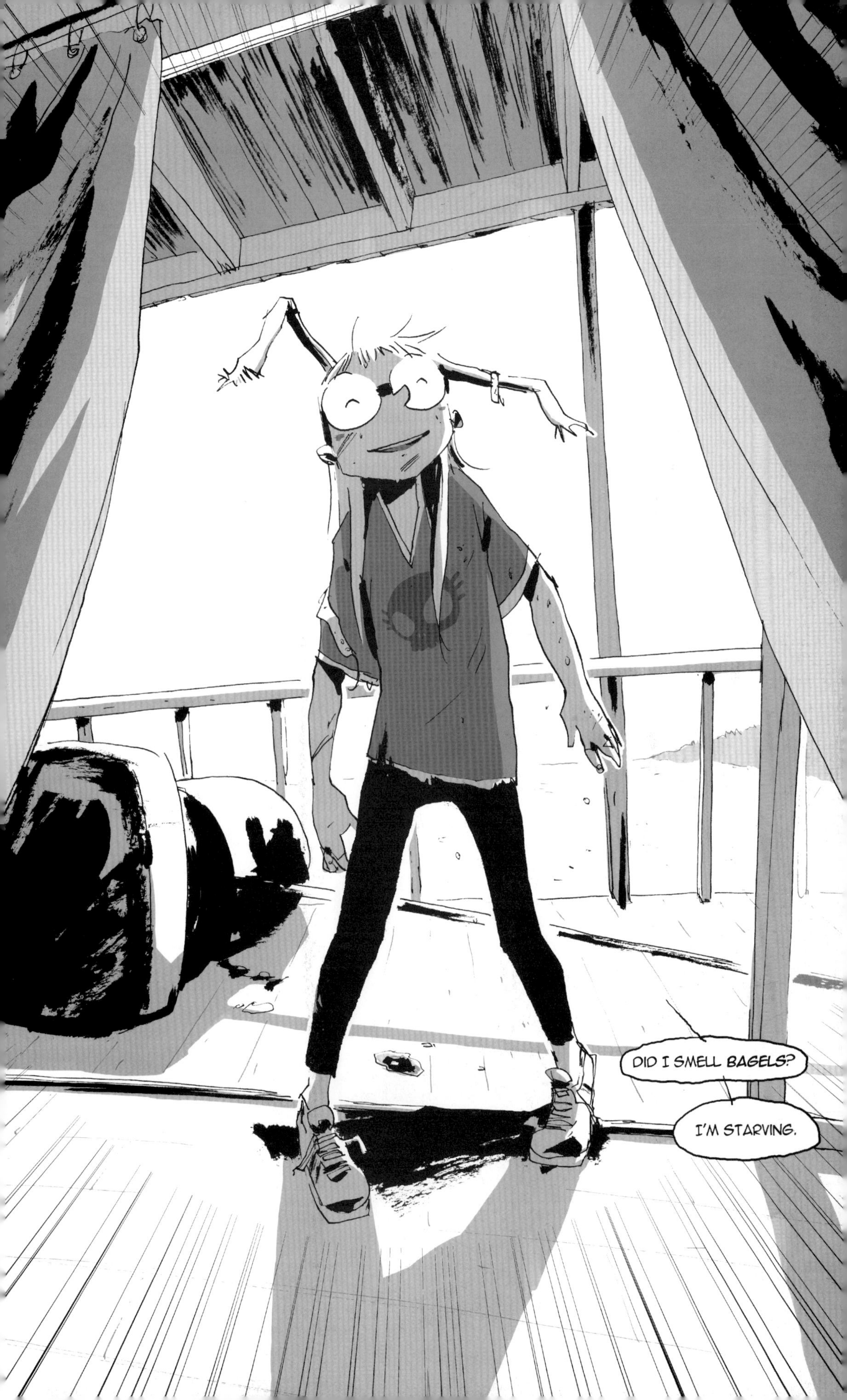
DID I SMELL BAGELS?
I'M STARVING.

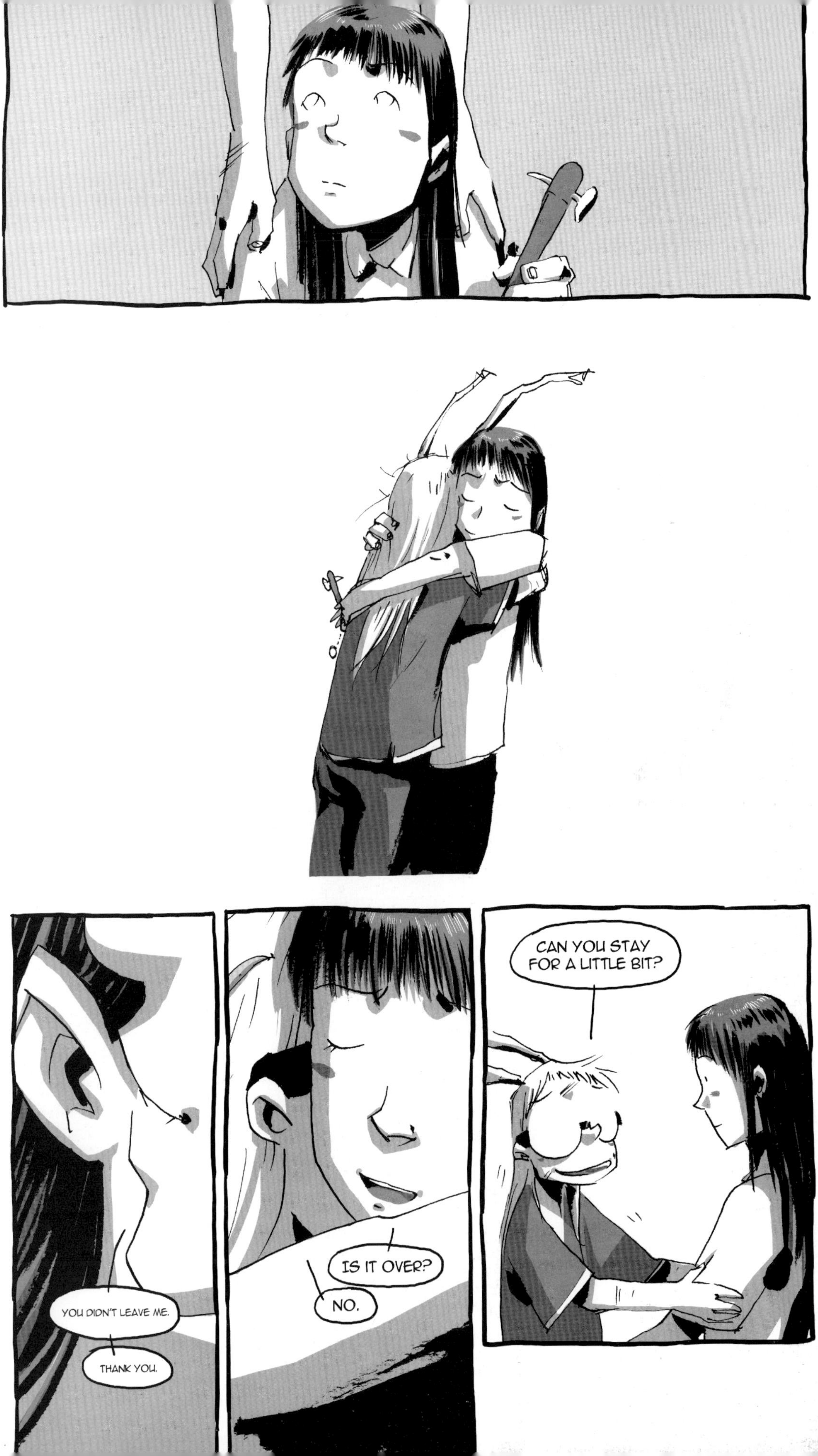
YOU DIDN'T LEAVE ME.
THANK YOU.
IS IT OVER?
NO.
CAN YOU STAY FOR A LITTLE BIT?

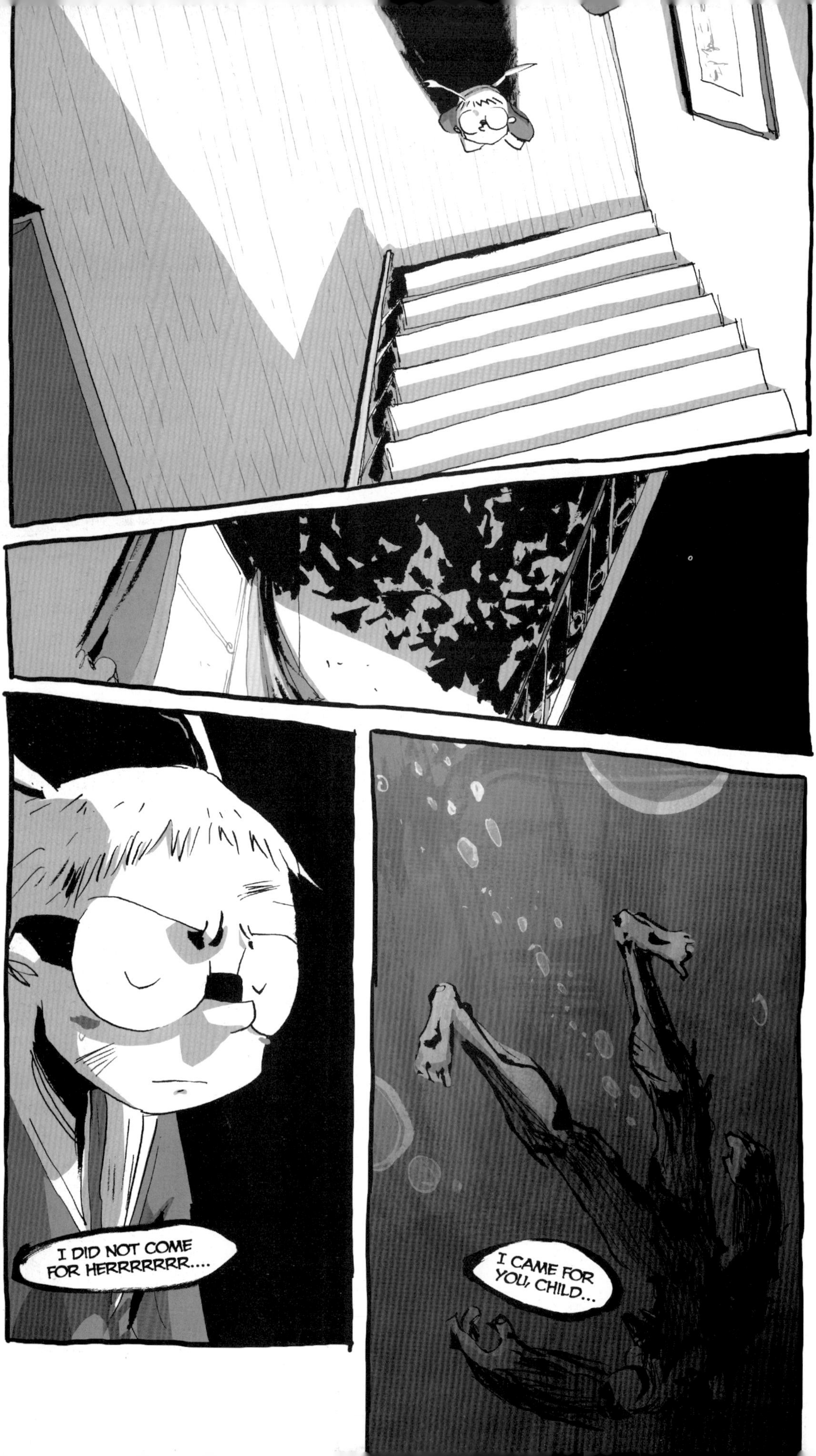
I DID NOT COME
FOR HERRRRRRR....
I CAME FOR
YOU, CHILD...

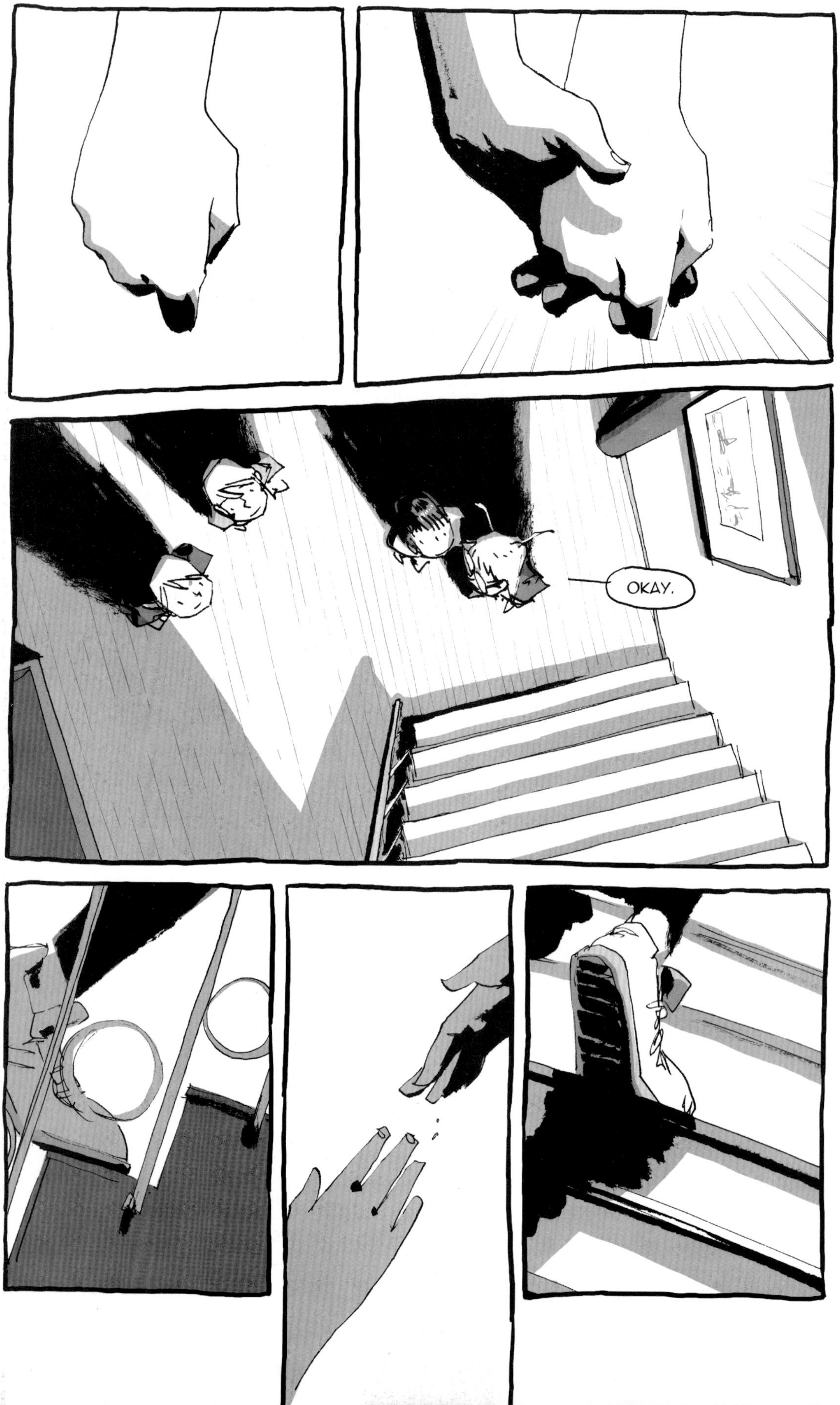
OKAY.

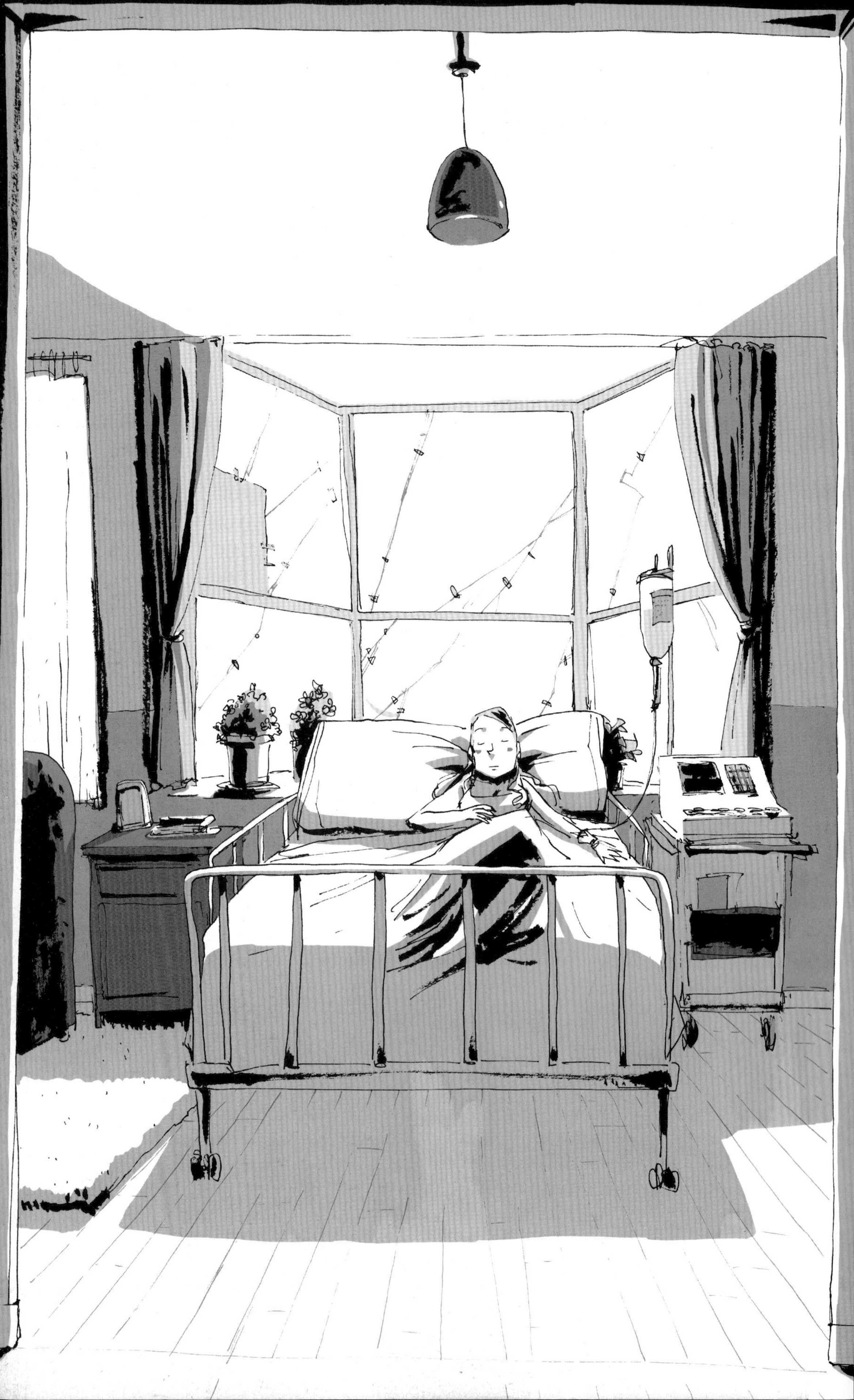

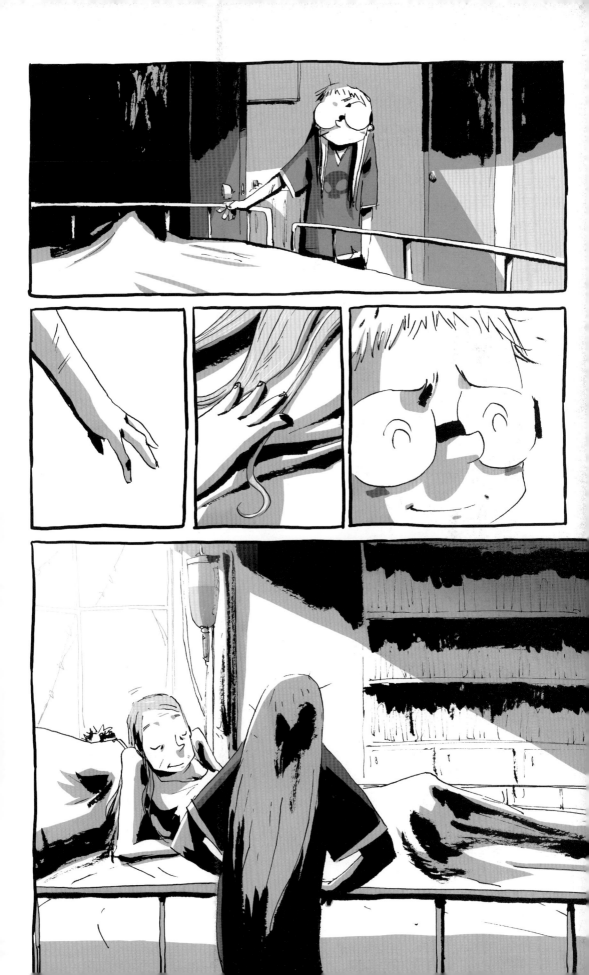

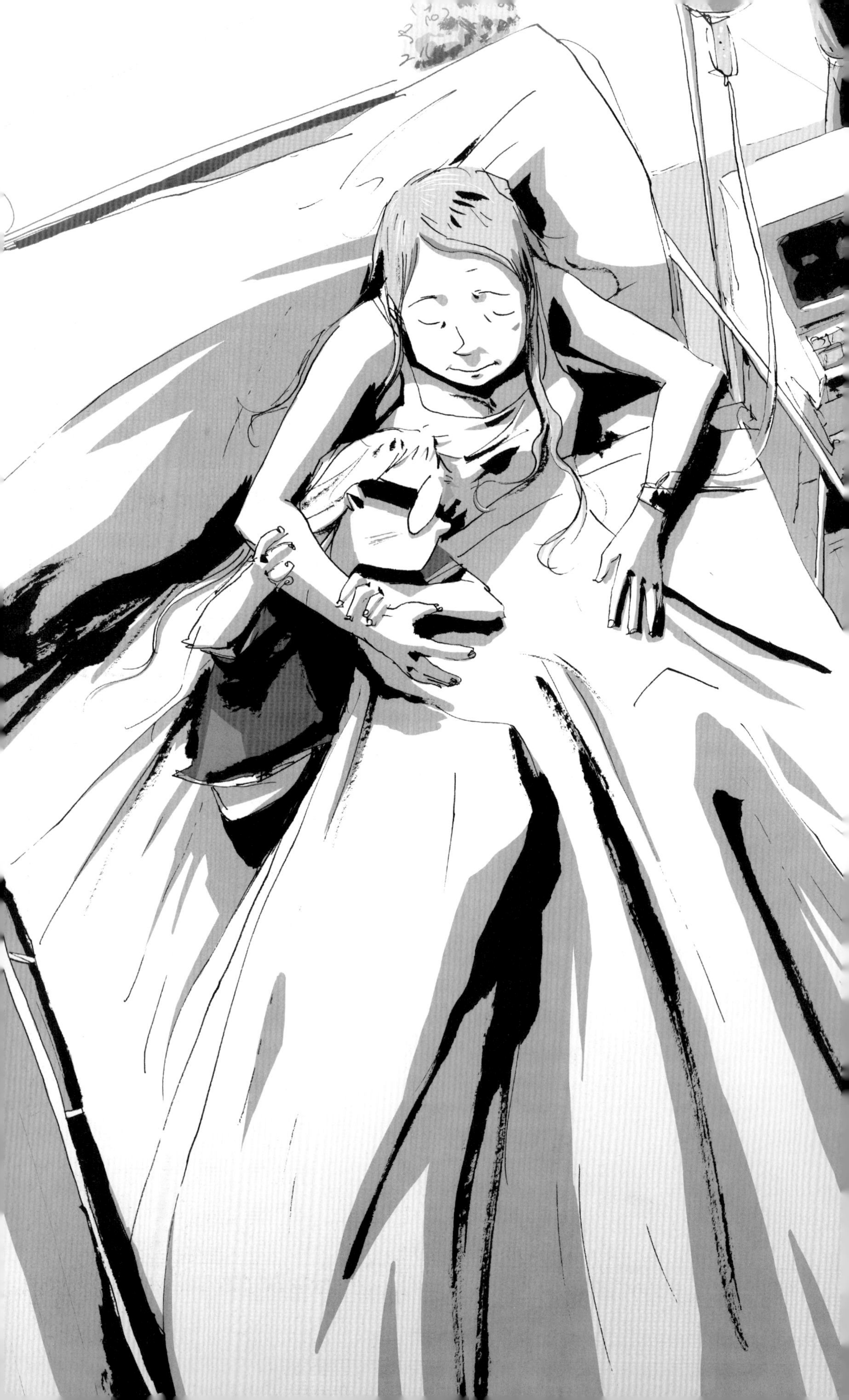

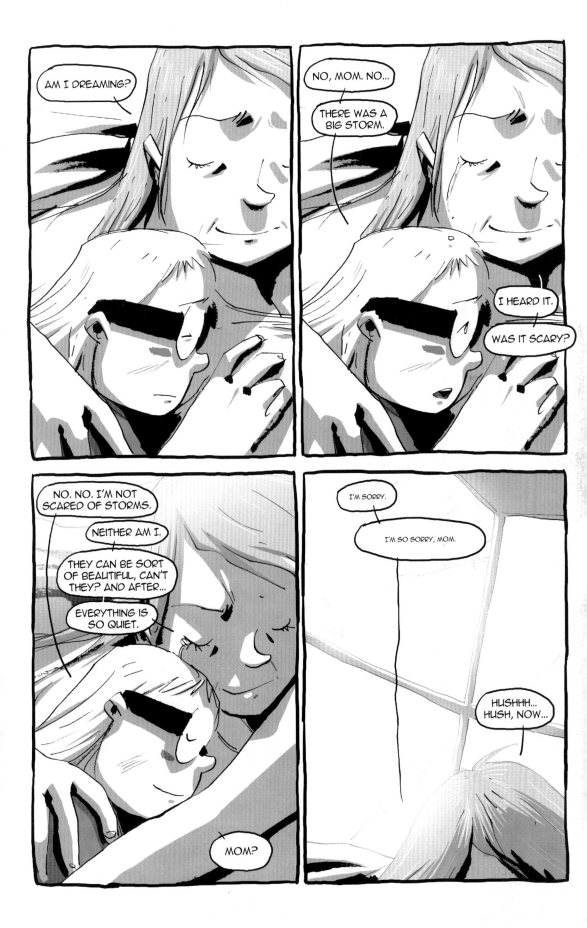

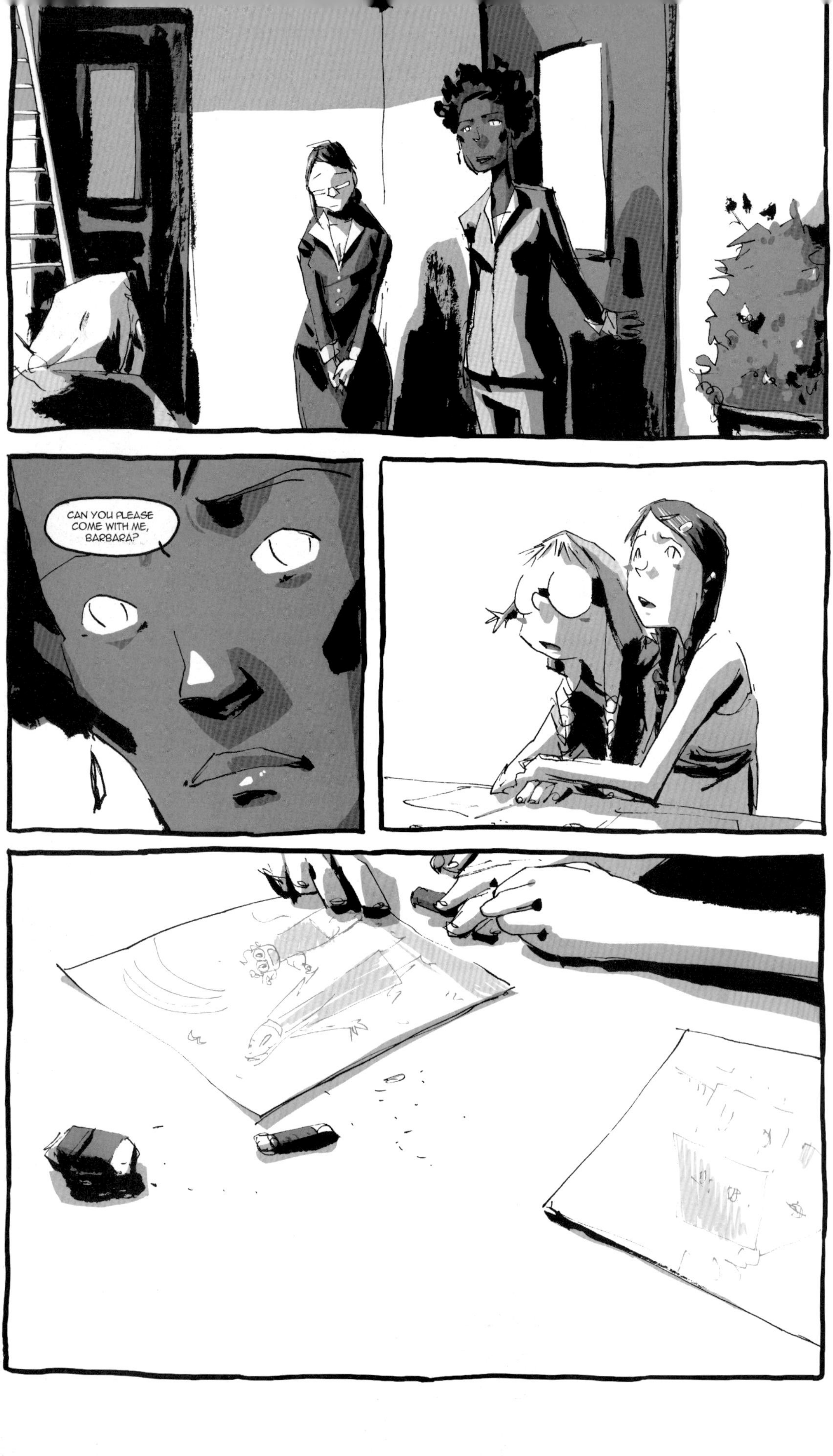
CAN YOU PLEASE COME WITH ME, BARBARA?

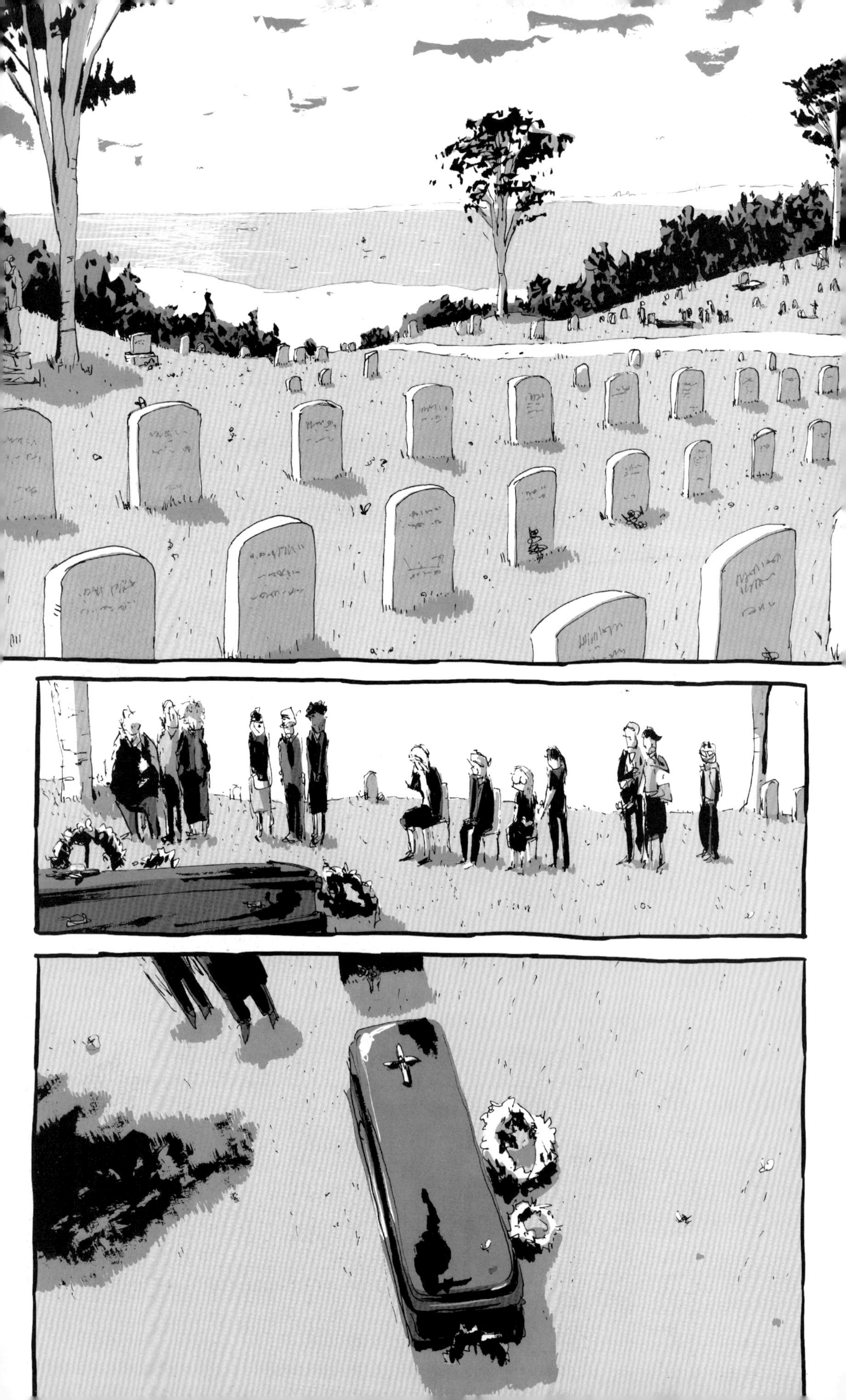

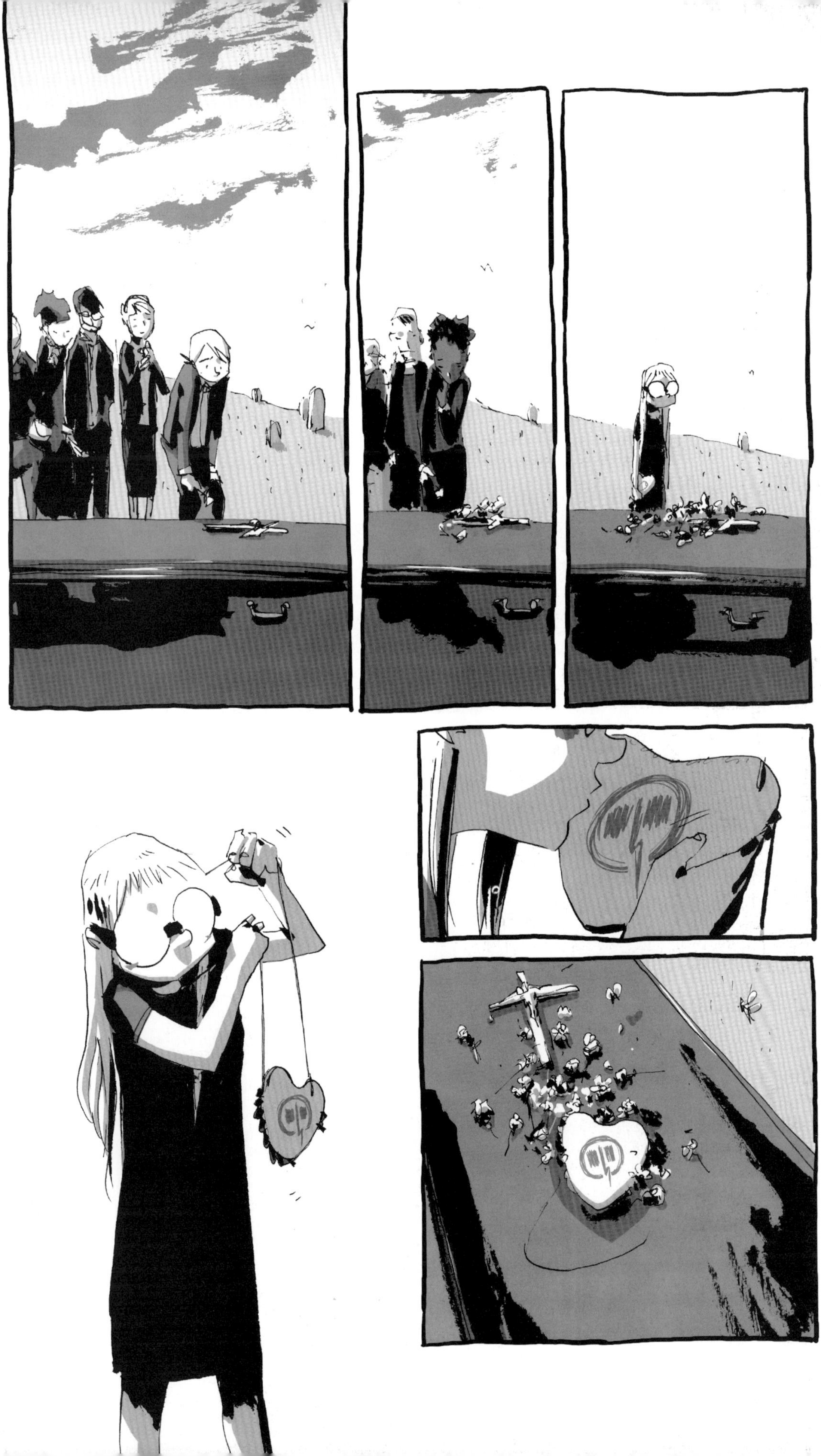

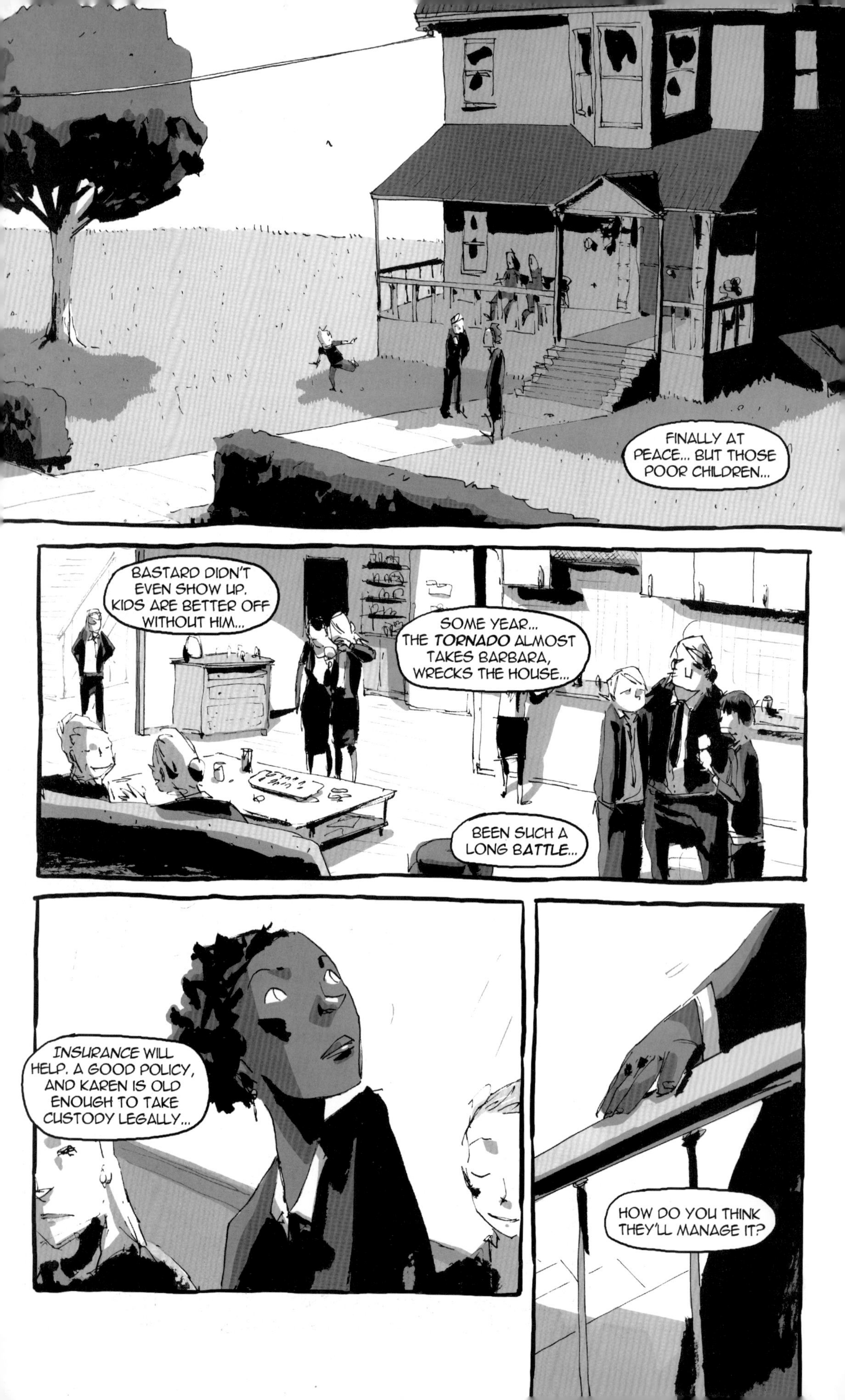
FINALLY AT PEACE... BUT THOSE POOR CHILDREN...
BASTARD DIDN'T EVEN SHOW UP. KIDS ARE BETTER OFF WITHOUT HIM...
SOME YEAR... THE TORNADO ALMOST TAKES BARBARA, WRECKS THE HOUSE...
BEEN SUCH A LONG BATTLE...
INSURANCE WILL HELP. A GOOD POLICY, AND KAREN IS OLD ENOUGH TO TAKE CUSTODY LEGALLY...
HOW DO YOU THINK THEY'LL MANAGE IT?

YOU DID A LOT FOR ME. THANK YOU.

DON'T GET ME CRYING AGAIN. I'M SUPPOSED TO BE THE STRONG ONE HERE!

I'M GOING TO SEE YOU A LOT IN SCHOOL, OKAY? BUT IF YOU NEED *ANYTHING*-- OR *DAVID* OR *KAREN*--

IT'S OKAY. WE'RE GOING TO BE OKAY.

I LEARNED IT... AFTER THE *STORM*...

MOM THANKS YOU TOO.

WE'RE A LOT STRONGER THAN WE THINK WE ARE.

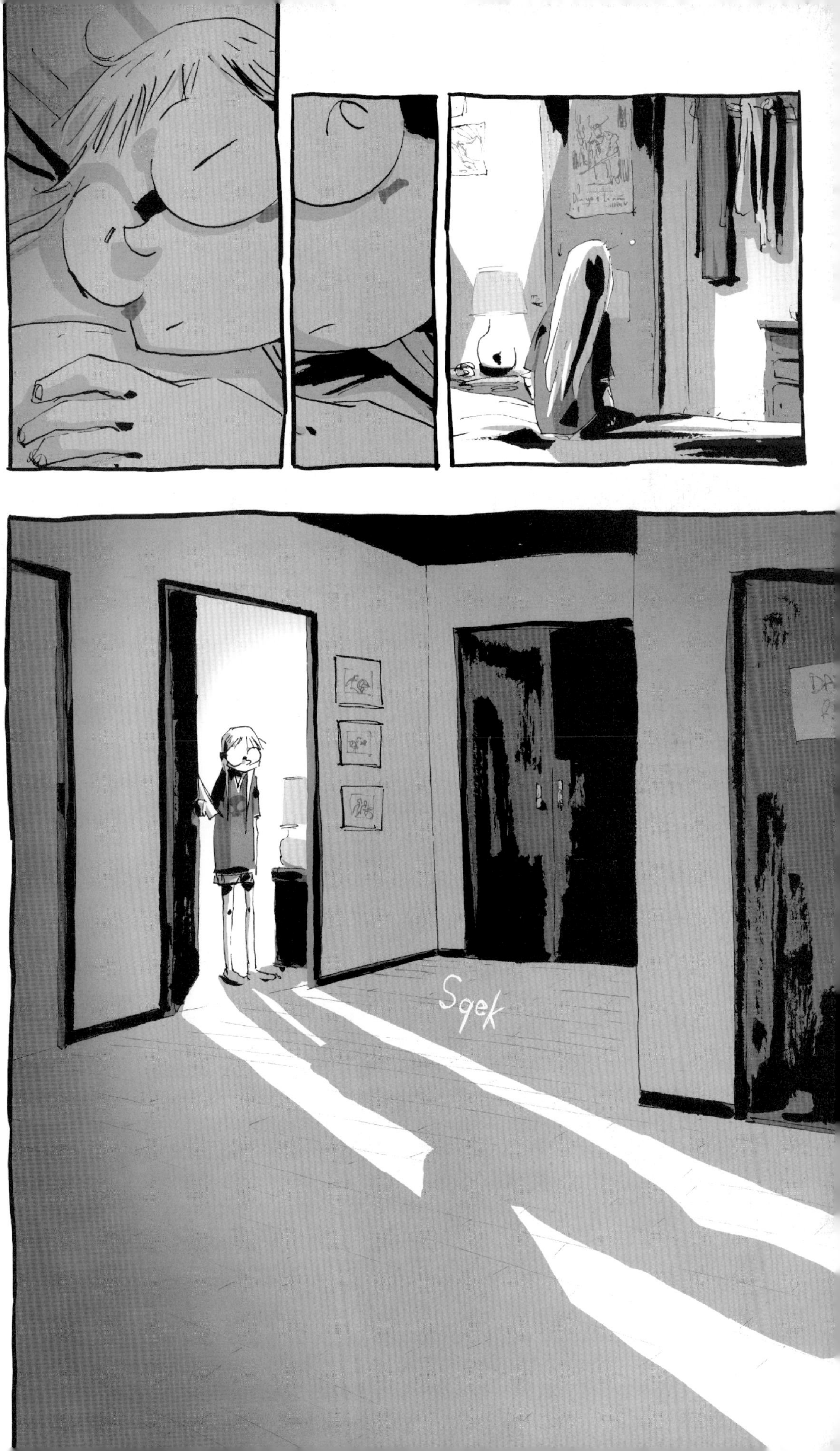
Sqek

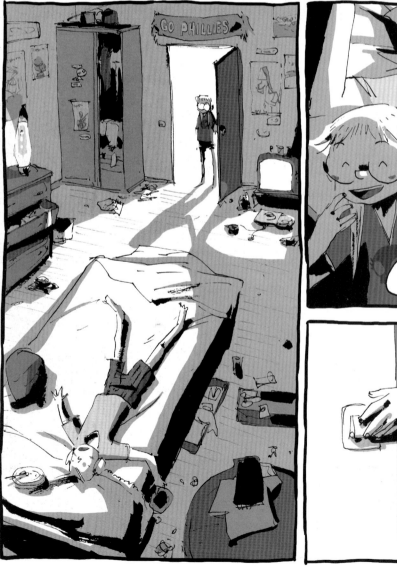

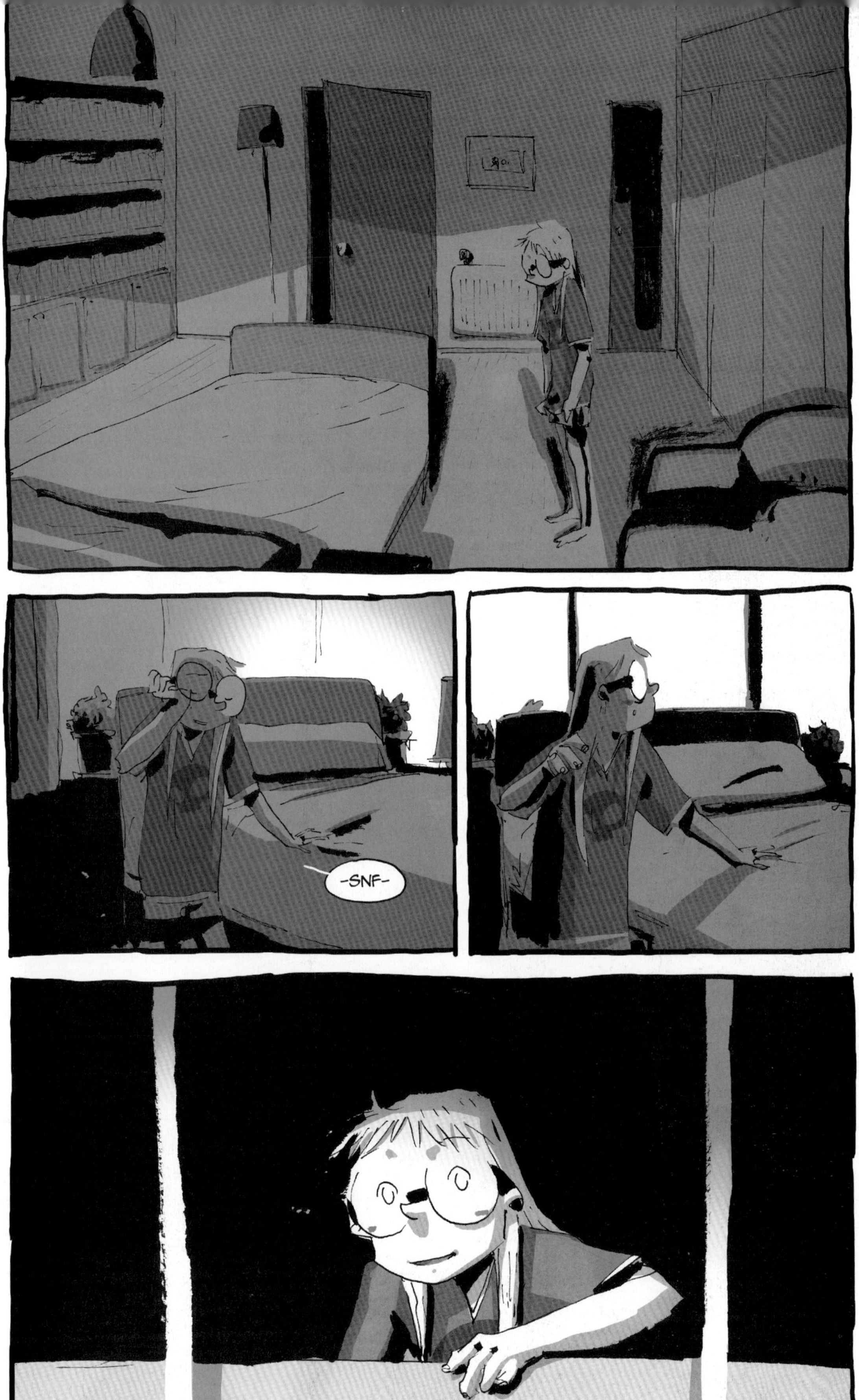
-SNF-

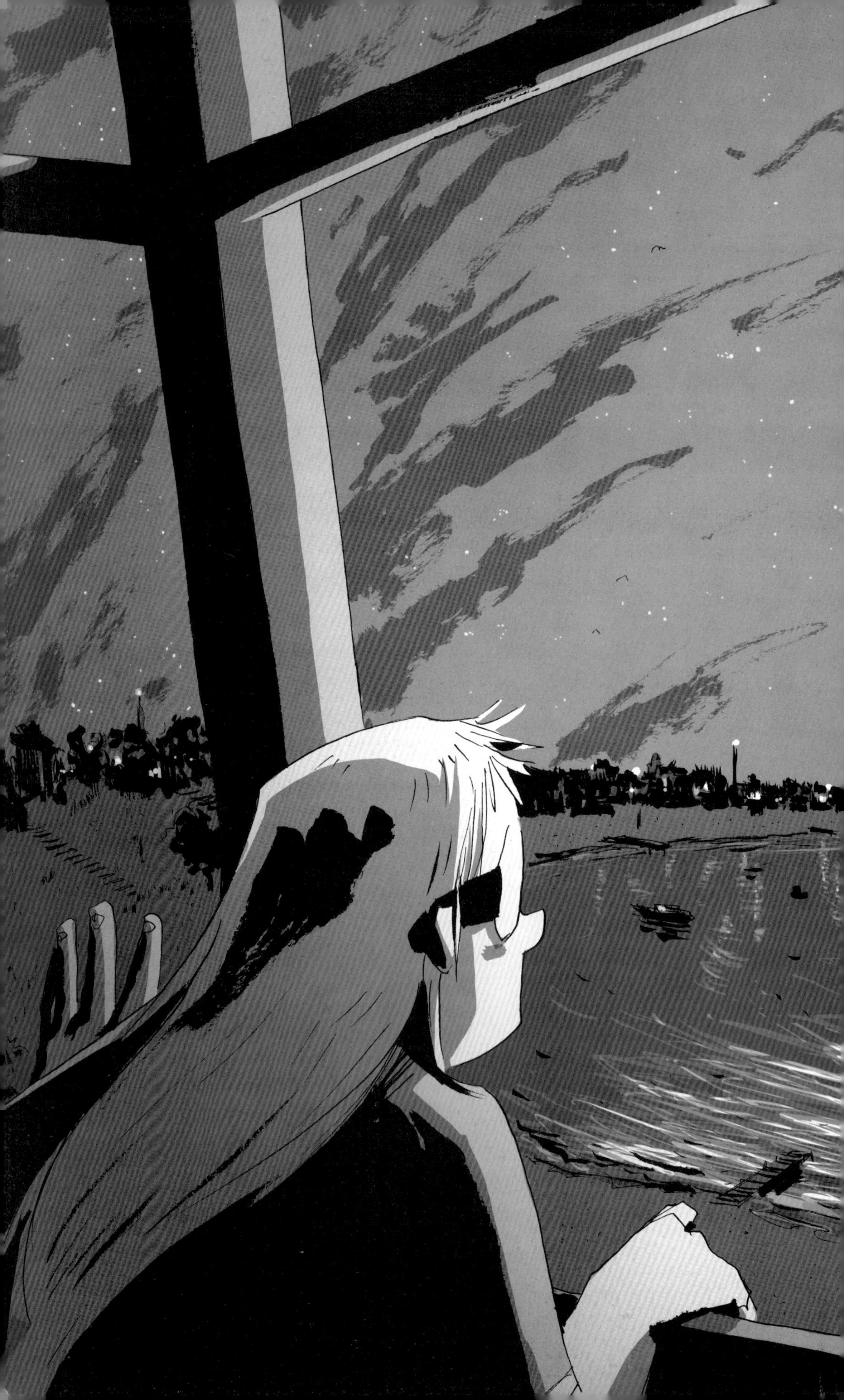

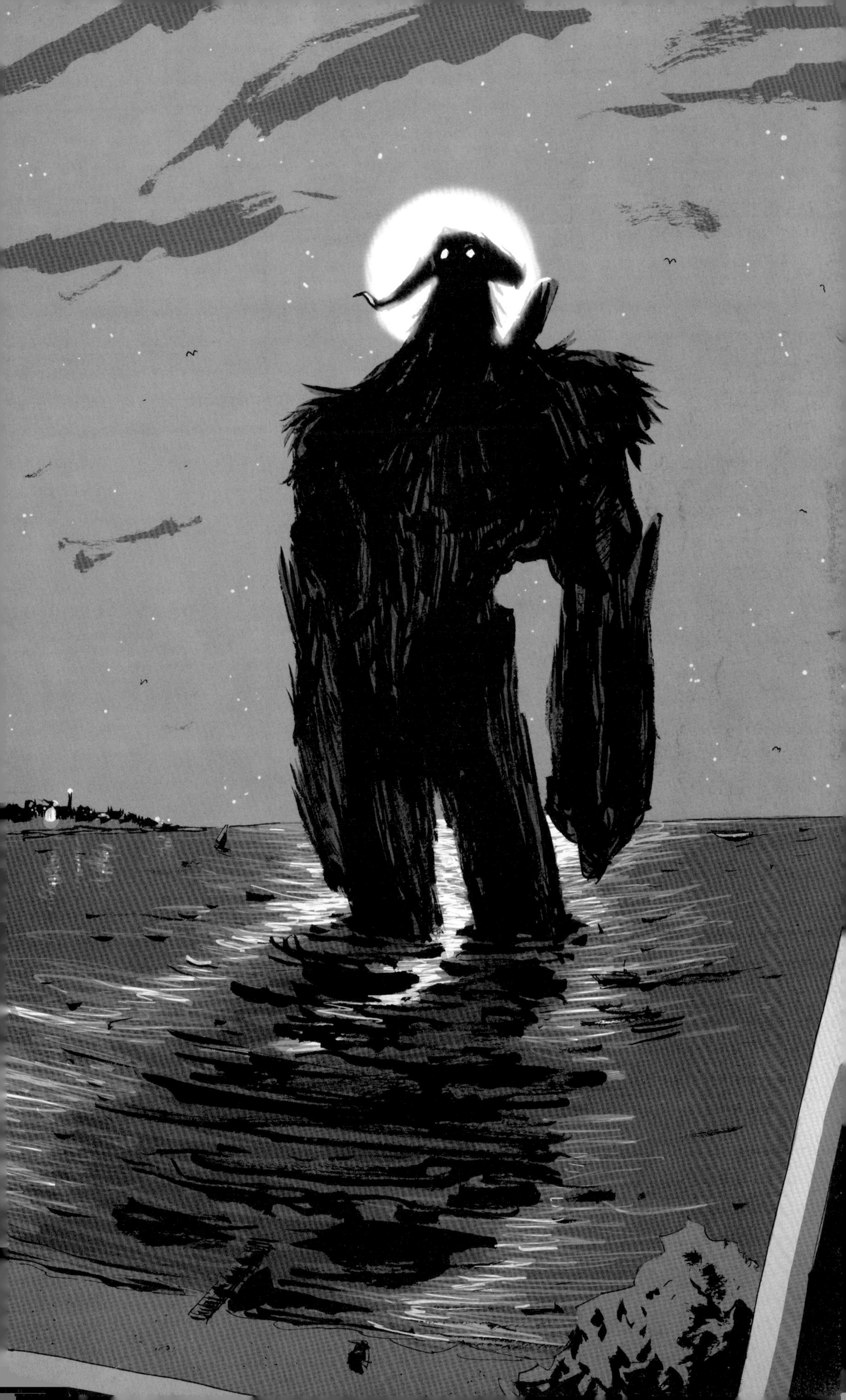

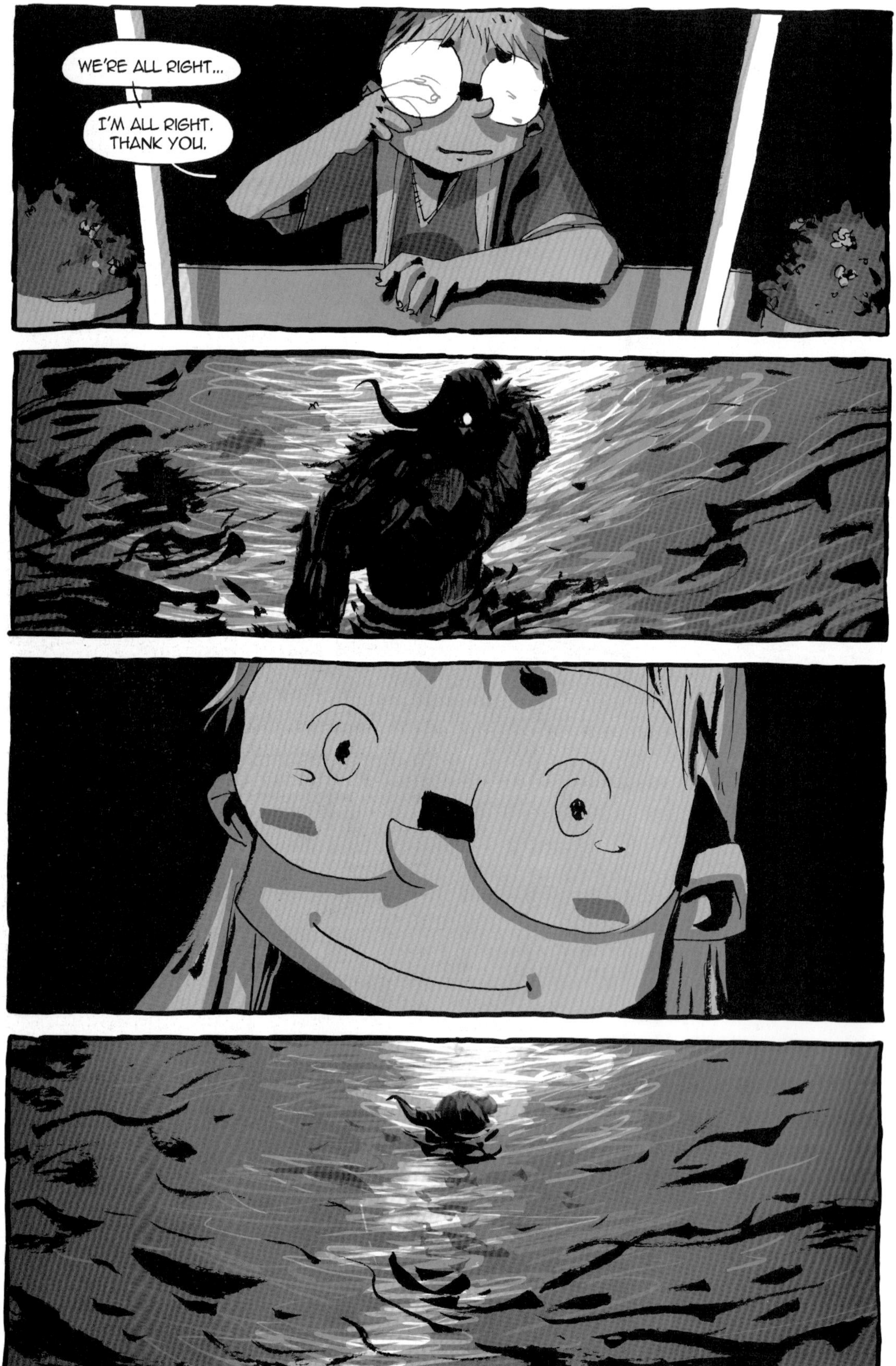
WE'RE ALL RIGHT...
I'M ALL RIGHT. THANK YOU.

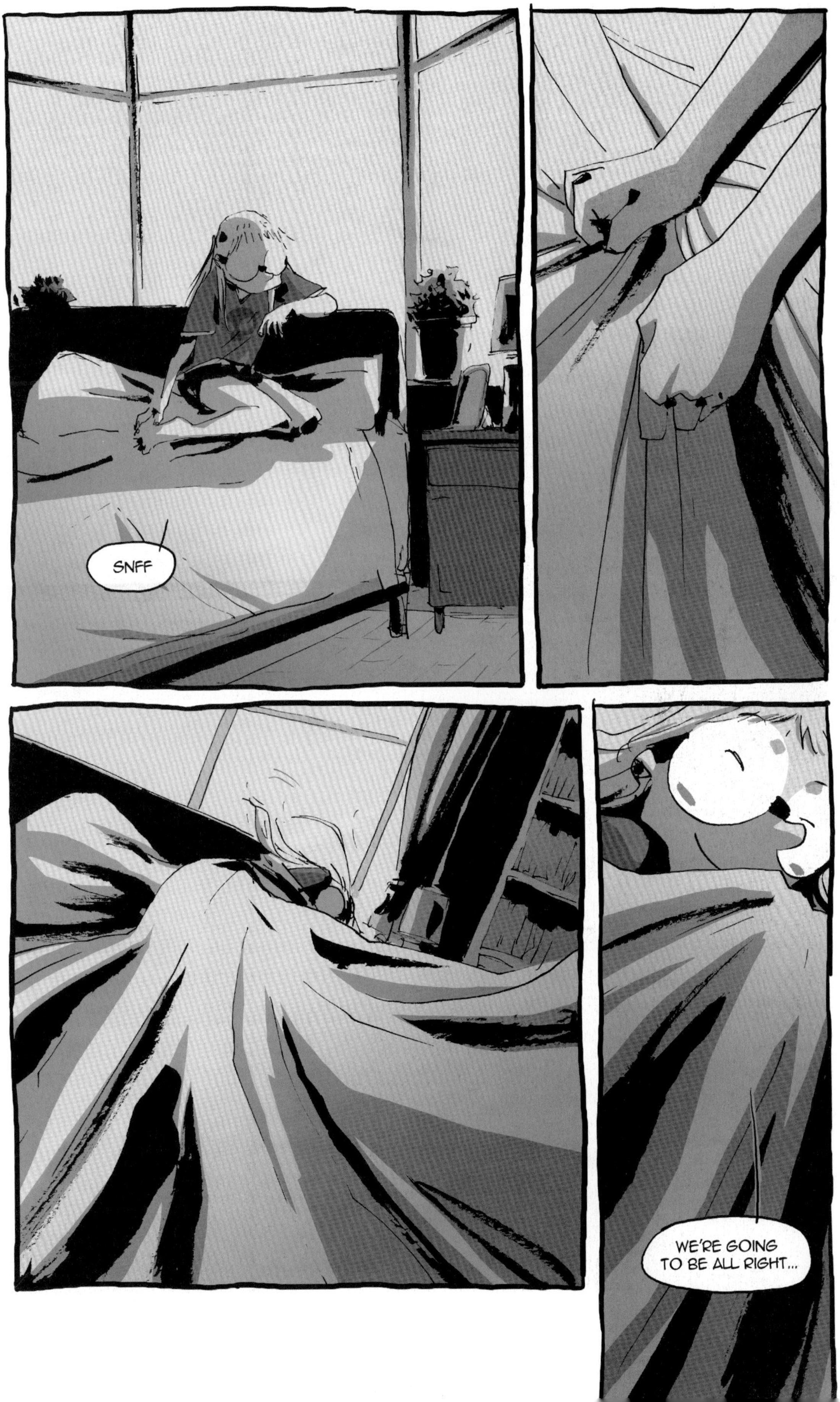
SNFF
WE'RE GOING TO BE ALL RIGHT...

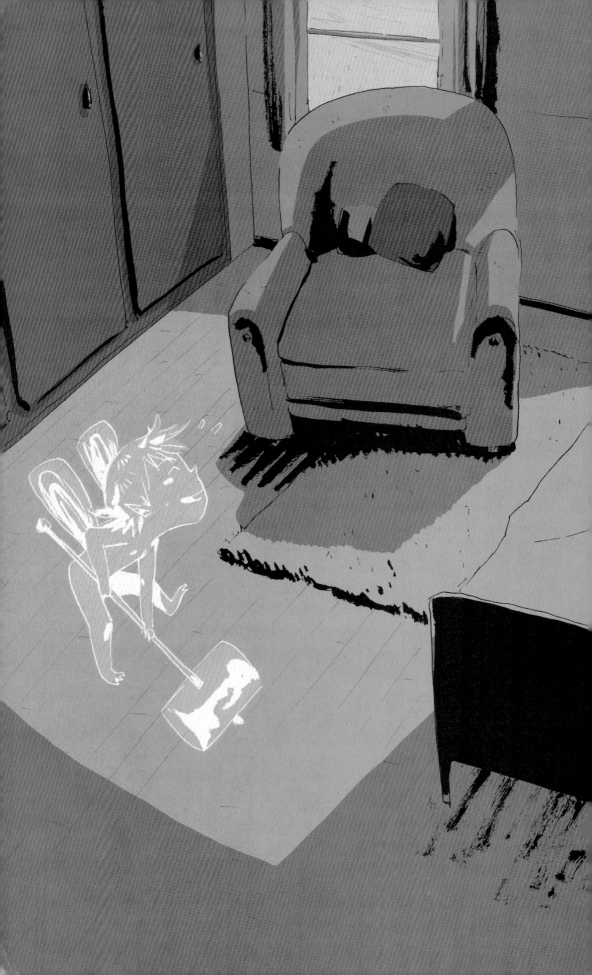

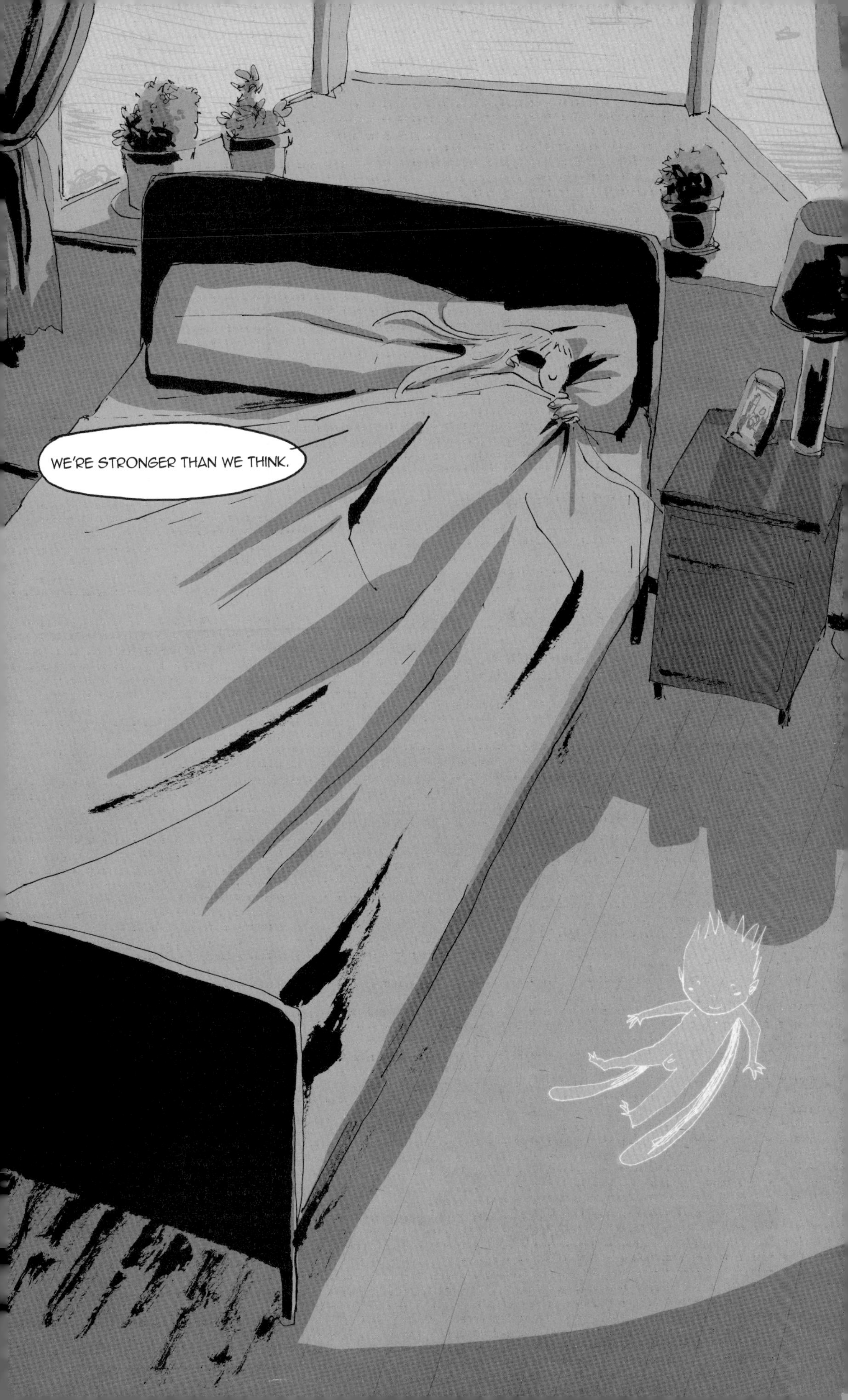
WE'RE STRONGER THAN WE THINK.

IKG: THE END

BEHIND THE SCENES

Writing is different for every person who's ever put pen to paper. For some it's a brutish, painful, bloody act of labor. For others, a methodical archeological expedition where bits of the whole are dusted off day by day until a civilization is revealed. After over a dozen years doing this professionally, I still don't know what my "method" is, unless you count guilty procrastination and overwriting as "method." However, I can always tell when a story is alive for me - because it literally claws its way through my guts and brains, consuming all other thoughts until I let it out in one furious burst. Invariably, when I get that feeling, I know I've uncovered a story I can tell the hell out of.

I Kill Giants was exactly that sort of story.

I scribbled Barbara's entire journey on a yellow legal pad in less than an hour while waiting for my dad to finish a physical therapy session. The idea for a story about a kid dealing with the death of a parent had been kicking about in my brain for a while, mostly because my Dad had spent a few months in the hospital for diabetes, which led to the loss of one leg - hence the PT session. Ironically, the year Giants finally saw print, 2008, was the year he succumbed to that same disease. (The last issue of I Kill Giants will hit the shelves almost exactly one year after his death.) Even though it took a few years for I Kill Giants to see print, the story never really diverged from those first dozen or so handwritten pages. Barbara aged up from her initial eight years. Scenes were moved. Thanks to generous and insightful notes from my friend Megan Casey, more of the "magic stuff" was worked through the story line and some of the "overtly sappy" bits were cut. But the spine was always there. More importantly, so was the heart.

As a general rule, I don't read my work once it sees print. I've lived with it for so long already - seen the layers of sinew, muscle, and skin added by my artists at every stage - that flipping through the printed final product doesn't hold much allure for me. Not so with Giants. Giants is a book I WANT to read, especially thanks to Ken's masterful drawing. I am not exaggerating when I tell you that Ken's breakdowns of the last few issues literally brought tears to my eyes, and each subsequent pass has only gotten stronger and stronger. I am fiercely proud of this book, and honored that Ken brought it to life with such care and affection. Barbara's story has become as much Ken's as it ever was mine, and, I hope, yours as well.

As always, thanks for reading.

JOE KELLY
New York, 2008

This has been my first long professional work in comics. Its mix of reality and fantasy has been the canvas on which Joe has kindly allowed me to work. I hope it was an enjoyable book to read.

JM KEN NIIMURA
Paris, 2008

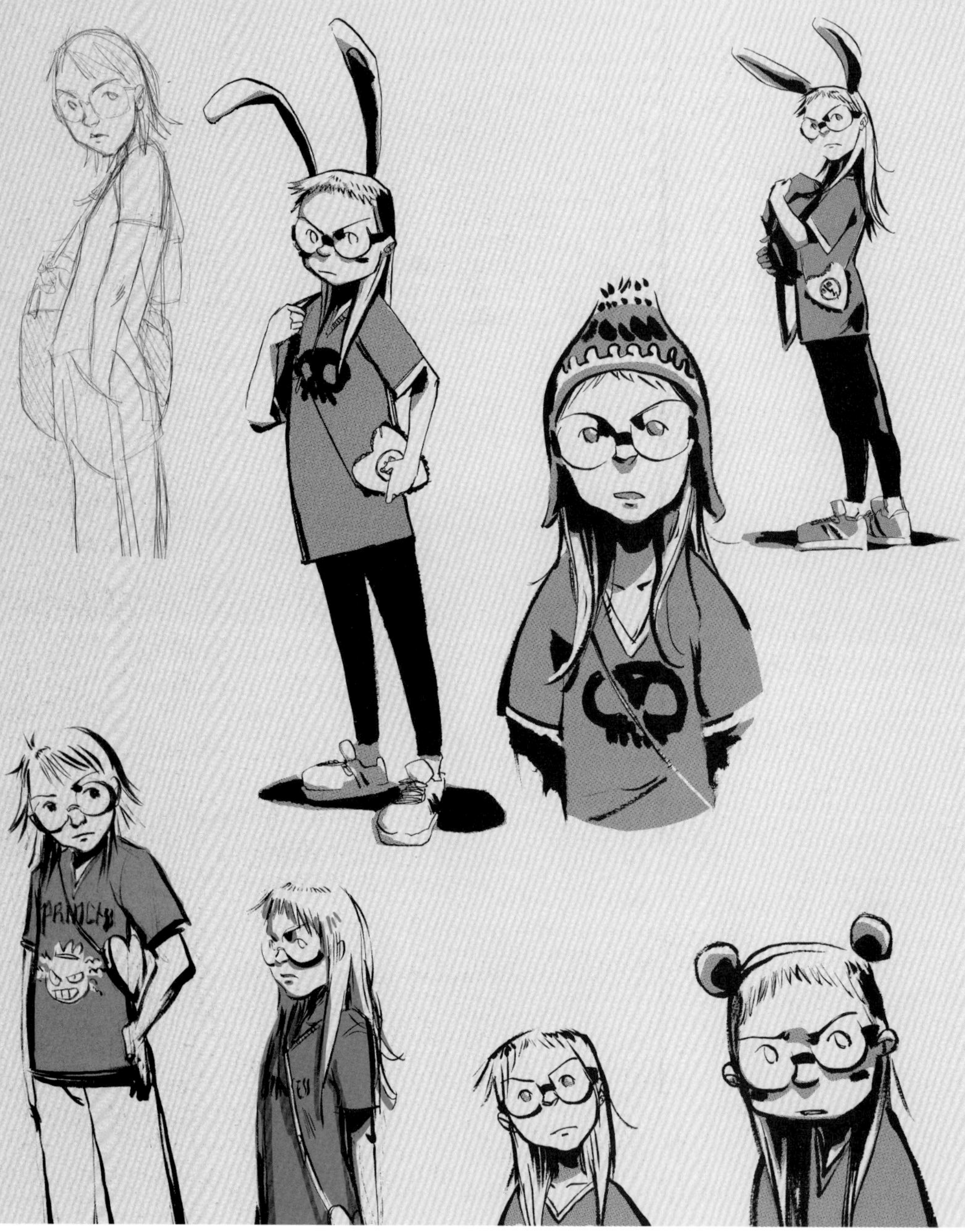

JK Barbara went through a lot of changes during the development of the book. She was loosely based on a 5th grade version of my daughter, who was in Kindergarten at the time I wrote the book. My daughter had a head of crazy curls, and I'd originally pictured Barbara with a barely managed head of flaming red locks. But when Ken started playing with her design, it just didn't sing to him. Especially in black and white, we both felt that the look lost something, and would just look like spaghetti. Being an insightful super-genius, Ken asked me what the hair was all about. I explained that I was gunning for an expression of Barbara's character, wild, unpredictable, a little weird. Since he was toying with the manga style anyway, Ken suggested "funny hats, animal ears really" to achieve the same goal. The second i saw those bunny ears in place, I was hooked.

KN I absolutely wanted Barbara to have a unique look, to have a something that with a single glance could tell us Barbara is a complete alien compared to the other characters. The animal ears were perfect for this: they allowed us to individualize her as well as making her much more expressive. Since the original script didn't say anything about this and Joe wisely didn't add any latter comment, all the characters seem to find it completely normal. That's precisely what I like the most, having this bizarre and somehow superficial element in a dramatic story.

JK I love the way Ken develops characters. He gives each one of them a ton of thought, experiments with styles, and ultimately collaborates with me to try and find the best expression of what I threw down on the page. In general, we spent a lot of time working out the ages of everyone in the cast, and he was extremely patient with all of my "help" in the designs.

KN This is my first attempt on a long story, and Joe's depiction of the characters was so accurate (both on a physical and psychological level) that it became a much easier task than I had thought. For months I made sketches of all the cast that we worked later individually. I came up with a first line-up that I found satisfying... but after a while, thanks to some of my friend's comments, I decided to make a second version of them all. It was also at this stage that I also brushed up the graphic style, becoming mostly what was seen on the comic. Sophia's character took very little to create, as well as Ms. Molle's, while Taylor took quite longer. I especially appreciate Mr. Marx, which is my personal homage to Finnish filmmaker Aki Kaurismäki: all the principals should rock as this one! There are of course friends that have been cast to appear on the comic, since it was much easier to imagine the character's body language if I had a real person as a reference. I hope they remain my friends despite their role!

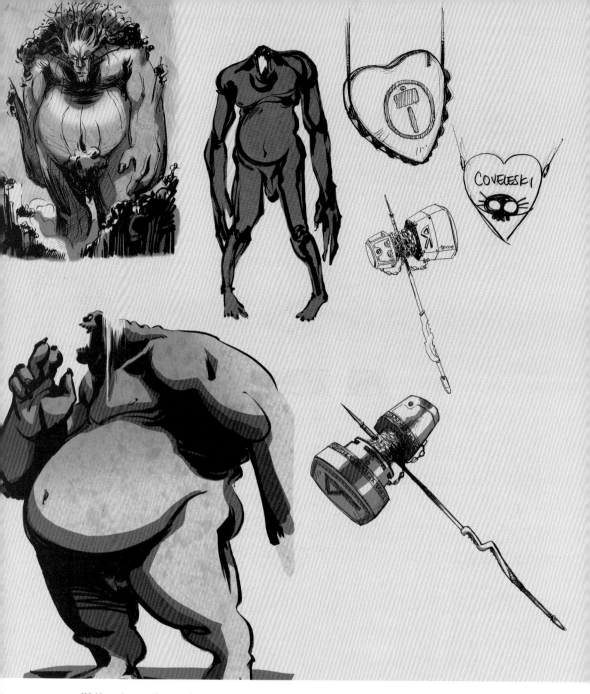

JK Ken threw down about a dozen Giant designs, even though they're really only used for one spread! But it was important to set the tone with them and show the depth of Barbara's imagination. A funny note, as you may notice, the giants are sporting... um... "little giants" of their own in the underpants area. I talked to Ken a bit about the difference in taste between the European and American markets - how here the wee wee tends to be a no no over here, silly as that is. Ken's response was something to the effect of, "Well, you wanted them to be scary, and I figured a monster chasing someone with a giant wang was pretty scary!" Scary indeed. We also put lots of attention on the designs for the pocketbook and

Coveleski, both of which are critical props in Barbara's story. He was extremely patient as I'd hem and haw, "Well, that's too girly... that's too rough... try leather... try denim... what if it was a wrench instead of a hammer... or a broom!?! No... a hammer..." The design he ultimately came up with was a great amalgam of both our ideas - with subtle additions from Ken like the handle (a lightning bolt if you look at it!), the rune on the head, etc. I could not have asked for a greater weapon of choice for Barbara.

KN Even though I knew they weren't going to be shown during the story, I drew lots of different giants. I'm absolutely unable to imagine a giant sewing clothes, not to mention underwear. Let them be naked, I say.

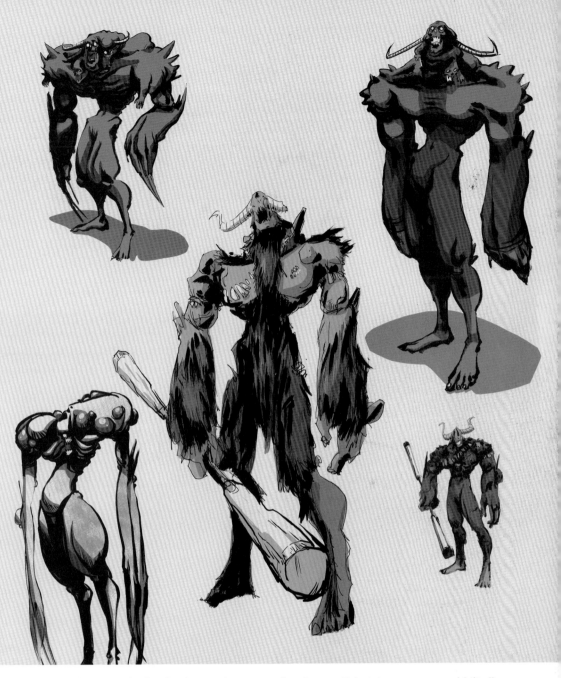

JK The Titan had to be the scariest giant we could come up with, and I think I asked Ken for about 50 versions. It was important to me that he be asymmetrical if possible, hideous and malformed. What's so cool to me about the ultimate design Ken came up with is that he's not only pee-your-pants scary, but on a second glance, especially in the context of the story, he's sort of cute in his monstrosity. That face can "act" and emote, which is critical for it to work.

KN This was quite a challenge to me. The key to a succesful story was in well portraying the Titan's character. Something too childish or too explicit would have killed its charm. I found it difficult since we're hiding its identity for almost all the story, so we couldn't allow his appearance to be deceiving. This was the same for all of Barbara's nightmares and visions, where rather than making them very specific, I thought a more abstract look would allow us to find common points with the readers on what is thought to be scary or dangerous. The Titan had also to be grotesque, deformed, but fought and moved a lot, so it had to be a figure that worked in different positions. I am aware that there could have been better possibilities for the Titan, but unfortunately found myself reaching my present limitations. Maybe in some years I'll be able to draw it as I imagine it. Meanwhile, I hope you all find it scary enough...

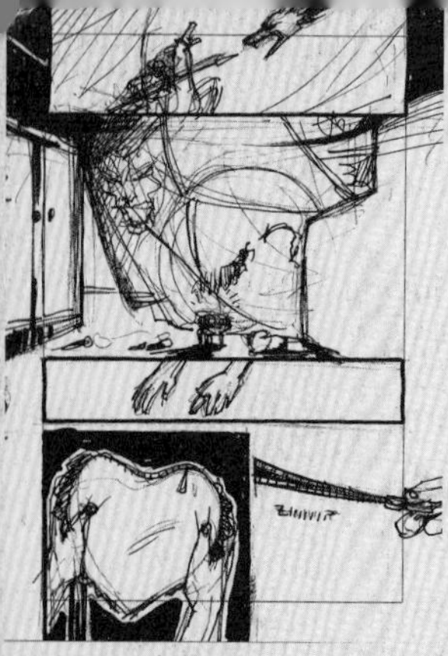

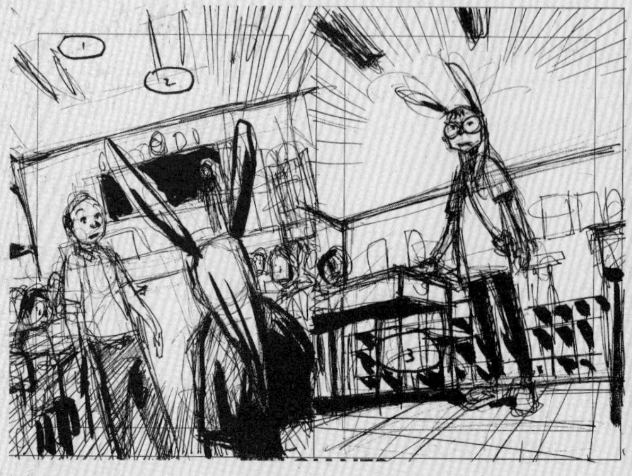

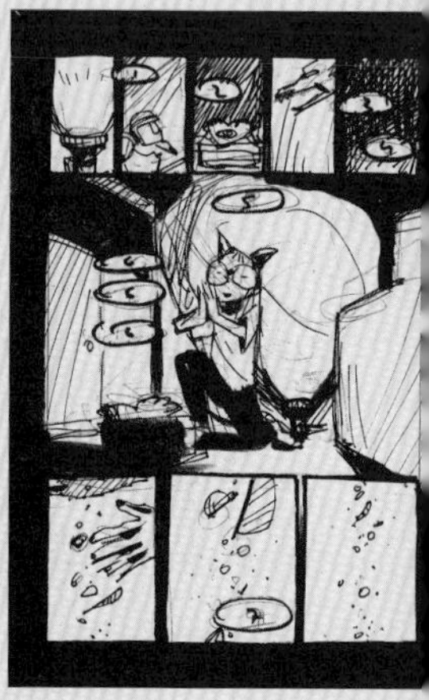

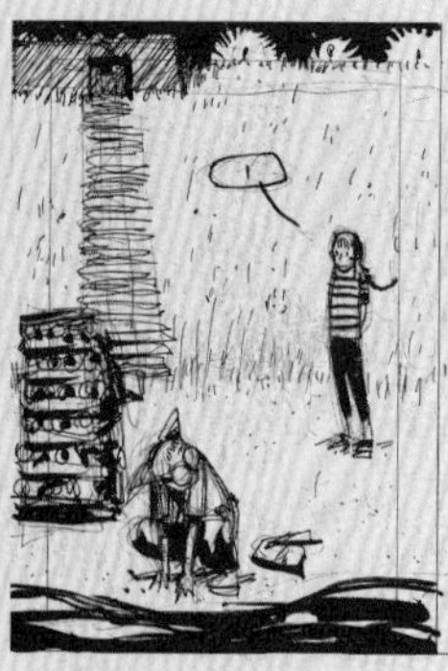

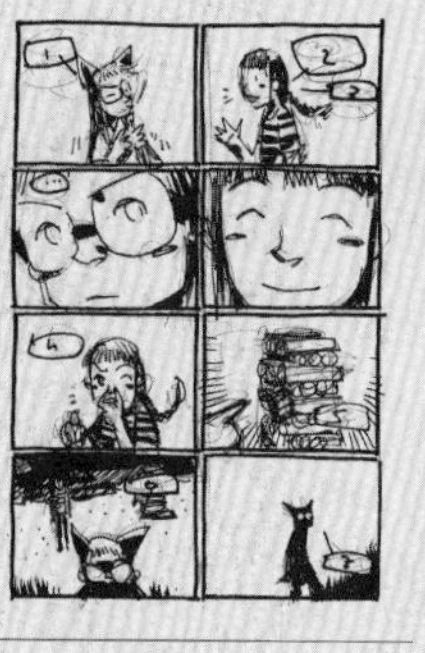

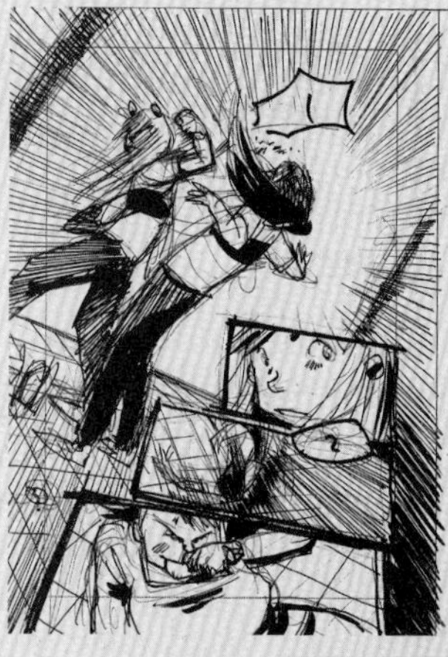

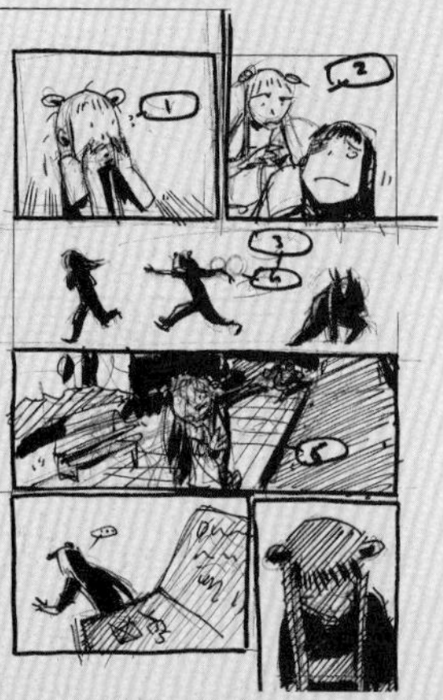

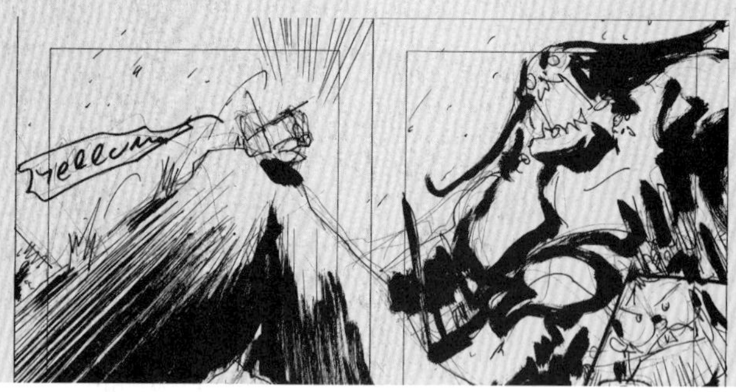

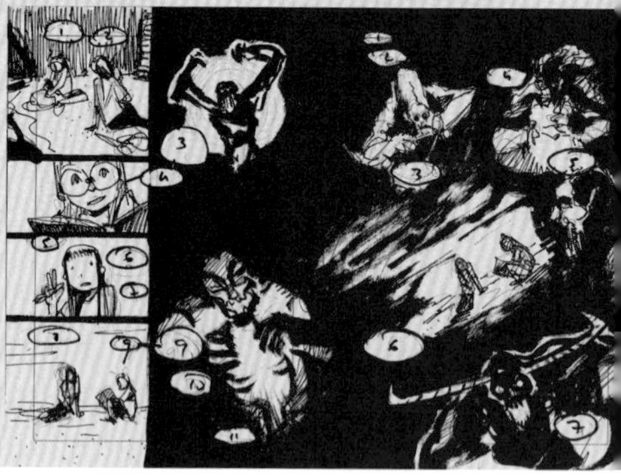

JK I'll let Ken talk about these, but one thing that continually amaze me was how accurate his breakdowns were compared to the final pages. Ken "sees" it all from the second he puts pencil to paper, it's just a matter of slow methodical construction to get everything just right. Even though his style looks "loose," it's a complete illusion. Ken is a perfectioinist of thie highest order, and it shows!

KN The way I make breakdowns is a good reflection of what I understand by comics. I very much appreciate those artists that not only take care on what they tell, but also HOW. As far as I am concerned, it doesn't mean drawing perfect figures or cool pin-ups, but rather being able to create a good reading rhythm, being able to suggest different moods and especially allowing the reader to flow from one panel to the other. Drawings only underline and help to complete the ideas thrown by the script and the breakdowns. I did thousands of versions of each page's composition before sending a final version to Joe. Being the first encounter between words and images, it was a great challenge to mingle them up to a point in which they become one. I also put lot of attention in making them very accurate. Funnily enough, the solution to most of the problems not only came from other artist's works, but also from the music I listen to (I need to have music all the time). It's all about rhythm!

JK Again, this is Ken's area of expertise, so he should discuss the process, but it's incredible to me how many layers of work he put into a B/W book! The subtleties are incredible and sublime as you move from one stage to the next.

KN My main challenge when I accepted to work on IKG was to create a black and white comic. So far I've been spoiled by being able to use color in my stories, so this time my personal goal was to achieve a good black and white drawing with which I could feel at ease. Some of my favourite authors in this field include Osamu Tezuka, José Muñoz, Nicolas de Crécy, Taiyou Matsumoto, Will Eisner, Hugo Pratt, Iou Kuroda or Katsuhiro Otomo, not to mention classics such as Goya or Hokusai. Unlike them, so far I haven't succeeded in drawing with only black lines as I firstly intended: suggesting textures, an atmosphere and movement by only adding black traces remains as a future challenge. At a given moment, I decided to add grey layers to help me complete the images. For the last year, I've been watching plenty of old movies, and it was there by chance that I found many solutions that I used on the panels. Special credit goes to Robert Wise's "The haunting" for its striking compositions and incredible tension. I kept all of these ideas for my working method while adapting them so as not to make as flashy as to eclipse the storytelling.

JK Ken's sense of design is amazing. I love watching him work through a visual problem as if it's a complicated mathematical equation - only to come up with a solution that at the same time feels organic and effortless. The graphic elements of this book make me smile every time - from the symbols on Barbara's shirts and pocketbook to the little glyphs on the IFC of each issue.

KN I come from a fanzine background where we had to do from the drawings to the graphic design and printing (and eventually selling and distribution). For some reason, I haven't been able to separate these elements from the comics I've done so far. A reader's experience with a comic starts from the very moment he looks at the cover and picks the book. Everything from the paper to the logotype, colors and compositionare part of the storytelling. I'm aware I'm not the best graphic designer ever, but I intend creating effective objects through the books I do. Working on a comic doesn't only mean doing the pencilling or inking, but developing a series of symbols, a graphic identity that's particular to this story. Some of my idols in this field include artists such as Chris Ware or Dave McKean, whose books not only are amazingly well done, but have a unique look to them that makes them especially appealling to me. I'm of course way far from them, but hope to modestly follow their steps from now on...